TO SEE
EVERY BIRD
ON EARTH

TO SEE EVERY BIRD ON EARTH

A Father, a Son, and a
Lifelong Obsession

DAN KOEPPEL

HUDSON
STREET
PRESS

HUDSON STREET PRESS
Published by Penguin Group
Penguin Group (USA) Inc., 375 Hudson Street, New York, New York 10014, U.S.A.
Penguin Group (Canada), 10 Alcorn Avenue, Toronto, Ontario, Canada M4V 3B2
(a division of Pearson Penguin Canada Inc.)
Penguin Books Ltd., 80 Strand, London WC2R 0RL, England
Penguin Ireland, 25 St. Stephen's Green, Dublin 2, Ireland (a division of Penguin Books Ltd.)
Penguin Group (Australia), 250 Camberwell Road, Camberwell, Victoria 3124, Australia
(a division of Pearson Australia Group Pty. Ltd.)
Penguin Books India Pvt. Ltd., 11 Community Centre, Panchsheel Park,
New Delhi – 110 017, India
Penguin Group (NZ), cnr Airborne and Rosedale Roads, Albany, Auckland 1310,
New Zealand (a division of Pearson New Zealand Ltd.)
Penguin Books (South Africa) (Pty.) Ltd., 24 Sturdee Avenue, Rosebank,
Johannesburg 2196, South Africa

Penguin Books Ltd., Registered Offices: 80 Strand, London WC2R 0RL, England

First published by Hudson Street Press, a member of Penguin Group (USA) Inc.

First Printing, May 2005
10 9 8 7 6 5 4 3 2 1

REGISTERED TRADEMARK—MARCA REGISTRADA

HUDSON
STREET
PRESS

LIBRARY OF CONGRESS CATALOGING-IN-PUBLICATION DATA

Koeppel, Dan.
   To see every bird on earth : a father, a son, and a lifelong obsession / Dan Koeppel.
      p. cm.
   Includes bibliographical references.
   ISBN 1-59463-001-1 (alk. paper)
   1. Bird watching—Anecdotes. 2. Koeppel, Richard, 1935– 3. Koeppel, Dan. I. Title.
   QL677.5.K614 2005
   598'.072'34—dc22   2005000476

Printed in the United States of America
Set in New Caledonia
Designed by Eve L. Kirch

Dedicated to Dad, Mom, and Jim.

ACKNOWLEDGMENTS

THE PERSON WHO IS MOST RESPONSIBLE for this book, of course, is my father. In the five years since we traveled to the Amazon together, he has spent more time on the phone with me than, I'm guessing, anyone else in his entire life. He was always willing to supply the information I needed, rushing across his house to look up some tiny detail—What was bird number 962? When did the American Coot split from the Andean Coot?—and provide it to me. When I asked him to list his favorite bird sightings, he did so (and made his deadline far quicker than I ever could have). When I needed more, he gave it to me.

If I have a sense of curiosity, I get it from Dad. If I have a sense of fair play, I get that from Dad, too. If I have an independent streak, he inspired it. I can only hope that I have a heart of gold, like he does.

When you tell a story of triumph, you also have to tell the stories of the pain and setbacks that led to that victorious moment. You can't have one without the other. I've tried to be as honest and unflinching as I can be recounting my dad's life. I'm sure there are things in here that he wishes I wouldn't have talked about, but I hope he'll see why they're here: because they're what make his story. They're what made him, and me, and my brother.

So there are no words, really, that can adequately say how much Dad has given me. I can only give thanks, and hope that I've done him justice.

I am also greatly indebted to my mother. Her candor in discussing very difficult issues was both helpful and cathartic; it moved me closer to a place of understanding and forgiveness. I know the past wasn't easy for her to talk about, and it was brave of her to do so. Mom has always encouraged my creativity, and I wouldn't be a writer today without having had her support. (Regarding personal information, as related by both my dad and mom—in several cases, I've changed the names and identifying characteristics of some of the people they've discussed.)

I WISH I WAS THE KIND OF WRITER who was supremely confident in his talents and instincts. But even when I haven't had faith in myself, Hanna Rubin has. There is nobody I've met who has been more supportive, more generous, and more decent to me than Hanna. Before I knew it was possible, she knew that this was a book, and she never wavered, even as I did. I don't know if I've ever told her how much she means to me.

Hanna introduced me to Laureen Rowland. Laureen started as my agent. She also saw a book in the story of me, my father, and birds, before I did. She spent a year waiting for an absolutely awful proposal, and many more months showing me how to make it better. When she founded Hudson Street Press, the first thing she told me was that she wanted to edit this book. Having her as my editor has been an absolute joy.

The second thing Laureen told me, upon announcing her career move, was that I needed a new agent. She recommended Laurie Liss of Sterling Lord Literistic. Laurie has been determined and protective, supportive when she needed to be, and as tough on me as (I know) she is on the folks she's negotiating with.

THE STORY ABOUT DAD'S SEVEN THOUSANDTH BIRD originally appeared in *Audubon* magazine, where it was assigned by Lisa Gosselin. It was the biggest and most personal story I'd ever done, and she shaped it expertly; I owe her a huge debt of gratitude for both conceiving the story and for showing me the right way to tell it. Other magazine editors—Jennifer Bogo, Peter Flax, Mark Jannot, Jim Meigs, Scott Mowbray, David Seideman, and Bill Strickland—were all supportive enough to listen when, during pitch meetings, I'd inevitably pull out "the bird story idea." Some of them even published portions—parts of chapter thirteen appeared in *Audubon* magazine, chapter eight in *Popular Science*, and the epilogue in *Backpacker*.

In the world of birding, Bret Whitney was liberal with his time and genius, inviting me to Brazil and to Austin, Texas, and patiently explaining the most complicated scientific concepts to me, guiding me through the world of modern ornithology. Peter and Kimberly Kaestner welcomed me into their home, and Peter kindly allowed me to interfere with his last big birding trip during his residence in Brazil. I spent a wonderful afternoon with Jim Clements at his home in the California high desert, and he never failed, after that, to answer my questions in great and helpful detail. Tom Snetsinger, Victor Emmanuel, Joel Abramson, and many others were also eager to talk, and took time out to help me understand how they see the world of bird listing. Dozens of birders and ornithologists consented to long phone interviews with me; many invited me into their homes. All of them have my thanks.

Finally, on a personal level, nobody has ever believed in me or cared about me more than Jocelyn Heaney. She was my emotional support during the hardest parts of writing this book. Similar thanks go to Alexis Amsterdam, Deborah Stern, Chris Ryan, Lisa Napoli, and Helen Kim, and especially to Leila Kuenzle. Other friends who provided support and encouragement while tolerating my malleable view of deadlines and bizarre moods were Tom Huggins, Matt Philips and Amy Colyar, Mark Riedy, and Zapata Espinoza. Friends who read parts of the manuscript and saved me from numerous mistakes include Lisa Jenio, Jess Holl, and Michelle Martinez.

I've listed most of my research sources in the bibliography that follows, but special mention goes to two books: Mark Barrow's *A Passion for Birds: American Ornithology After Audubon* and Joseph Kastner's *A World of Watchers: An Informal History of the American Passion for Birds*. Without those meticulously researched works, my understanding of how and why Americans learned to watch and count birds would have been even more meager than it is now; anyone who wishes to further explore the history of birding and ornithology that I briefly outline in chapters two and three would be well served to track down either of these books.

And though there are many people listed above who helped me, and many whose names I've neglected to mention, all of whom have enriched my knowledge and made this a better book, any errors or misinterpretations that appear in this text are 100 percent mine, and I apologize in advance for them. I extend the same mea culpa to any birders—especially Big Listers—who have made their mark on the activity and whose names I've left out. While I've done my best to find out who the world's best birders are, there are many whose names I'm certain I've neglected to include. I beg their forgiveness for the oversight.

CONTENTS

PROLOGUE

MY FATHER AND I WERE drinking champagne on a remote island in the Rio Negro, the dark river that flows into the Brazilian Amazon. I'd hidden the bottle in my backpack, along with paper cups for the other members of our group. The toast was brief. For Dad, this was the moment he joined an elite cadre—fewer than a dozen others, living or dead, have ever seen more than seven thousand bird species, the milestone he'd just reached. It was the culmination of fifty years of watching. For the rest of our group, the Amazonian Black Tyrant—a small flycatcher that shares the same coloration as the river we were traveling—was just another number.

But it's all about the numbers.

Dad and I had been traveling—up the river in creaky boats, along mud-packed roads, and through deep, wet forest—for nearly two weeks. I was on the verge of my fortieth birthday. It was the first extended period I'd spent with Dad since I was a teenager. Throughout my childhood, as well as now, our time together was focused on birds: Dad watching them, and me watching Dad watch them.

The group my father, Richard Koeppel, joined in Brazil is made up of people just like him: intensely dedicated, highly competitive bird watchers (or birders, as they prefer to be called) known as "Big Listers." Approximately 9,600 bird species are found on earth. About 250 people have seen 5,000 of them; about 100 birders have reached 6,000. Several of the twelve or so birders at the seven-thousand level are racing toward eight thousand, a mark only two birders—only one now living—have reached.

TO SEE MORE THAN SEVEN THOUSAND BIRDS IS A MASSIVE UNDER-TAKING. It requires extensive travel (only nine hundred species are found in the United States and Canada) to some of the planet's most remote destinations. And it requires a specific mindset: singular, focused, and obsessed, often to the point of blotting out any-thing—family, career, other pastimes—that might slow the quest. For most Big Listers, that arduous and all-absorbing mission seems to be borne of being pursued by circumstance, ambition, or personal demons, coupled with a barely submerged understanding that the only way to outrun those pursuers is to chase after some-thing else with equal determination.

If any air at all gets into the Big Lister's hunt, it's a compulsive need to count *everything*. My father counts books he's read and cheeses he's sampled. I've met Listers who tally the number of planes they've flown on, the states in which they've had Starbucks coffee, or their sexual conquests. Seeing every bird on earth is an eccentric pursuit. It can also be a tragic one. Phoebe Snetsinger, one of the two people to see more than eight thousand birds, be-came a Big Lister after receiving a cancer diagnosis. Given six months to live, she decided to forgo treatment and chase birds. She thrived and counted for seventeen years, and then was killed in a car accident on a remote road in Madagascar as she approached her 8,500th species. She'd talked about quitting because reaching numbers that high requires travel to distant and dangerous places, but she admitted that she was unable to stop. To my father, the only thing more important than his quest was cigarettes; despite the fact that he was a doctor, he couldn't shake the addiction until, just after seeing his seven thousandth bird, he was stricken with both cancer and heart failure. As he recovered, he took comfort in his list, reordering it, putting a half-century of bird sightings into cohesive form.

As I packed away the champagne in Brazil's Jáu National Park, the elation of the moment tempered, and I once again found myself—as I had all my life—becoming curious, trying to understand my father's consuming passion. Why? Why count? For the past ten years, I've been trying to find the answer. The search has led to more questions, about science, personality, and desire. My father is a brilliant man who has lived a life that, in so many respects, didn't turn out the way he wanted. He buried the sadness of his disappointments by watching birds, by tending his logbooks and checklists the way a gardener nurtures his blooms. On our trip, Dad and I connected in ways that were both lovely and difficult. I saw his self-destructive side, a part of him that for years has shut out family and love. And I saw his best qualities, a man with a gentle heart, hidden by pain, but not hard to detect upon careful inspection. The triumph of the list is the triumph of that hidden heart because it is proof not just of obsession, but also grace, and glory.

❖   ❖   ❖

DAD AND THE BIG LISTERS aren't just chasing numbers; they're chasing the definition of life itself. Not long ago, there were only thought to be six thousand bird species on earth. Ten years from now, most ornithologists believe, there will be three times that many. It isn't that new species are evolving; rather, scientists are arriving at new definitions of what species are. This advanced thinking—and birds are on the cutting edge of it—has profound implications for human understanding. Speciation *is* evolution. Evolution is at the heart of who *we* are, what life is on this planet. I hope that this book shows how the pursuit of birds relates to— and grows from—science's quest to explain our existence. I hope it shows what that science means to those of us who are content to simply watch at our backyard feeders. And I hope it shows why birds—especially birds—can lead to these understandings; the same reason Darwin chose finches to illustrate his theories—birds are active, colorful, and musical, all easy-to-differentiate evolutionary traits—are the reasons for the more general romantic love of birds. It shouldn't be a surprise that humans are fascinated by creatures that soar, sing, nest, and battle.

To see every bird on earth isn't easy. It requires strategy, money, and time; it is sometimes dull, and sometimes dangerous, and very often absurd. The underlying "game" of birding is a labyrinth of mechanics, rules, and rivalries. There are birders who've been shunned for cheating, internecine fights over what truly constitutes a sighting (seeing is *not* the only form of believing in modern birding— currently, many birders consider a "heard" bird countable). Birders' lists themselves are often moving targets, subject to frequent revision and categorization: You don't just start at one; instead, you create multiple tallies, delineated by year, region, species, genus, and just about any other category a person could think of.

My father says his listing is "an addiction, just like any other addiction." Though he spent a considerable portion of his medical career attempting to cure those with physical dependencies, I wasn't surprised that he didn't care to engage in analysis of his motivations: "I can't explain it. I can't even say it ever gave me a sense of euphoria. It's just what I do."

But I want to explain it. I want to understand. I know Dad won't agree with everything I've said in this book. I know he won't share many of my conclusions about what drives him. He won't be completely happy with some of the things I've revealed here. But that's the nature of love, especially between father and son. What Dad has given me, through all the trouble and pain, and finally through triumph, is his legacy. I didn't want it to be burnished and idealized. Dad's story is so much more beautiful when it follows the alternately tragic and elating course of a real life.

As I was writing this book, I spent hours on the phone with Dad. I accumulated hundreds of pages of transcribed interviews with him. I was, of course, using birds as a way to find out about him, as a door into his life. Sometimes the interviews were tedious. They were occasionally fun; often they were painful. Dad was in a big hurry to get them done. At first, I thought this was because of his typical impatience for introspection. But then he let it slip. He was nearing his seventieth birthday: "I was worried," he says, "that something would happen to me before you got the whole story. I wanted to get this done, so you'd have it."

He wanted me to get through the list, as well, he wanted to pass it on. Once it was safely in my hands, it was up to me to determine what, exactly, I'd been given. It was only when I began to read between the seemingly dry and formal lines of the tally itself that I realized what such a lifetime of counting contains: the desire to find one's own place in creation, pursued with a single-mindedness that so far has evolved only in humans. Seeing every bird is a way of seeing everything, of attempting to know everything. Such attempts mark human history, in religion and art as well as in science; they're seductive, and sometimes dangerous. The story told here is about finding a way into that seduction—and finding a way back.

A NOTE ON THE
BIRD STAMPS

IT IS POSSIBLE TO "WATCH" BIRDS only as they appear on your mail. Birds are the single most popular theme for postage stamps worldwide, and Chris Gibbins is the philatelic equivalent of a top bird lister. His collection, begun in 1970, contains more than 12,140 stamps, showing 2,950 species. Gibbins uses *A Complete Checklist of Birds of the World,* by Richard Howard and Alick Moore, to organize his collection. The stamps illustrating each chapter in this book come courtesy of Gibbins. They depict the particular species being discussed in the accompanying text, though the issuing country isn't necessarily the same nation where the bird in the text was sighted. The Gibbins collection can be viewed by stamp, nation, or species at www.bird-stamps.org.

TO SEE
EVERY BIRD
ON EARTH

CHAPTER ONE

THE BROWN THRASHER

❝ *This was the bird that really got me interested. My friend Mike Fitzgerald and I spent a lot of time wandering around the scrubby and swampy areas of Kew Gardens Hills, Queens. In May, we found several Brown Thrasher nests. They all had two eggs in them. The books said four eggs were usual. So we called the Department of Ornithology at the American Museum of Natural History in Manhattan. Of course, they didn't know why there were only two eggs, but whoever we spoke to asked where we lived and then suggested we check out the Queens County Bird Club. We did, and that was the beginning.*❞

—Brown Thrasher (*Toxostoma rufum*),
summer 1947, Flushing, New York, #24.

THE BOY DOESN'T YET KNOW EVERYTHING IN THE SKY. Because these are the days just following World War II, and because he is twelve—an age when anything buzzing through the clouds is cause for excitement—he knows the B-24s from the Republic Thunderbolts, both aircraft built a few miles from the woods where the boy is standing. But now, peering into the oak trees, human flight seems secondary.

It is a warm evening in the summer of 1947. Richard Koeppel— my father—has ridden his bike away from home, pedaling north through Queens, toward the shore, where the East River empties into Long Island Sound. He's been coming here for weeks now, to watch the birds frenzying in their nests. He comes back again and again to watch. He's fascinated, though he's not sure why.

What is it? He wants to know. He understands, somehow, that to understand it he needs to name it. John James Audubon wrote that the Brown Thrasher—because of its antics and crisp singing—is a bird "well known to children in the country." This bedroom borough of New York City doesn't quite match that naturalist's landscape, and Richard, as of yet, has no idea who Audubon was. He just knows that this bird, nearly a foot long, is interesting. It doesn't just sit there in the shrubs. It moves constantly, with energy that astounds him. And when he approaches, laying his bike against a tree, inching forward for a closer look, the bird begins to squawk, preparing to defend its nest.

What is it? The boy can name a few of the stars because he's recently become interested in astronomy, and the city's night sky has yet to be blown bright by haze and upflowing luminescence. One evening, he brings a friend, Mike Fitzgerald, to watch the nests. Now, both boys are interested. They make a plan. One Saturday, they pedal to the local library. They look through a few books, but they're overwhelmed. So many birds. How to tell which is which?

Richard has noticed the bird's yellow eyes and that it hops on the ground, pushing aside dry leaves. He's seen it snatch beetles and worms from the soil. He asks his parents—his father still remembers growing up on a farm in the Austrian countryside, and sometimes he takes the boy on weekend drives into the hills north of the city—and guesses that it might be a mockingbird.

Close. There's a picture in one of the books of a bird called the "Brown Thrasher." But the book says that these birds lay four eggs, and the boys have examined several nests, but they've never seen more than two eggs in any of them.

Could it be the Brown Thrasher?

Richard has an idea: He's been to the planetarium at the American Museum of Natural History in Manhattan. The museum has an entire room devoted to birds, where dozens of species are on display in real-life dioramas. The boys call the museum and are told about a place near where they live that can give them all the information they want about birds.

The boys pedal to the John Bowne House, the oldest home in

the borough. It was built in 1661 and stands beside an even more prominent landmark: the weeping beech, progenitor plant for every tree of its species now found in North America. Once a month, the Queens County Bird Club—each borough of New York City has such an organization, and they compete intensely, battling over which section of town has the most birds and the best bird-watchers—meets beneath the tree, scanning its arched branches before formally commencing inside the "House of the Weeping Beech." There's usually some comparing of lists, a display of photography, and a discussion of future outings. There's nearly always a new member or two. The boys are welcomed. Nobody minds that a couple of twelve-year-olds have poked in with questions; in fact, the club members are delighted.

Arthur Skopec, one of the group's founders, is a gifted shutterbug, and he often brings slides—he can make brilliant images using a recently introduced type of film called "Kodachrome"—to meetings. On that day, he thumbed through his portfolio and called for the lights to be dimmed. The image that flashed upon the hastily unrolled screen was crisply focused, perfect. The bird looked fierce, almost ready for battle. "This is a bird that is very active," Skopec says to Richard. "That's why they call it a Thrasher," he continued. "A Brown Thrasher." The lights go on, and the man shows the boy an oversized copy of Audubon's *Birds of America*, opening it to the page containing the naturalist's gilt-edged description. Richard reads it twice. Skopec shows the boys a pocket-sized book that names and identifies many, many species. He tells them that the club is open to anyone interested in birds. Age and experience are unimportant.

The boys are excited. They're quite sure the bird they've seen is a Thrasher. Except for one thing: What about the eggs? Why two, instead of four?

Skopec smiles: "That's the fun of watching birds," he says. "What's out there isn't always what you expect. You never know what you'll find. You might even discover something new."

YOU CAN STILL FIND THE QUEENS WHERE THE COUNT BEGAN, but you have to look hard. Imagine yourself in midtown New York. From Grand Central Station, board the Number 7 train and head east. You cross under Hell's Gate, tunnel beneath Jackson Heights and Astoria, emerging onto elevated tracks just before Queensboro Plaza, the city's busiest subway stop outside of Manhattan. Look out the window. You see apartments and low-slung factories; many of the industrial facilities are now empty or have been converted to residential lofts. Nearly all of them would have been visible—and active—fifty years ago as well. New York City's private transit agencies began building the route, then called the Woodside/Corona line, in 1917. It was completed, reaching the terminal at Main Street, Flushing, in January 1928. When the construction began, Queens was still a rather rural place, but the borough—the cramped living quarters for millions of immigrants passing through on the way to suburbia—grew around the newly constructed tracks.

Before you reach Main Street, take a short detour. Disembark at what today is called the Shea Stadium station. The big blue athletic complex, where the New York Mets play, sits adjacent to Flushing Meadows Park. The arena was constructed as part of the 1964 World's Fair (today's most visible remnant of that event is the skeletal Unisphere, a 700,000 pound, 140-foot diameter steel globe at the center of the old fairground). The spot was also the site of an earlier exposition, in 1939, that forms my father's first memories. Where the Unisphere now stands, rusting, a smaller globe, called the Perisphere, sat next to a towering ziggurat known as the Trylon. Together, the two comprised a town of the future called "Democracity." The utopian mini-village was, of course, hardly predictive—such things almost always represent an impossibly sterile optimism—but the 1939 fair did introduce America to dozens of items that would constitute the nation's future, including the first commercial television set, fluorescent lighting, and Borden's "Elsie the Cow."

I mention Elsie because the bovine mascot is central to my father's first recollection. He was impressed by the automatic milking machine demonstrated by Borden technicians, dressed not in farmer's coveralls but in sanitary lab coats; most likely he remembers this because my grandfather, always nostalgic for his own roots, for the cultivated pasturelands of Eastern Europe he'd left behind, lingered at the exhibit. But two additional memories may be more important than this demonstration of wholesome, scientific dairy production: The Hayden Planetarium, housed at the Museum of Natural History, had partially relocated to the fairgrounds, and offered a wide-ranging exhibition on space and astronomy. One of the pavilion's most impressive features was a "cosmic ray electric power generator": A Geiger counter at the main observatory was wired to the Queens outpost; the energy transmitted from one to the other powered the colored lights that flecked the projected starscapes. These so fascinated my father that he decided, at age four, to become a scientist (a decision also made by another child visiting that day, a Brooklyn five-year-old named Carl Sagan).

My father's final memory from the fair is of more symbolic import. It is of a room-sized map, a Mercator projection (a map that uses a mathematical formula to flatten a spherical surface; the notion was conceived in 1569 by Flemish cartographer Gerhardus

Mercator, and it effectively turned the rounded globe from a practical navigational tool into a decorative parlor object) that showed the entire planet, except Antarctica, which the U.S. Maritime Commission, whose cartographers had plotted the chart, considered unexplored. The map was as big as a tennis court, and my father stood before it in awe, staring at it for what seemed like a long time, before his father pulled him away. It was probably the first moment he was aware that there even was a world outside New York. A smaller Mercator map, dotted with dozens of colored pushpins indicating visits, stopovers, key milestones, and yet-to-be-seen destinations, now sits in the study of my father's Long Island home.

Returning from the fair, my father announced to his parents that he wanted to become an astronomer. He doesn't remember their reaction, but later, when his passion turned to birds, the way they'd regard anything that might distract him from their ambition, that he become a doctor, was very nearly hostile; that hostility would become a source of repressed desire, progenitor to obsession.

Today, that old World's Fair site is receding into history. The few buildings that remain are little more than skeletons. But the most important thing you'll see, as you reboard the subway and continue east, is what surrounds Flushing Meadows. Before the 1939 fair, the Willet's Point stop was tiny, with just a pair of stairways. Subsequent renovations equipped the stations with the facilities to accommodate tens of thousands of commuters. It was a reflection of what was happening throughout Queens. Flushing Meadows, even in the 1940s, was still surrounded by wetlands, streams, and a few remnants of forest. Skopec can recall dozens of spots—Parker's Pond; the Bayside Woods; sandy inlets covered in huge boulders, thrown by ancient glaciers—that were "as wild as anything you'd find up or down the eastern seaboard." New York's "undeveloped acreage," as the city parks department termed it, was home to an astonishing variety of wildlife: "Five species of gulls, a half-dozen ducks, and numerous songbirds," wrote John Kieran in 1950's *A Natural History of New York City*. They nested and sang on sassafras and Juneberry trees; the shorebirds picked their way across beaches lined with prickly pear cactus; in the spring, numerous ponds—called "kettles" because they were fed by the great aquifer that still underlies the region—would bubble with frogs and salamanders. From even before it became part of the city, descriptions of the area were highlighted by its wilder inhabitants: In 1670, Daniel Denton, a resident of the Jamaica neighborhood, a few miles east of Flushing, wrote of "Turkies, Heath-hens, Quails, Partridges, Pidgeons, Cranes, Geese of several sorts, Brant, Ducks, Widgeon, Teal . . . and many sorts of singing birds." (Denton also mentioned "innumerable multitudes" of seal and whale, just offshore.) Over two centuries later, Queens had changed little: Walt Whitman, exploring the borough in the 1870s, described it as a land of "sweet brooks and drinking water."

Change came faster in the twentieth century. By the time subway construction began, Queens was no longer backcountry, but it remained rural (over two hundred farms), though some industry—including the Steinway piano factory—could be found nearer to Manhattan. By the start of World War II, the borough was already in the throes of its greatest change. During the 1930s, Robert Moses built bridges into Queens and sliced the terrain with parkways. Between 1920 and 1930, population more than doubled, growing from 460,000 to 1,079,000. That meant more trains, more roads, more houses—but not yet fewer birds. "They were cutting into parks for roads," says Skopec, "but in the 1940s, there was still plenty of room." When my father identified his Brown Thrasher, Queens was bird-rich. Many of the species described by Denton were gone, pushed out by European imports, but the bird club's annual Christmas census routinely topped one hundred, a number proportionally far greater than today's tallies (which see more birds, but are conducted by scores more people).

Today the subway doors open at Flushing–Main Street. You step onto the platform and climb to the sidewalk. You're amazed by what you see. The neighborhood has become, as one current tourist guidebook puts it, "New York's *real* Chinatown." Not exactly: The Asian newcomers are from many more different countries than the Jewish immigrants, like my grandparents, who lived along Main Street in the 1930s and 1940s. Signs hang above stores in a dozen languages and multiple typescripts. Everything smells delicious and exotic, and everywhere, everywhere, there are people.

That's the difference. When I was a boy, and my grandparents were still living, my brother and I would walk to Main Street. Then it was surrounded on both sides by low-slung garden apartments and attached housing, and the storefronts—delis, kosher butchers, luncheonettes, and bakeries—were tiny; the neighborhood had an old-world feel. When I ask my father about Main Street, he recalls someplace between the modern era—those kosher markets are provenance to today's Vietnamese noodle shops—and the wild Queens described by Denton. "South of Main," Richard says, "where I lived, looks pretty much the same today—at least, the buildings do." But he smiles; I can see the nostalgia playing inside: "But north, it was nothing but woods and swamps. They were full of birds."

And hope. They were full of hope.

OBSESSION GROWS IN FRUSTRATION AND CHANGE. It also grows in duty. My father and his peers inhabited a world fixed between old and new, Promised Land and literal inferno, liberation and obligation. To understand what propelled Richard into a quest that would absorb—and sometimes suffocate—nearly every aspect of his being, one needs to take stock of that dual reality. It began with an even deeper bisection that took place with my grandparents: not global, but gravely personal, and kept secret.

The French-flagged ship *La Lorraine* arrived in New York Harbor on Christmas Day 1920, having made the Atlantic passage from Le Havre in nine days. Hundreds of immigrants, mostly Eastern European Jews, stepped out of cramped steerage and into the receiving halls at Ellis Island. Moses Koppel, twenty-four years old, was listed by an examining immigration officer as a member of the "Hebrew" race, a national of Poland, and a native of Vienna, Austria. His occupation was marked as "labor." All that is nominally true, and all certainly representative of the experience he shared, not just with the twenty-eight other men listed on the same page of *La Lorraine*'s manifest, but with millions. But the details are what we're concerned with because we're looking for clues—hints of what the future would hold for Moses, for his children, and for his children's children.

My grandfather's name and nationality changed three times. He was born in a region known as Galicia, then part of the Austro-Hungarian Empire, at the foot of the Carpathian Mountains (today, the region is mostly overlain by Poland and the Ukraine). He spent much of his time with horses—I remember, as a boy, hearing him talk about riding; I'd ask him if he ever thought about finding a farm, maybe upstate, and tending animals again, and he'd shake his head, as if that door had closed. Born Moishe Koppel, he'd fought on the Austro-Hungarian side in World War I. If his tranquil boyhood was something he'd locked away and viewed as an adult only from a wistful distance, then his experience in the infantry was beyond off-limits: He never spoke of the violence he'd witnessed, or how, dug in near the German border, he'd been exposed to dichlorodiethyl sulfide. (This was the first use of the chemical agent better known as mustard gas.*)

The war left Moishe restless, searching. For many German-speaking Jews, one answer stood above all others, even America: Vienna. A celebrated "Jewish Renaissance" began there in 1848, and was still under way after the turn of the century. Vienna Jews were allowed civil rights, even citizenship—an astonishing grant rarely seen in Europe since the earliest Christian era. Vienna's Jewish community included Sigmund Freud, Gustav Mahler, Franz Kafka, and, of notable importance to this story, the pioneering Zionist Theodore Herzl. Germanizing his name to Moses, my grandfather arrived in Vienna around 1917. There were nearly 185,000 Jews living there at the time.

But there were signs of trouble. In 1897, a nationalist named Karl Leuger was elected mayor of Vienna. By 1910—Leuger's fifth reelection—his philosophy of German purity began to influence another immigrant from the countryside: Adolf Hitler. Members of a Nazi precursor, the *Alldeutsch Parti*, were gaining political influence, being elected to increasing numbers in parliament. (Later, when Hitler was imprisoned in Germany, he described how his years in the Austrian capital crystallized his political philosophy: ". . . facing the question without whose solution all other attempts at a German reawakening or resurrection are and remain absolutely senseless and impossible . . . in my Vienna period I had leisure and opportunity for an unprejudiced examination of this question too, and in my daily contacts was

*This was a story that even my father hadn't heard; I remembered my grandmother's sister telling me about the mustard gas when I was in my late teens. My father isn't certain that it's true.

able to establish the correctness of this view a thousand times over.")

Hitler, who also fought in World War I and was also exposed to mustard gas, desperately sought to shift blame for their defeat to an ancient scapegoat: the Jews. He found plenty of company in hating them. Men like my grandfather quickly came to understand that Vienna would be no refuge; it would become, instead, a point of departure.

Nobody could mistake the gathering storm. My grandfather met a young girl during his time in Vienna, but, knowing that he'd leave, wasn't about to fully express his interest in Shoshana Purper. She was studying at the city university. (Her parents had been part of the great wave of Jews that had immigrated to Austria during the previous century, coming from Stanislaw, Poland, most likely after that city was destroyed by a great fire in 1868.) There's much my family doesn't know about the years when Moses and Shoshana were both in Vienna. We know that they met, "but they weren't a couple," my father says. Almost certainly, as he made his way by train toward the port at Le Havre, Moses would not have expected to see Shoshana again; she was part of the world he was leaving behind, making his way to someplace new and alien with little more than a suitcase and his uncle's Brooklyn address, scrawled on a scrap of paper. He wasn't sure what he'd do, but he understood that there was plenty of work. He believed that America would be good to him. He'd even reworked his name a bit: Morris Koeppel seemed more appropriate for the New World.

Shoshana, meanwhile, remained in Vienna. Her education was continuing, but one by one, her sisters—there were eight—departed, eventually leaving just her and Leonie, her youngest sibling, in Austria with their parents. Shoshana had thoughts of becoming a newspaper editor, but it was quickly becoming obvious that no such job would exist. In 1920, George von Schonerer—another Hitler mentor who'd cofounded the *Alldeutsch* group with Leuger—led a mob into the offices of *Neuss Wiener Tagblatt*, the city's Jewish daily, destroying it and injuring several employees. The truly discouraging thing about Schonerer's raid was that his capture and subsequent jailing only seemed to attract more adherents to his cause. No Jew who understood history could misapprehend the signal: It was time to leave.

On September 7, 1922, Shoshana Purper boarded the S.S. *Kroonland*, sailing from Antwerp. She was twenty-three years old, traveling alone, destined for her sister's home in Buffalo, New York. When she arrived, she gave her occupation as dressmaker, and made one more change: She told officials her name was Rose—it sounded sweeter, more American—so "Rosa Porper" is (mis)typed in the Ellis Island documents. Nobody in my family is sure how she traveled upstate, but one thing is certain: She was ambitious. She didn't know exactly what to expect, but she wanted success. It would be good insurance against whatever thunderclouds gathered and broke.

THERE WASN'T MUCH WORK IN BUFFALO, but Rose had studied some English, and quickly gained fluency. She spoke four languages—Polish, German, and Yiddish in addition to English—and that gave her a slight edge when she traveled to New York and applied for a job at a lower-Manhattan factory that specialized in brassieres and girdles. She wouldn't be sewing; instead, she'd translate packaging, product brochures—anything for a growing customer base of immigrants entering the middle class. It was a good position, and New York was an exciting place. Still, she was lonely. So the voice calling her old-world name—Shoshana—on the streetcar home from work one evening was welcome. She turned and saw, peering through thick glasses, an acquaintance from Vienna named Harry Schechter. Rose was delighted to see him, but she was especially excited when Harry told her that another old friend was in New York: "Morris—Moses, I mean—is here," Harry said. "He's got a clothing store, right here in town. You should go see him!"

Rose went to visit immediately. And the young man she'd met years ago hadn't forgotten her, either.

Over the next few months, Rose and Morris grew closer. They were a good match: Morris was a hard worker, but still a bit of a country boy; Rose would help him navigate the new world.

What did my grandparents want, when they were married in June 1924? It's an important question because the roots of my father's own ambitions grew from what his parents desired for him—as did the events that led those two things to diverge so wildly. First of all, they wanted to be safe. But as the Depression took hold, leading to the failure of Morris' business in New York, and as they heard news of increasingly virulent anti-Semitism overseas, they also wanted the *world* to be safe. It isn't hard to understand that they became nearly obsessed with security, that almost every decision they made was based on the desire to remain safe. My grandfather took a job with Metropolitan Life, selling insurance. My grandmother became one of the first life members of Hadassah, a Zionist women's organization, in the United States. The idea of a Jewish homeland, and the couple's nonstop work toward that ideal, helped satisfy their desire for universal protection.

In 1926, Rose learned she was pregnant. The couple was hoping for a boy, and even before the pregnancy could show, they'd decided two things: that he'd be named Theodore—after Theodore Herzl, the Austrian founder of Zionism whose oversized portrait hung on the wall of the couple's small apartment in Astoria, Queens—and that their son would become a doctor.

"My son, the doctor" is such a culturally Jewish concept that it has grown to nearly comic proportion. But the notion dates back to the Middle Ages; medicine, like finance, was a profession open to Jews, whose written traditions allowed sophisticated skills to be preserved and passed on (in some places, Jewish doctors were even granted extra rights and exemption from persecution). The flowering of the Jewish medical tradition took place during the Austrian renaissance; nearly 60 percent of Vienna's doctors were Jewish, and four of the first fifteen winners of the Nobel Prize for Medicine were part of that Austrian community. Add to that tradition Rose's own frustrated ambitions—she'd avidly attended Sigmund Freud's lectures in Vienna, and had always wanted a career—and it is no surprise that the first Koeppel born in the United States was expected to become a physician.

In December 1926, Morris rushed Rose to the hospital. She was a tiny woman, and the last few months of her pregnancy had been a strain. But she was tough, and her husband probably worried more than she did; she trusted the doctors who were waiting for her.

But medicine, for all its marvels and the admiration the couple had for them, was unable to help. The story is rarely told in my family; when it is mentioned, it is as something secret, nearly shameful. This is the way my father relates the story: "They told her that she'd given birth to a monster. They told her not to look at it." My grandfather was given the infant and told to leave it in an empty room. I don't know how Morris felt, or how he reacted. I don't know whether the stoicism I saw him exhibit when I was a boy was the thing that helped him do what he had to do, or whether his sober nature was a result of that terrible day. But he did as he was asked and returned to his wife.

The baby might have survived five, ten, twenty minutes. It was a boy. They named him Teddy.

HOW COULD ROSE AND MORRIS LAMENT THEIR TROUBLES? Not during the Depression; not when darkness began descending on Germany and Austria and threatening the rest of Europe. Rose was told to never again become pregnant. Her heartbreak was something that was never discussed in my family.* It's hard to imagine that she didn't think of Teddy, but it's also possible that Teddy's death signified the beginning of ever more terrible times, that the magnitude of that event shrank in the shadow of what came after.

In 1930, Hitler's Nazi Party won 18 percent of the vote in Germany's parliamentary elections. Two years later, that total doubled. A sense of panic set in among American Jews; they knew what must lie ahead. A race against time began: Relatives had to be extracted, loved ones rescued. Rose and Morris turned their attentions toward community; through Hadassah, they worked toward establishing a Jewish state in Palestine, helping refugees find their way to the earliest settlements in that nation, raising funds, and especially—in Rose's case—helping build what she saw as pinnacle evidence of emergent nationhood: hospitals.

The idea of their own family faded. In 1934, Franklin Roosevelt took office. His New Deal brought hope for economic recovery. For Jews, though, Roosevelt's arrival was overshadowed by Hitler's election to the German chancellorship a few months earlier. The world was still in chaos, but November might have been the one

---

*Rose died just before I graduated college. I visited her in the hospital, and she clutched my hand. I didn't know about Teddy then.

time that year when life in New York seemed normal: A welcome heat wave brought summer back, even as autumn was supposed to be ending; Fats Waller scored a huge radio hit with "Honeysuckle Rose"; and one of the fastest-selling books in the city was *A Field Guide to the Birds*, a slim text written by Roger Tory Peterson, a painter and naturalist associated with one of the New York bird clubs.

My father isn't sure how his parents were getting along then, but it was earlier in 1934 that Rose did something audacious: She returned to Nazi-dominated Austria and retrieved her sister and parents. Perhaps it was because the mission was so dangerous, or perhaps it was something else, but when she got back to New York, Rose and Morris seemed to lift themselves out of the sadness they'd felt since losing Teddy. Just before the new year, Rose found out she was pregnant again.

This time, no name was chosen in advance; they didn't dare hope. Besides, there was work to be done. Rose continued with Hadassah, writing the group's newsletter. My grandfather had settled in at Metropolitan Life's Long Island City district office—a Queens landmark built to resemble, on a smaller scale, the company's deco skyscraper in midtown. By spring 1935, Rose had been advised to take to bed, to remain as still and quiet as possible. Her sister Leonie's arrival from Austria couldn't have been more fortuitous: She ran the household while Rose waited.

On August 13, 1935, Rose delivered a healthy baby. At the same time, in Germany, Hitler and his aides were drafting what would become known as the "Nuremburg Laws," created to "preserve the purity of German blood." The new regulations stripped Jews of citizenship, of employment. The Austrian renaissance was finally, completely halted. And from that day, no direct kin to that newborn—they named him Richard—would arrive from Europe.

The baby was the first of a new generation. His duty would be to honor, by his success, those who'd been unable to follow him.

A PICTURE OF MY FATHER AT AGE TWO used to sit in my grandparents' house, on a small writing desk also decorated by a photograph of Herzl and a commemorative medallion, about the size of a soup-can lid, that my grandfather received after completing fifty years with Metropolitan Life. With flowing, blond curls, Dad looks, as nearly everyone in my family used to joke, "like Shirley Temple." Rose, Morris, Leonie, and their fair-haired, blue-eyed two-year-old moved, in 1940, to Kew Gardens Hills, a new neighborhood of redbrick row houses attached to each other in blocks of four, south of Main Street.

My father doesn't remember the exact moment he became aware of the sorrow that gripped the world during his early boyhood. His recollections are fragmentary: people staying in his house, speaking odd languages—refugees who my grandparents housed. There were always strangers; planes flew overhead, and sometimes they'd take cover for air-raid drills. At the World's Fair, Rose and Morris made sure Richard saw the science exhibits, and that he knew this was all part of the training for his medical career. At four, he was too young to perceive it, but by grade school, my dad says, "I knew what my parents wanted me to become."

Going into the woods wasn't, at first, an act of rebellion. It was just play, fighting imaginary Nazis in the trees or hunting for a mysterious creature known as the "swamp tiger." The woods were just the woods, and the animals in it were just animals. Until the Brown Thrasher.

"The bird was so interesting," Dad recalls. Interesting enough for him to go back every day. Interesting enough for him to want to find its name.

My father pedaled home from the House of the Weeping Beech. Brown Thrasher. Perfectly descriptive. Almost exciting. What were the other birds called? He was thinking about this as he rolled down the alley and leaned his bike against the garage. There were people on the patio above. They were smoking, talking. The farms and forests where Moishe Koppel had tended horses and seen mockingbirds were stolen away, forbidden by history. There could be no return. There could hardly be memory.

Richard climbed the narrow staircase. He sat at the broad oak desk his father had built for him and opened up a notebook. On a blank sheet, across the top, in fountain pen, he wrote:

Birds

He thought about the birds he'd already seen. Should he include the ones he hadn't officially watched—the common sparrows and robins—but could now identify? It was an important decision, he felt. The best way to go about it was to look through the book the bird club had loaned him and see how many others he could remember. By the time he was finished, he'd written down twenty-four names. The first twenty-three were birds he knew he'd seen in the past. So the Brown Thrasher—the bird that sparked his interest—came after that. It was a meticulous start to a lifetime devoted to a most meticulous activity. Brown Thrasher, number 24.

Thousands to go.

CHAPTER TWO

WHY BIRDS?

❝ *In 1949 I saw the European Goldfinch in Massapequa, Long Island. It had been established there since 1910, and had been introduced to the United States in 1878. The earliest large populations were found in New Jersey, but Allan Cruickshank noted in his guide,* Birds Around New York City, *that there were considerable numbers where I saw it. Sometime in the 1960s or 1970s, the goldfinch disappeared from the region, and occasional sightings since then are probably attributable to escaped caged birds.*❞

—European Goldfinch (*Carduelis carduelis*),
May 14, 1949, Massapequa, New York, #208.

IT IS A COLD DAY, and small boats bob on Little Neck Bay, a tiny inlet that juts south at the edge of northeast Queens. Richard walks toward the water, through a forest of beech and oak. The woodland gives way to a vast marsh of reeds and cattails, then a tiny beach, where horseshoe crabs emerge onto the sand.

It is November 1948, and Dad is just past his thirteenth birthday. The waters surrounding what was then called the Bayside Woods are filled with birds: ducks and gulls, sandpipers darting in and out of the gentle surf. Members of the Queens County Bird Club are pointing out different species to the young prodigy accompanying them. Richard raises his binoculars, challenging himself to spot birds as quickly as they can.

RICHARD IMPROVED QUICKLY. He'd always been fascinated by the sky: the World War II planes; stars; even butterflies (he gave up on that, he says, because he felt bad having to catch and pin the small insects). In the years following the war, Long Island began to open, and a teenager with a bicycle could, without too much trouble, find himself at some fairly wild locations. Richard and his friend Mike Fitzgerald quickly enlisted Morris, who'd drive out to Jones Beach or the Rockaways, where he'd patiently sit for hours behind the wheel of his black Chevrolet as the boys wandered the shoreline, searching for seabirds. (My grandfather always had mixed reactions to Dad's birding—on one hand, he didn't want it to get out of hand, to become more than a hobby; on the other, he enjoyed the country excursions the pursuit required.)

Richard was also free to bird, to read about birds, to make lists of the birds he saw because other topics occupied Morris's and Rose's existence. In 1947 and 1948, the newly formed United Nations had as its headquarters not the gleaming, landmark skyscraper that now towers above New York's East Side, but a smaller facility, right in Flushing Meadows Park—not far from the old World's Fair site, not far from where Dad had seen his Brown Thrasher. The organization was created with many ideals in mind, but the one that most occupied the thoughts of my grandparents was "the Jewish Question." Did the people who'd suffered at the hands of the Nazis deserve a homeland? If so, where would that be? Though other places were considered—Saskatchewan, parts of South America—Rose and Morris, and most other Jews, believed that the nation should spring from the Middle East, cut from their biblical homeland in the areas known today as Jordan and Palestine. It was this cause to which my grandparents devoted their lives, so much so that the moment turns both poignant and volatile as Dad describes my grandfather's willingness to wait in the car on those weekend excursions, back when the pursuit of birds was just a childhood diversion: "He was a good father," Dad insists, his voice trembling. But another emotion quickly surfaces: "What did their Zionism mean to me?" Dad repeats the question, slowly, before answering. "It meant that my mother would get Hadassah [the women's Zionist organization] phone calls during dinner. The food would get cold, and we'd never eat together," he says.

I ask Dad how he felt when my grandmother devoted her life to the cause of a Jewish homeland. He answers curtly, in a way that begs for more information but also seems to shut the door on further discourse: "Israel," he says, "was more important to my mother than I was."

IN THE SUMMER, MY GRANDPARENTS WOULD ALWAYS visit a small hotel in the Catskills. Traditionally, these places were seen as part of the semi-absurd, semi-romantic borscht belt phenomenon—where Jewish comics and musicians entertained in a style originating somewhere between the shtetl and the Statue of Liberty. My grandparents had no time for such merriment; Maud's Summer-Ray, their chosen resort, was a place for the serious-minded. An old postcard I have of the place depicts a pleasant-looking structure, sort of a largish country home, tucked into the woods. On the back, various diversions are promised: Maud's is "the ideal place for your vacation, equipped with all modern improvements including a gymnastic outfit, tennis courts, bathing, fishing, and dancing pavilion on premises." The only sign that this place is a different species from its better-known neighbors is the final sentence: "Special accommodations for vegetarians."

Maud's welcomed folks with different ideas. In an essay called "Borscht Belt Red," historian Louis Proyect notes: "When people think about leftist resorts, three names typically come to mind— Maud's Summer-Ray, Chester's Zunbarg, and Arrowhead Lodge." Maud's guest lists, Proyect continues, included "socialists, communists, and Trotskyites." From my father's recollection, Maud's seems a bit more dour than even its competition in the ideological resort category; the Zunbarg often featured concerts by politically active entertainers, including Woody Guthrie and Paul Robeson. At Maud's, dance pavilion notwithstanding, Dad remembers most of the time being occupied by chess matches.

I was surprised that Maud's turned out to be a tough topic to discuss with Dad. "Don't write about my parents going there," he said at first. I learned later that Proyect experienced similar hesitation: "I started asking around to see if any old-timers wanted to be interviewed in relation to their radical past. They were still too frightened." I wondered whether Rose and Morris had been communists as well as Zionists. Dad denied it vehemently: "It was a left-wing hotel filled with communists and fellow travelers, but my parents were neither." So, what drew them to Maud's? "They just liked it," Dad replied.

But why? Dad can't say, won't remember. His key recollection of Maud's is, of course, birds: The environment was just far enough removed from the seaside ecosystem of Queens to yield several new species. Once more, the sky provided escape from a stern interior. During the summer of 1947, Dad netted five new species at Maud's. They're marked in his life list as occurring in Port Jervis, the nearest Catskill community. When I passed through there recently, the woods and the birds were still there in large numbers, but nobody I spoke to could tell me where Maud's once stood; no one even remembered it.

THE QUEENS I GREW UP IN WAS FAR LESS WILD. The rural landscape had nearly vanished. An expressway bisected the Flushing Meadows, turning it into Flushing Meadows Park. I spent plenty of time there as a teenager, but it was watching baseball games at Shea Stadium, which had been built right on top of Dad's favorite birding area in 1964.

But pieces of the Bayside Woods still remained—just a few. I know because I grew up right across the bay from them; I didn't know, then, that the scant stands of trees that lined Little Neck Bay—a thin strip of green between the waterfront and the Cross Island Parkway, the city's last major highway project to be completed, which I could see from my bedroom window—had been Dad's wonderland, a place even more magical than the Flushing Meadows.

The forests of Bayside, Dad recalls, "were magnificent."

Through the late 1940s, Dad visited the Bayside Woods over and over, pedaling his Rollfast bike or taking the Q12 bus down Northern Boulevard. The place fixed itself in his mind, especially during spring and fall migration, when the bay was covered with birds: ducks, heron, and teal, sometimes floating peacefully and other times exhausted, attempting to regain their energy after what birders call a "fallout," when a storm forces flock after flock of northward- or southward-bound avifauna toward land. As Dad grew up, the Bayside Woods dwindled in reality. But they idealized in Dad's subconscious.

It is no wonder that, as an adult, raising a family, Dad's first major decision was to move us there. We'd live in his dreamland. But his dreams would be forced in another direction.

THERE IS A PART OF THE BRONX, the borough that rises just across Little Neck Bay, where you can recapture New York's pre-urban landscape, even today. Follow the highways west, then north, and you'll reach the Bronx River Parkway. Despite the name, you might not notice that it winds along the banks of a waterway.

The Bronx River begins at Westchester County's Davis Brook,

then meanders mostly through rusty industrial complexes and scrap yards before it empties into the East River, flowing into Long Island Sound. But there is one spot where the river changes character, making such a startling transformation that it seems nearly miraculous. Deep, nearly hidden, within the Bronx Botanical Gardens, a place that mostly comprises manicured flora amid pavilions and greenhouses, sits New York's last remaining patch of precolonial forest.

If you bird here, you'll walk amid oak and hemlock. You might see several warblers that were common in the 1940s—there are over forty species of this bird found in the eastern United States, and identifying them can be quite difficult; it's one of the skills that separates an advanced birder from a backyard hobbyist. Dad visited here with an older birder on several occasions; they'd find each other in the woods by mimicking the alliterative call of a bobwhite (like the cuckoo or Brazil's Screaming Piha, the bird's song spells its name). On his first visit to the Botanical Gardens, which were then called Bronx Park, Dad saw the Pine Warbler (yellow-breasted, with white wing bars), the Parula Warbler (yellow-breasted, with white wing bars, but with a gray-blue head), and the Canada Warbler (yellow breasted, gray-blue head and back, but with black markings on its neck). A bird Dad never saw there that you would almost certainly see today is the Red-Bellied Woodpecker, a new (and noisy) arrival to the Northeast. The larger variety has been extending its range from the South for several decades now, especially as hemlock trees, victims of a blight, begin to vanish, and are themselves replaced by other species that the Red-bellied Woodpecker typically favors as habitat. (Dad's first Red-Belly was seen in the South in 1962; I was an infant, and he and my mother were passing through South Carolina on the way to Florida. Today, there are plenty of the species in his Long Island backyard.)

The constant ebb and flow of ecosystems, linked to changes in nature both organic and man-made, is part of the appeal of listing—whether you're counting birds, or butterflies, or orchids, or spiders. Everything newly found or recently departed must be named and tallied. Less obvious is that these tidal movements—decline, abundance, migration—also mimic the things we humans prize most, the currents that form the framework for our own definition, if not of life, then of living.

THE SWAMPS, WOODS, AND WETLANDS OF MID-CENTURY NEW YORK didn't just give birth to Dad's birding habit. They sired the activity itself, turning it from an activity for the educated elite into an almost gritty, urban phenomenon: a sport. The transformation of bird observation began in the late 1920s with four boys, all living in the Bronx. None were particularly well off. Most had immigrant parents who worked long hours, usually in Manhattan, in factories and restaurants, as small merchants and day laborers. Left to themselves, the boys roamed freely through the neighborhoods, along the shoreline, and especially in the garbage dump at Hunt's Point, where they'd climb mounds of trash, searching for anything valuable. But they found something else, every time they went exploring: birds. They soon began to compete with each other, testing to see who could come up with the quickest identifications, and becoming very exclusive in the process: To join their Bronx Bird Club, you had to be a top birder, and from the borough.

WISE-MOUTHED TEENAGERS FROM THE BRONX don't just show up at the American Museum of Natural History and tell the assembled and generally well-heeled ornithologists and birders of the New

York metropolitan area (at the museum for a meeting of the Linnaean Society, then and now the city's premier ornithological organization) that you've seen this rare species or that one, just as you can't just say you've seen six or seven thousand birds. The sport relies primarily on the honor system, along with what might best be described as impromptu interrogation. You'd be asked to say exactly what you saw, where, and to provide key details: How did it fly? What songs did it sing? How big was it? Some of the questions are designed to trip up an amateur; others are just to test knowledge. (Many of today's competitive birding events are contested by teams; judges verify tallies by questioning each team member individually. In Big Listing, the test is a bit less formal: Since you have to go to many remote places to see thousands of birds, you usually need to hire an ornithologist-guide or join an organized trip. Your rivals will be along, too, and they'll be watching to make sure you're doing the work. Slip up, exaggerate a sighting, or fabricate—claiming birds that absolutely don't appear in the habitats you visit—and you're blacklisted, out of the game forever.)

The boys of the Bronx Club, now numbering nine, had an especially formidable inquisitor. Years before, Ludlow Griscom had helped start the movement that led birding away from guns—and carcasses—as primary identification tools. By the 1920s, Griscom had become the guru of New York's birding elite. He was assistant curator for birds at the American Museum of Natural History and author of *Birds of the New York City Region,* a 1923 book that listed the best places to find local species. Griscom was what has since become a rarity in the ornithological world: a respected scientist and a fanatic counter. Griscom repeatedly set records for the most birds seen in a single year in the metropolitan area, and he kept detailed files that extended beyond birds—he was fond, as many birders are, of logging weather records. And he couldn't stop. In 1941, when his annual count first topped three hundred, he declared he'd had enough: "I trust this will be written up as a record of a way of life and a technique of bird study." For his part, Griscom vowed, "I will never again try to duplicate 1941."

At least until 1946, when he saw 307 birds. He continued to not try to duplicate and surpass his records, somehow managing to do so anyway until the 1950s. (When my father's birding became over-sized, he said he'd stop, as well: At five thousand. At six thousand. At seven thousand.)

THE PRODIGY BIRDER, the lonely boy who finds himself hypnotized by the avian world, wasn't a new phenomenon when the Bronx teenagers turned it into a more raucous, urbanized, and competitive phenomenon. Though you wouldn't know it by his rather stodgy and rarified image, America's most important early birder fell into the category that would eventually snare my dad. Fougère Rabin was born in Haiti in 1785. Rabin's mother was a Creole slave; his father was a French slave trader. Rabin's mother died when Fougère was six months old, leaving the boy to be raised by relatives. Prospects were hardly optimistic. It took four years for Fougère's father to finally acknowledge paternity; the boy then moved to France and was baptized. "Legitimacy" couldn't change the olive color of Fougère's skin, but it could provide him with a new name: Jean-Jacques Fougère Audubon.

Even then, the plot would seem to lead only to a better life on the continent. How could a teenage Frenchman, living in an era when being of mixed race was considered a sign of inferiority, become the father of American wildlife study? Again, it was timing as much as anything else. A few months after Jean-Jacques's religious initiation, France was swept by revolution. As the fighting raged, more and more young French citizens were called up for military service. At age eleven, Audubon began naval training. It was practically a death sentence, and the young man's father sent his son to the United States, ostensibly to manage property the family owned in Pennsylvania.

Far from the reach of fighting and conscription, the teenage Audubon encountered, in Pennsylvania, something he'd never imagined. It is also something many of us today can't conjure: the vast woods of the pre-agricultural American northeast. Arboreal Pennsylvania was dense with hemlock, pine, and spruce, and brimming with wildlife: turkey, bald eagle, mountain lions, and wolves. Audubon's job, as a planter, was to tame that landscape, to banish the dark groves.

He didn't. Instead, Audubon—by then in his twenties, with a wife and child—preferred to develop a hobby he'd taken up during an 1803 visit to France. There, he'd begun to make pencil sketches of birds. Back in the wild country, Audubon began to paint, using a remarkable and novel technique: He'd shoot his subjects and then pose them in lifelike positions on wire skeletons.

The early Audubon work was a sensation. Alexander Wilson— who published the nine-volume *American Ornithology* in 1808— praised the young painter (who was grateful for the compliment, but privately derided Wilson's paintings as stiff and unnatural). Even so, Audubon still felt an obligation to succeed in the family's farming business, or at least some business. He found this difficult to accomplish. He moved his family around the young nation, painting only as a hobby and failing to earn any sort of living. Then, in 1819, bottom fell out. The United States was in a depression. Audubon's daughter, Rose, died. Deeply in debt, Audubon declared bankruptcy and served a brief term in debtor's prison. When he was released, the family moved west, settling in the then-frontier town of Cincinnati.

The humbling seemed to provide Audubon with the impetus to move forward on his true ambition (there was little else left for him to do). Earning his living as a taxidermist and painting on the side, Audubon grew more and more confident. As with most who are afflicted with avian obsession, he set a grandiose goal: He'd paint every bird species in America. For the next five years, Audubon wandered. The resulting watercolors were absolutely revolutionary: natural-looking, unposed, and painted with scrupulous attention to accuracy. Audubon supported himself by selling subscriptions—advance reservations—to the book he intended to ultimately produce, which he'd determined would be called *Birds of America.**

Audubon had no publisher. He painted, sent samples, sold subscriptions, and waited. Nothing. The work was good, but life was almost impossibly hard. Finally, in 1826, Audubon placed *Birds of America* with a Scottish press. It took another thirteen years to complete the project, during which time Audubon continued to work as a taxidermist and sell advance copies of his opus. The first printing of Audubon's book, in 1839, contained 435 color plates. The images were astounding. Until then, other painters and naturalists had paid attention to birds, even captured their likenesses. But this was the first time so many stunning and realistic images of birds were available to the general public, complete with detailed, firsthand species descriptions. Audubon's sumptuous color

---

*Birds of America is an incredibly popular book title. Over fifty authors have published volumes using that name. But Audubon's is still the most popular, available today in versions ranging from costly folios of glossy prints to functional and inexpensive reprints.

and precision set a standard for wildlife portraiture that continued through the 1930s, when another young bird painter, Roger Tory Peterson, invented a simplified method of bird representation, designed not for study but for instant field identification. But even with the advent of the field guide, photography, and hundreds of other avian artists that followed, Audubon remains ascendant, the indispensable pioneer.

AS WITH STARS AND SNOWFLAKES, there's always one more bird to tally. Counting birds is like attempting to calculate the highest number; if you can reach a centillion (a one with six hundred zeroes after it, the highest "known" integer), you can certainly reach a centillion and one. The number of known bird species on earth when Dad began was about eight thousand; today, that number is on the verge of surpassing ten thousand, and climbing.

Nobody can count everything. But you can try, even while knowing that the number that equals everything is, itself, not fixed. You've found, in that case, a list that stretches into the future. It has no end. But the listing game does have winners. With Ludlow Griscom taking on the role of mentor, the boys from the Bronx Bird Club set out—and usually managed—to beat their adult rivals at such censusing events as Christmas tallies and the twenty-four-hour counting marathons known as Big Days. They knew the best spots, had the most stamina, and acted with the unity of a real team.

The Bronx birders were all good, but the group definitely had a star: He was the first—and only—member of the group admitted without having origins in the borough. The skinny nineteen-year-old came from upstate New York and was attending school in Manhattan. He was quiet, nearly bashful, and in love with birding.

The teens subjected the newcomer to a withering interrogation, just as Griscom had done when they'd first appeared at the Linnaean Society with their sighting records: Where did you see it? How did it fly? How big was it? Are you *sure*? They headed into the field, where their guest identified dozens of species at lightning speed. One club member put it simply: "Roger Peterson," he said, "was a better birder than any of us."

Many of the original members of the Bronx club had gone on to prominent careers in science by the time Dad arrived. Was Dad on a par with them? In May 1949, the Bronx squad called Dad with an invitation: He was to join their team for a Big Day in the city's outer boroughs. It didn't matter that he was from Queens. The group saw over one hundred birds from dawn to dusk.

ROGER TORY PETERSON WAS A BIRD PAINTER, but his work is so stylistically different from Audubon's that—looking at the reproductions of his oils in Dad's 1942 edition of *A Field Guide to the Birds*—you might hardly notice that Peterson, like Audubon, committed bird images to canvas. Audubon's magnificent scene-setting and classical perspective are completely absent. Peterson's images are simple, sparse. They're also revolutionary.

Try to identify a bird. Ask a deceptively simple question: What bird is that?

It seems appropriate, to answer that question, that we visit Flushing Meadows Park. For the sake of argument, let's say it's around Memorial Day. The particular glade where Dad saw his first bird is gone, but, surprisingly, as we pick our way around the park's public structures, we arrive at a pair of surprisingly extant lakes, undisturbed remnants of the park's prewar wetlands. As we approach, we'll go over Peterson's most subtle innovation: the way he arranged the birds in his book. Until Peterson, nature texts listed birds in "systematic" order—by scientific family. This was inconvenient, since birds don't necessarily appear in the wild according to human-imposed taxa. Peterson's notion was to order birds in what he called "visual categories." Birds that looked like each other would be placed near each other so watchers could quickly tell the difference between them.

A few feet from the lake, we see a small group of brown birds. They're hopping in the trees. That's the first clue. These birds aren't water-borne or chicken-like. What Peterson category do they fit? They don't seem to be hawks. The key is what the birds are doing: branch-sitting (officially, perching or passerine) birds are one of the Peterson types. We open the book to the section devoted to passerines, and we're quickly presented with an array of species: birds like the Brown Thrasher, as well as mockingbirds, wrens, finches, and warblers.

Which is our bird? Peterson offers several ways to figure it out. Size is important. Beak shape and color are also crucial. But our judgment is most aided by Peterson's painted illustrations. By creating artwork that was unadorned, almost generic in its simplicity, Peterson was able to highlight key features that distinguished one bird from another. These "field marks" were slightly exaggerated in each image, and were pointed out by thin, printed arrows. By confirming (through the binoculars) whether these easy-to-spot markings existed, an amateur could quickly narrow his guess down to the most likely candidates.

Peterson's illustrations are so simple they serve little documentary purpose. Instead, they possess a kind of meta-realism that sums up the parts of an individual species, and in doing so creates a "perfect bird" that can't possibly exist in the wild, but which functions as a visual template for accurate spotting. Peterson took bird identification away from the high priests of the laboratory and museum and offered it to an urban public that was interested in nature, but knew little about it firsthand. His method was to identify a bird from just a fleeting glimpse, which was often all you could get; Peterson made these glances satisfying. They were fast-paced, like city life; the speed made the activity feel more competitive and exciting.

Back to Flushing Meadows. The illustrations in the passerine section distinguish these birds by their large eyes and slim bills, but especially by their spotted breasts and brown backs. We quickly narrow our choices down to five—all thrushes that, like the common robin, we note, resemble each other. Which to pick? There are several ways to zero in on the correct answer. First, the Peterson guide includes range information, telling which birds are found where, and during what time of year (in early editions, this information was presented textually; color-coded maps were a later addition). Of the five birds, according to Peterson, only the Hermit Thrush and the Wood Thrush are regularly found in the northeastern United States in the month of May. Another possibility, Swainson's Thrush, is rarer. Which is it? Again, narrow the choices. If you can hear the birds singing, you might be able to distinguish them using Peterson's mnemonic sound transcriptions (the Hermit Thrush, Peterson said, makes a "scolding *tuk-tuk-tuk*," while the Wood Thrush's call is more like a "rapid *pip-pip-pip*"). But the field markings are the best method of telling them apart. Arrows point to the strongly spotted breast of the Wood Thrush; the Hermit Thrush has fewer spots and less red; the Swainson's Thrush has an eye ring, something neither of the other candidates possesses.

The real contest is in the final conclusion. Peterson gets the average watcher more than halfway there. He brings us to the brink of naming—as if he's driven a golf ball perfectly to the green, but left the most satisfying and precise part, making the putt, to his readers.

ROGER TORY PETERSON's work created a world booming with birders: "Bird clubs that numbered a hundred members 25 years ago," Peterson wrote in *Birds of America*, a 1948 memoir, "now have more than 1,000 . . . as a lecturer, I have been astonished at the sizes of the audiences that filled the halls." Eighteen hundred people turned out to hear Peterson in Daytona Beach, Florida; fifteen hundred arrived in Kansas City. Annual attendance for the Peterson lecture circuit, as estimated by its sponsor, the National Audubon Society, was estimated at over a million.

Peterson veered between giddy approval and slight unease with the mania for pure counting he seemed to have launched. (This came even as Peterson carefully tallied attendance figures for his own speeches; another Peterson project was to calculate the total number of birds in the United States. His final estimate, arrived at by what he described as "simple mathematics," was exactly 7,612,866,560.)

Listing wasn't the pinnacle of birding to Peterson. He imagined a progression from looker to lister to scientist. The final phases would arrive when the ability to tally was exhausted, allowing true curiosity to emerge. This is a possible scenario, but for many birders, the final two elements either reverse or live in parallel. There's little doubt that many of today's Big Listers possess scientific knowledge. But there are an equal number who know little, care only about the numbers, and rely on the ornithologists who accompany them to make the actual identification. (Dad falls into the dual category of true birders and obsessive listers, with skills developed on both ends of the pastime.)

Peterson had his own opinions regarding the reasons for birding's growing popularity. Referring to its emergence at the dawn of atomic warfare, he said, "Life is getting more complicated, but it seems the more artificially complex man's affairs become, the more he yearns for the fundamentals, the things of earth." The "boom in birds," Peterson concluded, "seems to be an antidote for the pressures and artificialities of the modern world."

From Peterson's 1948 perspective, this makes sense; it is the traditional "nature as remedy" idea that inspired Thoreau, John Muir, and Walt Whitman. But in retrospect, I'm not so sure birding's popularity rose because it cured any inherent illness in the modern world. Rather, it seems to me that listing is one of the most earth-friendly examples of manifest destiny—it doesn't solve the problems of modern life, it brings a measure of control to them. Yes, birding was (and is) an antidote, but its efficacy comes not by providing a sylvan counterbalance to that uncertainty, but by adding to a chaotic world an element of power and control. Counting birds is an assertive way for the average person to gain mastery over nature. A heating-up of the Cold War could have ended the world in a flash. That danger is gone, but birders now race against a different kind of clock: the dwindling of wildlife habitats. Amid such insecurities, to see every bird could be a true comfort—and a true calling.

ONE THING YOU'LL NOTICE ABOUT SERIOUS BIRDERS is that they don't carry field guides around, at least not in areas where they're familiar with the avifauna. The bird-obsessed usually have remarkable memories, knowing—usually through the Peterson field markings, which they've absorbed, early on—hundreds of local species by sight, song, or behavior. Dad knew what most of New York's birds looked like by his early teens. His mission was to find them and mark them off. So the book that is most important is a tattered volume that still sits on a metal shelf in his "bird room," the part of his house that's filled with almost six decades' worth of reference volumes, notebooks, and maps, along with one taxidermied Great Horned Owl and a bronze plaque of Theodore Roosevelt. That book, written by another Bronx club member, Allan Cruickshank, was my dad's birding bible.

Allan Cruickshank's *Birds Around New York City*, published in 1941, was a follow-up volume to Ludlow Griscom's 1920s guide. It didn't offer any help identifying birds, but it was indispensable in finding them—and, therefore, so much more useful to the count. The book began with explanations of seasonal migrations and what different birds might be found at different times of the year; then, it listed every species in the area—often with the exact spots birders might find them. "I knew that book by heart," my dad says. "Month by month, I used it."

THERE'S NO HINT OF PRIDE or the seductiveness of the chase in Dad's copy of Cruickshank. Instead, you see the footprints of a boy, approaching adulthood, who loves his hobby. The preciousness of the document and what it represents are evident only when I ask Dad if I can borrow the book.

"No," he says. "I can't let you do that."

"Can I make a copy of it?"

Dad allows that, but to safeguard his treasure, he insists on accompanying me to the copy shop—a forty-mile drive from his house. Dad's book is filled with check marks and date records: the Brown Thrasher, marked retroactively—Flushing, Summer 1947 (he bought the book in late 1947)—or 1948's Red-breasted Merganser, which Cruickshank described as "a bird of the ocean, the Sound, and the larger bays." Sure enough, Dad saw it where the Atlantic meets the farthest reaches of Queens—you've flown over the exact spot if you've ever landed at Kennedy Airport—"Dec 1948 Rockaway Pt."

Plain check marks don't distinguish one moment from the next. How to read between those few angular lines? By understanding that the apparent lack of ecstasy is a clue to a growing obsession. When counting birds, once the tick mark is earned, the bird itself hardly matters. The job is done. The next "target" bird (to use the sport's vocabulary) is waiting.

How birders count varies as well. Some share their tallies, publishing them online or registering them with birding organizations. Some don't. For Dad, birding has always been escapist, mostly solitary. He's never felt a need to officially compare his numbers with anyone else's. This doesn't mean he's not aware of his rivals. It's just that obsession, in his case—and in many others—has been primarily used to construct a private world.

Even so, if to list is to count, you can't truly go it alone, no matter how hard you try to imagine it's just you, your binoculars, and the birds. Why? Because the list isn't a list of birds—it's a list of bird names. God may or may not have created the hawks and doves, but people decided what to call them. People—other birders, ornithologists, guides, friends, daughters, and sons—know what you're doing; they know you're tallying things we have admired enough to classify, paint, and give names to.

Do the birds care, or know? On some level, perhaps, since

species identification primarily involves choosing a reproductive partner. But the list? That's exclusively human.

AT THE END OF HIS FIRST DAY in the Bayside Woods, Dad counted up the new check marks in his copy of Cruickshank. He'd seen dozens of birds, and four lifers (birder slang for a first-time encounter). On the water, he saw three new species—Red-throated Loon, Common Goldeneye, and Bufflehead Duck. Toward the end of the day, he saw a fourth: a Red-tailed Hawk, soaring above the bay. New York City was then filled with raptors like this—predators like the hawk, which patrolled the marshlands; and Peregrine Falcons, which quickly adapted to the urban habitat that Manhattan became, roosting on skyscraper ledges and sconces, diving toward busy sidewalks for pigeons. At the end of the day, Dad's life total was nearing one hundred.

The game had begun.

CHAPTER THREE

THE GREATEST YEAR

" *This was the first really rare bird that I found on my own. It was May 1, 1949. I had been birding virtually every weekend day that year. My father drove me to Jones Beach that morning, and we visited the Tobay Sanctuary, a freshwater pond on the north side of the highway between Jones Beach and Gilgo Beach. We parked in the rear, and I walked west, toward the pond. North of the trail was a salt marsh with lots of relatively high bayberry and poison ivy thickets. There, perched atop a shrub, was a Louisiana Heron (now called Tricolored Heron). I knew what it was immediately because of its distinctive color pattern and very snaky neck. I also knew that it was very rare. (There were nine Long Island records for the century as of the publication of Cruickshank's* Birds Around New York City *in 1942.) Although I had seen some uncommon birds that year, this was the rarest, by far, and I found it on my own."*

—Louisiana (Tricolored) Heron (*Egretta tricolor*),
May 1, 1949, Jones Beach, New York, #178.

R ICHARD'S SIGHTING OF THE LOUISIANA HERON was so unusual that it could not be taken at face value, even though the
bird—standing over two feet tall, with a blue-gray back and a white
belly—is impossible to miss. It was beyond exciting, and the boy
knew what he had to do: Tell the world (which, for a young birder,
meant announcing the discovery at the next meeting of the Linnaean Society).

The assembled elite of New York's birding community regarded
Richard's report with rigorous skepticism, as Ludlow Griscom had
two decades earlier, when the Bronx club members announced
their presence. The most intimidating questioner was John Elliot,
who wrote the weekly birding column in the *Long Island Press*.

"How big was it? What color? Describe the plumage!"

Dad aced it. He knew what he was seeing. It turned out that the
sighting was the first in a gradual shift in the Louisiana Heron's status: The bird had begun moving north, and by 1964, it was breeding in New Jersey—and can now be seen quite often during the
summer at the marshes and wetlands surrounding New York City.

What made the Louisiana Heron so wonderful?

Dad doesn't hesitate: "It was the first one," he says, "that was truly mine."

As the 1940s came to a close, Richard's parents became increasingly worried about with his birding. The pressure was subtle, but intense. When he mentioned ornithology as a career, he recalls it as the only time his mother seemed to be actually interested in what he was thinking—if only to insist that his ideas were foolish. Richard was a star at math, biology, and chemistry, receiving frequent awards and honors. Today, parents might encourage a child so gifted to choose his own path. But for a Jewish teenager in postwar New York, such talents had to be put to a single, noble use: "You'll be a doctor," Rose said. "A great doctor." (I can easily envision the intensity of my grandmother's urgings: I remember her not so much as a stern woman, but as an intellectually potent one, who read constantly; refused to pull punches when she challenged her young grandchildren to Scrabble; and saw herself as a proud Viennese, even decades after she'd left the city of Freud and Goethe. I recall my grandfather as a much quieter man, who always had a roll of peppermints to hand out to my brother and me. Though Rose remained intense, she was tremendously sorrowful after my parents divorced; on our weekend visits and rare sleepovers, she made sure we felt that we were absolutely at home and taken care of, whether it was showing me how to write with a fountain pen or carefully folding the *New York Times*' television section to the Saturday-morning cartoons she'd always watch with us.)

My father had his bar mitzvah in June 1948. That was the year he truly began listing, and it was less than one year after the United Nations, at its original headquarters in Flushing Meadows, not far from where Dad had seen his Brown Thrasher, voted to partition Palestine, creating Israel. It was a triumphant time for Zionists, especially the New York community, where anxious crowds broke into spontaneous cheers and traditional dances when the results of the vote were announced. (The Zionist passion my grandparents held was all-consuming; I remember being given blue-and-white Hadassah collection boxes. Going door to door in my Protestant/ Catholic neighborhood for such donations was a profoundly isolating and absolutely unproductive experience, but even returning with a few pennies was met with approval from Rose and Morris; they were profoundly thrifty people, and Dad has bitter memories of being forced to eat rotten food—especially eggs, which to this day he can't stomach—in order to save a bit for the Zionist cause.)

The United Nations decreed that the new partition would become official just around the time of my father's thirteenth birthday. But even before that, cause for celebration diminished. In Palestine, riots broke out, with casualties reaching the thousands on both sides. Through the winter of 1948 and the following spring, negotiations to "save" the partition agreement took place; these talks were held against a backdrop of increasingly severe guerilla fighting and displacement of people who'd lived in the region for centuries. Bloodshed—including several horrific massacres—increased on both sides. My grandparents were more and more preoccupied: "They'd been so happy when Israel was created," Dad recalls, "but became more and more overwhelmed with worry." On May 14, 1948, Israel declared "independence" (*existence* is probably a better word). Arab armies invaded immediately. The first full-scale war in the modern Middle East had begun.

During the summer leading up to my father's coming-of-age celebration, birds again became a constant, a refuge; on a personal level, they provided a more visceral thrill than the aggressive studies his parents encouraged him to undertake. Dad worked hard, and was always at the top of his class in math and science. Birds were an escape, a way to leave the house, a way to explore, safely, a world that during my father's lifetime had seen a cascade of horrific events. Now, as Dad's own manhood was about to be confirmed, the dream my grandparents had put ahead of their child's future appeared to be crumbling. Assam Pasha, secretary of the Arab League, called for the fight against Jews to be a "war of extermination." Three years after the liberation of Auschwitz, genocide was again seen—at least by some—as an acceptable "solution" to, using the then-in-vogue shorthand for the post-Holocaust issues that faced the world, "the Jewish Question." For my grandparents and their Zionist comrades, this was an unearthing of demons that had seemed, however briefly, to have been put to rest. The existence of Israel—and, by extension, the Jewish people—again appeared tenuous. David Ben-Gurion, Israel's first president, estimated that the new nation, to which the U.S. State Department had strictly prohibited arms sales, had less than a 50 percent chance of survival.*

The day of my father's bar mitzvah, then, was one where anxiety and sadness mixed with joy. What kind of world would Richard inherit? For many Jews, the State Department's neutrality indicated that even America might not be safe. Dad spent most of that autumn searching the woods for birds; his parents were preoccupied and didn't notice. They weren't terribly aware of his hobby, or of the fact that he was beginning to keep a list of the species he'd seen. He didn't make any special announcement when, on Novem-

---

*One of my grandfather's cousins was in Israel at the time, fighting. David Kopel—also a doctor—had been close to Ben-Gurion; he'd been in the running to become the nation's first health minister. When this didn't happen, possibly, I've been told, because of David's violent and intense single-minded commitment to the cause, he vanished into the jungles of Central America. How was he "rediscovered"? By Dad, of course—on a bird-watching trip.

ber 13, after a trip to Valley Stream State Park, he saw his one hundredth species, the Greater Scaup, a compact, yellow-eyed diving duck. Dad continued to bird as the weather got colder. By the end of the year, his life list stood at 126. He was just thirteen years old.

THE FIRST OBSESSED BIRDERS OF THE MODERN ERA actually were doctors. When I tell Dad this—mentioning the names of nineteenth-century ornithologists (like most serious birders, his need to list is supplemented by a compulsion to amass reference materials, and his bird-book collection numbers into the thousands)—he's surprised; he knows these men only as bird folk.

The young doctors of the post–Civil War era figured out a way to use their chosen profession as a means to what they really wanted to do: count birds. The ringleader of the physician-listers was Spencer Fullerton Baird, who'd given up his medical career to become assistant secretary of the Smithsonian Institution. Baird, like most of the birders of that era, measured his obsession not in checkmarks but in collected bird skins and eggs: The sports of ornithology and oology were driven by competition and acquisitional mania. You didn't just get a single carcass or a couple of eggs. The idea was to collect everything you could. (Baird's own cabinet of avifaunal artifacts filled over two railroad boxcars when it was moved, upon his appointment to the Smithsonian, from Boston to Washington.) Baird came up with a nifty scheme that would allow him to send his emissaries—all top birders—to the farthest reaches of the newly expanding United States. He volunteered the services of the Smithsonian to military expeditions that were planning and building the railroad lines that would eventually stretch to the Pacific. Being part of the medical profession was essential: There was little room on such voyages for bird men, but medical assistance was a requirement for the surveying parties. Over a decade, Baird's medical/birding corps collected millions of samples and records, resulting in what would become the continent's first birding checklist, the weightily named *Reports of Explorations and Surveys to Ascertain the Most Practicable and Economical Route for a Railroad from the Mississippi to the Pacific Ocean.* (Listing 738 species, the volume quickly began to be called by the easier-to-utter title *Baird's General Report.* Later, it was issued under a more Audubonesque name: *The Birds of North America.*)

Science was important to the young doctors, but, as today, it was really all about the numbers. Two of Baird's protégés, Elliot Coues and Robert Ridgeway, became such bitter rivals in their quest to out-collect one another that they ultimately forced Baird to chose between the two; the arguably more brilliant, but more difficult, Coues lost.

Just as Roger Tory Peterson's methods popularized birding with the general public, including my father, nearly a century later, so did the lists published by the Smithsonian explorers launch the world's first birding craze. Scientists begat hobbyists begat adventurers, who took more and more risks to best their rivals. Magazines and newspapers whose counterparts today publish the exploits of mountaineers and extreme athletes chronicled the exploits of what were, at the time, considered the most radical of all swashbuckling outdoorsmen: egg collectors. An 1889 article in Newfoundland's *St. John's Evening Telegraph* detailed the exploits of John Cahoon; he'd begun collecting at age fifteen, and within a decade had traveled much of the continent. The newspaper account told of the "Daring Act of an American Ornithologist . . . He Scales a Perpendicular Cliff Three Hundred Feet High. Shuddering Fishermen Lean on Their Oars and Witness the Dangerous Ascent." The article went on to compliment Cahoon on being a "man of splendid nerve power." A few years later, on the very same palisade, Cahoon was searching for raven's eggs when he lost control of his ropes and tumbled to his death; his corpse hung above the waves for several days before it could be retrieved.

Ornithologist and Oologist magazine celebrated the fallen birder as both "a dead shot" and having a "kind and joyous disposition." He was, the eulogy noted, "a typical American collector."

If the risk of personal injury represented a sort of tragic-yet-heroic aspect of the activity, there was an even darker side to collecting's obsessional nature: Birds were killed by the carload. It was thought then that nature could renew avian resources indefinitely. Possessing a single sample of a species was good, but real status came if you gathered a series—three or four dozen carcasses of the same bird. Some ornithologists actually thought that killing as many birds as possible was a sacred duty: Louis Agassiz, founder of Harvard's Museum of Comparative Zoology, brushed off suggestions that his amassed specimens, numbering into the hundreds of thousands, represented a diminishment of nature: "It is with museums as with all living things," he wrote. "What has vitality must grow. When museums cease to grow, their usefulness is on the decline."*

But in the air, the evidence argued otherwise. Majestic birds like the Ivory-billed Woodpecker and the Snowy Egret began to vanish. But no diminishment of species was more powerful than the loss of the Passenger Pigeon. It is almost impossible to describe how many of these birds flew over North America until the

---

*It should be noted that commercial harvesting—the commercial gathering of Snowy Egret feathers for hats, for example—killed far more birds than scientists ever did. Nevertheless, the voraciousness of the academy could hardly have set a good example.

late 1800s; scientists today estimate their population into the billions, some asserting that there were more Passenger Pigeons on this continent than *all other bird species on earth combined.* The decline of the Passenger Pigeon began with the loss of woodland habitat, but the bird's fate, like that of the buffalo, was sealed by a nearly inexplicable frenzy of killing that swept across nearly every corner of the United States through the nineteenth century. The Passenger Pigeon hunt was possibly the nation's most popular sporting pastime; winners of some competitive shoots bagged as many as *thirty thousand* birds in a single day. The final blow came in April 1886, on a single, bloody afternoon. Just one flock of Passenger Pigeons remained, numbering about 250,000 birds. A group of technologically adept Ohio hunters—they communicated by telegraph—managed to kill over two hundred thousand of them, and to wound nearly all the others. The last wild Passenger Pigeon was killed in Ohio in 1900. A bird named Martha lived in captivity until 1914.

The formalization of ornithology as a science brought the debate over collecting into relief. Hobbyists were excluded from the newly formed American Ornithologists' Union, which saw a need to professionalize in order to keep the kill-and-collect rights scientists required for their studies. Though some amateurs felt insulted by the separation, others enthusiastically embraced their new status. Charlie Pennock began as an egg collector, but by 1900 was enthralled by the numbers. He was one of the first to come up with the idea of a "Big Day," where birders try to see as many species as possible in a twenty-four-hour period. (Pennock varied from modern practice by tallying *every* bird he saw. On one wintertime excursion, Pennock counted 1,714 juncos.) Pennock's obsession took a bizarre turn in 1913, when he simply vanished, leaving behind a wife and three children. Mrs. Pennock remained hopeful for several years, but ultimately donated her husband's egg collection to the Philadelphia Academy of Sciences. A few years later, a group of birders in Florida welcomed a dedicated newcomer. John Williams kept meticulous records and possessed uncanny endurance. Soon the editor of a regional bird publication noted that the handwritten notes submitted by Williams looked suspiciously like Charlie Pennock's. A brother-in-law was sent to investigate, and Williams confessed. He'd suffered a mental breakdown and had spent the previous six years traveling south, taking the birding cure. But he was ready to come home, and his family welcomed Williams/Pennock back as if nothing had happened.

One sign of amateur birding's emergence was a division between those who saw it as a sport and those who preferred to view it as a gentle hobby. The issue was taken up in the November 1894 issue of *Oology*, which published an article titled "Oology vs. Philately." (Although today's birders despise being compared to stamp collectors, back then, to be held up alongside that honored pastime was a legitimating act.) Bird books—idealizing tomes, often including long and colorful narratives of the lives of adventurous species*—began to appear. They were designed to help amateurs quickly identify the birds they spotted. And the spotting itself became easier: Several European manufacturers of fine crystal began using their expertise to create prisms; mating these with magnifying lenses resulted in binoculars that actually worked. They were bright and sharp, and they brought distant birds eight or ten times closer. "The glass is winning over the gun," wrote Ludlow Griscom.

Equipment was available. Identification was becoming easier.

---

*The most significant of these is Florence Merriam's *Birds of Village and Field*, published in 1898. In many ways, hers is the first attempt to do what Peterson successfully did almost four decades later. The book specifically aimed, the author wrote, to help those "unembarrassed by knowledge" name birds in the field.

What was missing were rules. In 1900, Frank Chapman, editor of *Bird Lore* magazine (still published as *Audubon* magazine) made a proposal: a counting contest, based in New York, but held concurrently across the country. "Put in a day," Chapman exhorted, "taking a census of all the birds found in village . . . farm . . . or, if in a city, the neighboring park." The inaugural Manhattan Christmas count was a modest success. Twenty-seven birders participated. A total of ninety species were recorded. But the idea took off. By 1910, such events were attracting hundreds of birders and netting thousands of observations. Today, the holiday tally remains one of the most popular forms of competitive birding; it has morphed into dozens of variations, including species-specific contests (like Brackendale, British Columbia's annual bald eagle census) and avian-totaling marathons—New Jersey's twenty-four-hour "World Series of Birding" and the five-day, no-sleep, "Great Texas Birding Classic." These events are possible because of the rule structure—relying on cumulative expertise, reputation, and the honor system—that Chapman formulated for his initial event.

THE MOST EXCITING YEAR of Dad's early birding life, 1949, symbolically began a few days earlier, on December 26, 1948, when Dad joined the Queens County Bird Club for the forty-fourth edition of Chapman's New York Christmas count. Below the Jewel Avenue Bridge—the highway interchange that leads to my grandmother's old house is just beyond the overpass—Dad had his first taste of a genuinely triumphant bird find: the "common" yellowthroat, which, as Dad notes, "isn't common in winter." It was the moment he began to realize he could bird independently; until then, "my skills weren't there—I wasn't sure, on my own, that I could make identifications."

From that moment on, birding became something that didn't require anyone else. Company would be by choice, not necessity. "The idea that I could do it all by myself, that I learned how to do it on my own, made me feel really good," Dad says. "And it was all I wanted to do."

To BUILD A LIST REQUIRES AUTHORITY. For U.S. birders, the highest power belongs to the *Checklist of North American Birds*. Containing approximately one-fifth of the planet's avian species, it is larger than a Manhattan phone book—829 pages, filled with descriptions of 2,030 birds—and covers the farthest reaches of the continent. The checklist sweeps from the frozen islands of the Bering Sea, home of the Arctic Tern, which migrates farther than any other creature on Earth, flying, each year, from the South Pole to remote nesting grounds at the top of the world; to Panama's impenetrable Darien Gap, where the master of the air is the Harpy Eagle, which twists through the trees at 50 mph, picking off monkeys.

Today's checklist is published by the American Ornithologists' Union. Its precursor (the book is now in its seventh volume) was written by Elliot Coues. His 1874 *Check-List of North American Birds* was 137 pages long and listed 637 species. In his introduction, Coues wrote that demand for such a list was "urgent." More and more people were looking at birds, and needed a way to record, if not identify, what they'd seen. But Coues knew that his nascent endeavor would not be something eternally fixed. Even as the number of birds one person sees in a lifetime increases, so does the list itself. One of the biggest ways bird lists change, even today, is with differing views of whether birds are full-fledged species or subspecies. Over the past century, there has been an ebb and flow between "Lumpers," ornithologists who'd combine several species into one, and "Splitters," who'd do the opposite. Coues knew that the list was subject to constant change, and that any single tally would, he said, "before long, become obsolete."

The rules of the game are strict. But as with any contest in which humans dare to pit themselves against nature, the rules shift. Constantly. As the most remote parts of the world became known, numbers of birds began to increase, a process that continues today. The early lists, developed by committed hobbyists, paved the way for these changes, and for the advent of professional ornithology. And as scientists expanded the global tally of birds, hobbyists would always follow, searching for one more bird—just one more—to increase their total.

Coues knew from the start that there would always be more kinds of birds. Life, he understood, was nothing if not a process of evolution. But one thing stood fixed: the way the most enthralled undertook the chase. *How many birds do you want?* Coues asked his readers. He answered his own question with an exhortation: *All you can get!*

THOUGH THE LOCATION OF THE UNITED NATIONS in the spot where my dad started birding is a nice bit of personal symbolism, the mundane phenomenon behind the choice of that historic site had an even more powerful result on Dad's activities. By the 1950s, Robert Moses—New York's legendary "master builder," who'd insisted that the UN be situated in Flushing (until the Rockefeller family donated the current Manhattan location)—had begun slicing Queens up, crisscrossing the landscape with new highways. Mazes of interchanges, overpasses, and the residential districts that inevitably sprung up around them turned Queens, according to Arthur Skopec, "into a much less productive place for birds. The entire character of the area changed."

Development meant more development. Flushing's meadows became Flushing Meadows Park. The "swamps" on the other side of Main Street, where Dad had seen many of his first birds, were filled in and layered with row houses and garden apartments. "Birders were very aware of the changes," Dad says. "By the nineteen fifties, nearly all the habitats we'd explored a few years earlier were gone." But post–World War II expansion also had some positive effects, at least on Dad's listing. New highways made more distant birding areas easier to reach. Getting to Jones Beach, once a rugged excursion, became a simple matter of defying my grandparents' wishes and hitching a ride. When I asked Dad how it happened that so many birders would happen to pick him up, he replied: "Well, if it was early on a spring day, there weren't many other people heading out to Jones Beach. You wore your binoculars and stuck your thumb out and you were almost guaranteed a ride."

Dad's birding excursions worried my grandparents. I think they generally saw the entire pastime as perverse. They were suspicious of some of the single, older men who pursued the hobby, especially one who Dad met in Bronx Park; they'd find each other by making bird calls. Dad says that the sexual orientation of the older men was never something he worried about: "We were birding," he says. These concerns piled on top of his parents' constant fretting that he wouldn't fulfill the medical destiny they had planned for him. Morris and Rose tried, with varying degrees of force and persuasion, to make sure their son viewed birding only as a hobby. But Dad was getting better and better at it, especially as he began to venture out on his own. That built his confidence in the activity, and brought it increasingly to the forefront of his ambitions.

His moment of truth came after spotting the Louisiana Heron. "I was so nervous about announcing what I'd seen," Dad recalls of his visit to the Linnaean Society. "But I gathered the courage and spoke." After his sighting was accepted, it was noted in the *Audubon Field Notes*, a regular publication that alerted birders to unusual local sightings. (By the time I was a teenager, the notes had become a recorded telephone message called the "Rare Bird Alert." Today, that function is performed with far greater efficiency by the Internet.) Dad had been reading the Audubon notes in his local library for several years; he was especially fascinated by reports of sightings far away, in places he could only dream of going. To be in the notes was something that made him feel incredibly proud. Dad doesn't remember his parents sharing that pride.

The Linnaean meeting was a turning point for Dad. "I finally felt like I was really good at something," he says. In 1949, he birded constantly, was invited to compete at several listing events, and by year's end had added 116 new birds to his tally, bringing his total to 242. "That year," Dad said, "was one I thought I'd have many more of. It was exactly the way I wanted my life to be."

My father's newfound seriousness about birding took its toll. It suddenly appeared on my grandparents' radar screen, and they began to more actively discourage his birding. Dad was unwillingly enrolled in violin classes as a way to wean him toward a more "sensible" hobby; he is repulsed by memories of trudging into Manhattan with his violin case and being forced to practice, over and over again. "I hated it, hated the instrument, hated practicing," he says. It isn't that he isn't musical; he's quite a good saxophone player. The lessons, he says, were just another public demonstration that "what I wanted simply didn't matter to my parents."

An even more symbolic message against the hobby was sent on Dad's fifteenth birthday, a year later. To this day, Dad becomes hesitant and distantly angry when he mentions the present he received. He'd asked for an Argus telescope; he wanted it to spot birds, to stare at the stars, to see distant—maybe calmer—vistas. Instead, what he unwrapped was a microscope, another push along the safe path, a way not to open horizons, but to contain the world. A tool for a future doctor, not for a young dreamer whose head was, quite literally, in the clouds. He remembers feeling instantly deflated, suppressing his anger, feigning—as a dutiful son should—gratitude.

"I was shown," he says, "in no uncertain terms that I was going to do what was expected of me."

What happens when the people we love and depend upon expect from us that which we don't want to supply? The choices range from rebellion to quiet acquiescence. Over the next few years, Dad would sway between those extremes. Later on, he'd go too far, too dangerously, in one direction, then careen, as though pushed by an unseen hand, the opposite way.

IN 1950, DAD SAW ONLY NINE NEW BIRDS. "I was easing off," Dad says, "because everybody thought I should try to get interested in other things." His early birding triumphs and the accompanying confidence and commitment to making birds the focus of his life suddenly evaporated, under the pressure from his parents and the mechanical forces that were changing the landscape of Queens. Dad's favorite hangout became a local candy store, the High Spot, on Main Street; the woods he'd roamed just a few years earlier had been right across the road. Dad silently watched as stand after stand of oak and maple vanished and was replaced by rows of houses and apartments. Dad began playing sports and listening to jazz. "I was also getting interested in girls," he says, "though I was kind of backward with them. I didn't really date during high school." Even so, his life felt strangely conflicted: His two favorite books at the time were Irving Shulman's *The Amboy Dukes*, a novel about alienated, tough New York teenagers, and Thoreau's *Walden*.

He didn't go out, but he did take notice. Rosalind Brenner lived in Forest Hills, a couple of miles away, and she was five years Dad's junior. One of Dad's buddies, Mike Glantz, had a younger sister; Rosalind was her closest friend. How Dad fell in love with my mother is one of the hardest things to get him to discuss. But Rosalind, even at twelve, was beautiful, with long, dark hair, brown eyes, and a tiny, perfect nose. She was a constant winner of popularity contests in school, and smart—consistently at the top of her class in English—as well. But she was miserable at home; her parents were constantly battling, often over the money that they constantly seem to have been losing, and so Rosalind was all the more happy and voluble at her friends' relatively more stable home. "She was always there," Dad says. "I liked her, even as a kid."

It might be an exaggeration to say Dad loved my mother from the start. But knowing him, it might also not be. He won't discuss it, but what he does say, thirty-five years after their brief union ended, is more than a clue; it isn't so much a confession of feeling as a bottom note, a tone that's barely audible if you listen only briefly, but which, when you pay attention, you discover is always, always there.

"Your mother," he says. "She was beautiful."

Dad also knew that his future wife was having troubles at home; it was the first time he'd felt what would become one of the driving patterns of their relationship: "She seemed very nervous," Dad says, "and I liked playing the part of the rescuer who could calm her down. It made me feel good."

But their brief and dramatic life together was still years away in 1950. Rosalind was barely a teenager, and Dad, whose parents had enrolled him in an accelerated science program, was thinking about college. Though he'd pushed birding into the background, it continued to grow in silence. "Deep down," he says, "I wanted to be an ornithologist. So badly." Some of Dad's friends from the Queens club, slightly older teens, were already making names for themselves: Walter Bock (who went on to become a highly influential bird scientist; he's now emeritus chairman in biology at Columbia) had chosen Cornell University, and the school seemed like a good option for Dad, as well. Cornell's Ivy League status made it acceptable to my grandparents, who probably didn't know that the school's ornithology program was then—and still is today—one of the best in the world. Dad began spending time in the library, reading about birds, studying them. It was an activity he purposely kept low-key, especially from his father, who "exerted tremendous pressure to not be an ornithologist. He didn't approve, and I knew that if I became one, it would make him very unhappy." A more subtle attack on his ambitions came when Rose consulted a psychologist about her son's birding. The resulting diagnosis remains a tart memory for my father: "She told my parents I was a voyeur," he recalls. "That I had a problem with 'peeping.'"

Something curious happened then, something that, despite ten years of probing, reflecting, questioning, and connecting the dots, I haven't quite figured out: Dad almost did it. With all the pressure being applied to quell his ambitions, he still got so close. But even though he brought himself to the right place, he never allowed himself to hit the target.

Dad initially entered the agricultural school at Cornell. This was the wrong place for a budding ornithologist or a future doctor to be; in either of those cases, one would attend Cornell proper, most likely majoring in biology. He could easily have taken the biology major's path. It would be safe, since science and medicine traveled virtually the same road for entering students; he could gather his willpower and make the choice later.

But he didn't.

He chose the agriculture school—a subject he had zero interest in.

Why? Dad says he received "poor advice. Nobody told me how to become an ornithologist, or anything. Nobody told me what I needed to do." But between his own predilection for meticulous research, his acquaintance with Walter Bock, and his exposure to the Linnaean Society's dozens of ornithologist members, Dad must have known what his options were. He must have known that the agriculture school was absolutely the wrong place to be. When I ask him to explain today, he can't fully do so. "My father was a little panicked that I wasn't completely committed to becoming a doctor." Almost offhand, Dad adds: "There was some talk that it would be acceptable—barely—if I became a veterinarian."

Future animal doctors did go to Cornell's agricultural school. So the choice looks like a compromise, though one that would clearly have been unsatisfactory to all concerned: Dad wouldn't be a doctor, nor would he study birds. Picturing it, I can practically see my dad, torn between his own dreams and his sense of duty. But there's another twist: Dad never entered the agriculture school. Again, he made a brief parry toward his own ambitions. The summer before college, my father worked on a farm—the Cornell farming program required in-the-field experience—and "hated it. Getting up seven days a week at five in the morning, without a second to look at birds, even though I was in the country." He decided that whatever being a veterinarian might do for the desires of his parents (or himself) wasn't worth it. Halfway through summer, Dad quit the farm job. And again, he almost took matters into his own hands. He almost did what he wanted to do. Without telling his parents, he called Cornell, determined to move from the agricultural school to liberal arts, where he could choose biology. It wasn't an easy change to make; the two schools are considered different entities, and moving between them isn't generally allowed. But Dad managed to talk university officials into it. The move to liberal arts was one his parents approved of; he was that much closer to being a doctor.

But Dad didn't want to be a doctor. And finally, he rebelled against his parents. He finally chose something for himself.

Pre-med, he announced, was not going to happen.

The surprise is that he didn't choose ornithology.

At the end of his freshman year, Dad declared English as his major (he ultimately changed his focus one more time, emerging from college with a degree in philosophy). From his parents' point of view, it was absolutely the worst choice; even birds would have been better. They were furious. Dad explains that he was so confused that he simply gave up. It was as if he knew he had to break free of his parents, but his guilt over doing so forced him to make a choice that was, in some ways, a form of self-punishment. He was genuinely interested in literature and poetry—"It was something I'd never been exposed to"—but he also admits now that the choice was a way to "completely deny my interest in science." Dad had closed the book on his most passionate ambition. "From that point on," he recalls, "I had no idea what I'd do with my life." He pauses. "But I knew I would never be an ornithologist."

✵   ✵   ✵

DAD DIDN'T GIVE UP BIRDING IN COLLEGE. He and his roommate, Joel Abramson, pursued the activity intensely and competitively (today, Abramson is also a Big Lister, with a lifetime tally exceeding 6,500). But most of Dad's college years were spent drinking and getting his heart broken. His first love, a woman named Barbara, ping-ponged between two paramours, falling back on my dad when neither was available. "I somehow always was attracted to women," Dad says, "who didn't have the ability to stay with me." Instead of focusing his desires, college made him feel even more aimless, as if repressed ambition had flattened his entire being. The wandering continued after graduation. Dad's account of his life during the late 1950s is an odd contrast of spectacular achievement and utter paralysis. He began hanging around in Greenwich Village, with the idea of becoming a writer. He considered himself a beatnik, while at the same time searching for what he describes as "the ultimate sell-out job" in advertising. Knowing that he'd soon be drafted, Dad applied and was accepted at Harvard Law School. He began classes in 1956. Six weeks later, he dropped out. "I realized I really wanted to be hanging out in the Village, walking around with books of French Symbolist poetry under my arm, being very intense," he says.

Nineteen fifty-six was the first year since Dad began birding that he added nothing to his life list. He can't explain why he didn't bird, at least not specifically. It was a vague feeling: "I just had no idea what I wanted to do or be," he says. By the end of the year, Dad had moved back into his parents' house in Queens, though he'd stay out for days on end, with his hidden anger usually drowned in downtown bars, and occasionally erupting. The looming draft made the pressure feel even greater: he just didn't feel cut out for military service. "I knew I had to do something," Dad recalls.

He finally gave in. In 1957, he began taking classes at Columbia University, filling in the missing science courses he'd need to enter medical school. He kept what he was doing from his downtown friends. "I made the choice only out of frustration and fear of the army," Dad says, "but I didn't want them to know." There were no new birds in 1957. In early 1958, Dad was accepted to New York University Medical School. He still hated the idea.

The summer before classes were to begin, I think, was the last chance Dad had as a young man to take a path of his own choosing. With a copy of Kerouac's *On the Road* in his pocket and Peterson's *A Field Guide to Western Birds* on the passenger seat, Dad signed up with a drive-away car transporter company and traveled cross-country. When he talks about this trip, even today, you can hear the joy and excitement in his voice. There's no sense of loss, just visceral travel back to a time when, briefly, an idyll was embraced. "It was glorious," Dad says. "I saw so many amazing things." He loved life on the road. He loved the sights—the Great Plains, the Grand Canyon, the Rockies.

And he saw sixty-three new birds.

In his back pocket, Dad carried his medical school acceptance letter. Traveling south along the Pacific Coast, Dad was enthralled. San Francisco, Monterey, Big Sur—and birds he'd only read about, that he'd dreamed of seeing, a decade earlier, as he'd pored over sighting reports in the library. On a warm August evening, Dad arrived at Ventura Beach, north of Los Angeles.

It was a gorgeous sunset. Dad stood there with his binoculars. The fall migration had started, and waves of birds, moving toward warmer terrain, filled the sky. He saw nothing new that evening, but it didn't matter. At that moment, the list didn't matter. "It was the most beautiful thing I'd ever seen," Dad says. "It was paradise."

For a few minutes, he thought about not coming back. About taking the letter from his back pocket, tearing it up, and scattering it in the wind. But he didn't. Was it a girl who'd been on his mind—Rosalind, just about to turn eighteen? Was it a sense of duty? Was it fear? I wish I knew. I wish Dad could tell me, but he's unable to explain, and attempting to open the topic always leads me to a closed door. All I know is that, just as writers talk about reaching junctures—when key choices are made, when one path closes, when everything from that moment on transforms—my father, standing in perfection on a Pacific Beach as night fell, had reached a juncture of his own. Were the birds warning him, somehow, of looming obsession? Or were they drifting out of his reach, taking his dreams with him?

Or maybe it was a more routine choice. Maybe, as it does for all of us at some point, convention finally seemed like enough. Go to school. Marry the girl. Accept responsibility.

He bought a bus ticket home.

Time to move on. And, for now, maybe for the rest of his life, no time for birds.

CHAPTER FOUR

JUST A HOBBY

" *I saw seventeen lifers on the way to California, and in California, mostly routine birds, but one that I found in the San Diego River Valley, a Yellow-Green Vireo, is very rare and distinctive. Over the years, it has been lumped and split alternately with Red-Eyed Vireo. I found it the day before my medical internship began. It's not that easy an identification, but a good look and the song should confirm it. Nevertheless, I wanted to show it to someone else. A friend had given me the name of a San Diego birder, and I showed it to him, but he turned out to be almost totally deaf, and could not hear the song at all. I ended the year with forty-three lifers.*"

—Yellow-green Vireo (lumped, then
split, from Red-eyed Vireo, shown—
Vireo olivaceus), June 28, 1962,
San Diego, California, #467.

WE WERE DRIVING DOWN A TEXAS HIGHWAY. The sky was dark blue—it might have been dusk—and streaked with orange. Gravel rumbled beneath us; chunks of dirt and stone pinged against our bumpers and doors. Dad was at the wheel, Mom in the passenger seat, my brother and me in the back. Even as he drove, Dad stared intently at the horizon, peering through thick, black glasses. His hair was close-cropped, and his face—unlike the primary image I carry of him in my mind—was clean-shaven. My brother had just turned three; I was nearly five. Jim and I don't resemble each other. I've got my mom's face and dark hair, and my brother has lighter hair; it was blond, then, like Dad's. Neither of us has Dad's blue eyes, but vision-wise, Dad and I are the same. I wore glasses that were miniature versions of his.

What did I see, as Dad peered through the dirty windshield? Maybe I was staring at my mother, nervous and beautiful all at once, who seemed frightened, sometimes angry, and who—even now, as this is being written, over thirty years later—always existed apart from the car's other three occupants. Maybe I was staring out the window, too, reading road signs. Much of my childhood seems like an endless car trip, sometimes to amazing places, sometimes to tedious locales. Dad had finally been drafted, and he was undergoing twelve weeks of basic training in San Antonio. My memories of Texas are fragmented, but I remember that motel, and that pool. And I remember that drive. There was a bird.

It was a hot afternoon. Sometimes, Dad would just stop, we'd pull to the side of the road and he'd rush out, grabbing his binoculars. Mom usually waited. Dad would bring me out—later, my brother, too, when he was older—and point at something: a tree, a fence post, or a patch of cloudless sky. This road, in my recollection, seems endless. I don't remember hills, I don't remember trees. I remember telephone poles, stretching into the distance.

Dad maneuvered to the edge of the tarmac. He opened the car door, stepped to the passenger side, and trundled me out. He put his arm around me and pointed upward, toward the overhead wires.

With my glasses—always smudged—I could make out that the bird was quite a bit larger than the other ones we'd seen today. Not larger the way a hawk is bigger than a sparrow; the bird's body was average-sized. But it had a long tail. A very long tail.

A truck rumbled by, tossing up more dust. I clung to Dad as it passed. Then, when the air settled, he knelt down and steadied his heavy binoculars for me. Dad turned the focus wheel and guided the lenses upward, toward the wire.

Telling flycatchers apart can be very difficult. There are over 350 species of the bird, of which 35 are found in the United States. The most challenging to identify are the six members of the Empidonax family. Kenn Kaufmann, author of *Birds of North America*, a modern field guide that many consider to be today's successor to Peterson's pioneering work, simply notes that Empidonax is "best identified by voice." They all look nearly the same. For one pair of Empidonax, the Pacific-slope Flycatcher and the Cordilleran Flycatcher, Kaufman simply advises birders to throw up their hands: "Usually," he writes, "it is better to call them 'Western Flycatchers.'"

But the bird we saw wasn't one of those delicately obscure species. In my worn copy of Peterson's *Field Guide to the Birds of Texas* (Peterson published a stand-alone Texas guide because the state is so huge and so much a place where geographic zones—western mountains, eastern woods, coastline, and tropics—collide), the flycatcher I saw is described almost gleefully: "A beautiful bird, pale pearly gray, with an extremely long scissorlike tail. Usually the 'scissors' are folded. The sides and wing-linings are salmon pink. No other bird in its range has such streaming tail feathers."

If that description had been read to me then, I'd have thought it an understatement. The feathers were huge; the bird was so strange, so awkward. I looked for a long time. I stared long enough that Dad let me hold the binoculars while he lit a cigarette. I can remember the feeling of the rubber eye cups on the binoculars, pressed against my thick, horn-rimmed glasses. I remember that my glasses got a little fogged, and that, when I handed the optical instrument back to Dad, he wiped the lens with his handkerchief, then used the same cloth to clean my glasses.

Finally, it was time to go.

"Scissor-tailed Flycatcher," I kept repeating to myself, imagining (wrongly) that the tail was the apparatus used by the bird to catch those flies. I pictured it slicing through the air, snagging insects with decisive chops, pink feathers moving rapidly. I pictured my dad and me, the rugged discoverers of this unusual bird, two men who had managed to pluck it—at least visually—from the sky.

✿   ✿   ✿

A BIG BIRD LIST, in the early 1960s, was more a matter of conjecture than reality. There were thought to be about eight thousand species on earth back then, but there was no single, accepted master list. For the parts of the world with the most birds—Africa and South America—there were no field guides, no Peterson revolution. Peterson himself was chasing big numbers: he established a rivalry with Stuart Keith—later listed in the *Guinness Book of World Records* as the world's biggest lister—in races to build the biggest annual lists. Keith had actually come to the United States from Britain specifically to beat Peterson's single-year record; he stayed, and went on to cofound the American Birding Association.

But Peterson kept returning to a goal he'd given a simple name to: "My own personal hope is to see, during my lifetime, half the birds of the world," Peterson wrote. That objective—Peterson and his colleagues abbreviated it to *Half*—was something Peterson finally reached, but not until the mid-1980s. His rival, Keith, arrived there a decade earlier.

Could anyone have imagined seeing that many birds in the early 1960s? Even Dad's life list—420 when I was born—was a lot. Though records weren't kept during that decade, by 1974, only 129 U.S. birders had bigger tallies. For world birding, only eleven watchers had surpassed 2,500. Today, that number is still fairly rarified territory—the American Birding Association's list says 256 birders have passed that milestone, only about one percent of that elite group's membership.

So when Dad says that he couldn't have had such huge goals because, back then, "they were unheard of," he's right.

But it wasn't out of the question. Peterson and Keith believed that getting to Half would take decades. And yet it took Dean Fisher—probably the first true Big Lister, and one most have never heard of—only a few years.

When I first heard about Fisher, I didn't believe he really existed, mostly because he's not mentioned in the early accounts of listing that I'd seen. I was told that he and a friend had, over the space of thirty-five months, driven a battered Jeep across every continent; Fisher looked for birds, and his buddy, Noble Trenham, tagged along for the adventure.

Fisher and Trenham met on an aircraft carrier in the Pacific. Both were finishing their military service. Neither was quite ready to settle down once their enlistments were up. Trenham suggested that the two of them travel the world.

"I wanted to learn about other cultures, and look for business ideas," Trenham says.

Fisher, who is exactly Dad's age, and today is a retired biology professor living in Nacogdoches, Texas, had already built a life list of about nine hundred birds and had a different idea: "I wanted to get to four thousand," he says. "I wanted to do something nobody had ever even thought of." He wanted to be the Jack Kerouac of birding.

The two left Pasadena, California, in January 1959.

Fisher's achievements in the coming years were so radical that he's almost disqualified from listing history—not because he didn't see thousands of birds, but because what he was doing was so presumed to be impossible that even conceiving it is difficult. He and Trenham drove through Mexico, took a freighter around Panama, and headed to the tip of South America; they had their vehicle shipped to Africa, then Europe, then Asia. They traveled the world's highest road, in the Andes, and the lowest, near the Dead

Sea. They had no bird books to speak of, and only the most thread-bare resources.

Fisher knew that he'd be unable to identify many of the birds he encountered, but he kept detailed notes, recording habitat and behavior along with physical characteristics. Over the next three decades, he scanned the literature, identifying his mystery birds one by one. His final identification—closing the book on the journey—happened in 2001, forty years after he'd sighted the small, puffy, perching bird in the Kenya's Kakamega rain forest.

That Gray-chested Illadopsis was just one of over three thousand birds Fisher saw on that trip. When added to his life total, Fisher estimates that he was the first to top four thousand, though he never bothered reporting it (and there was nobody, really, to report it to). Why?

"Well," he says, "so much happened. I met my wife on the last leg of the adventure. So I was busy being a newlywed. It just didn't seem important."

As Fisher told me his story, I found myself wondering how much of what we end up doing—or being—is inevitable, and how much is choice? Dad told me that he had to accept responsibility. Most of us have met that moment where we suddenly realize the things that we once sought are now falling into a different order of priorities. Sometimes, we have to find a way to change our lives, to re-embrace that which seems to be vanishing.

Other times, we simply abandon our dreams.

As Dean Fisher was chasing thousands of birds, Dad was pushing birds away. In 1958, Dad says, "I stopped entertaining ideas of going back to ornithology." When I ask him why, his reply is typically stark: "The possibility had," he says, "been eliminated."

Dad entered medical school. He began dating my mother.

Mom's parents weren't as comfortably middle-class as my father's folks. I remember my maternal grandfather, Murray, as a fun-loving, handsome man who'd frequently talk about the fortunes he'd made and lost; his favorite pastimes were golfing and visiting the racetrack.

My mother describes growing up in a household filled with conflict: my grandfather's attempts to find his way back to wealth, and my grandmother's explosive temper. (My grandmother is a sharp-tongued individual, always capable of coming up with what seems to be the most bitingly cruel statement imaginable; I remember her calling me a "Nazi" when I got a shorter-than-normal haircut during college. When she was younger, her verbal abuse was matched by physical assaults; Mom describes a home where the slightest missed chore or complaint could lead to violent punishment. It shouldn't be surprising, then, that my own mother was, at her weakest moments, sometimes incapable of preventing herself from similar actions toward her children.)

As with my father's parents, Murray and Betty were formed by the primary experience of their lives: leaving home, in a Russian-speaking part of Poland, and coming to America. A few years ago, Betty was interviewed by a historian at Ellis Island. She describes being torn from an idyllic existence just after her fifth birthday: "We were poor," she says, "but we lived in the country. I didn't have toys, but we didn't need them. My brothers and sisters and I had the flowers to play in." The whole Nebelkopf family emigrated in 1916, and after that, Betty was thrust onto the overcrowded streets of Williamsburg, Brooklyn, just after she began grade school. The transition from ideal to reality led to fantasy: She would be a movie star; she'd have riches and luxury. Her parents were not the intellectuals Rose and Morris were; Betty and Murray were scrappers, struggling to get by, and constantly looking for a way out. (My grandmother's oldest brother, Jack, joined the army prior to World War II, and never came home. Today, in her nineties, Betty sometimes mistakes me for him, and asks me if I've finally "come back from Texas," where Jack apparently was stationed.)

When Betty's dream of fame and fortune failed to materialize, her frustrations boiled over and were directed toward my mother. It made things worse that Mom seemed close to the things Betty wanted: Rosalind was voted prettiest in her Forest Hills High School graduating class; her yearbook picture shows a dark-eyed, smiling girl, but she was hiding a desperate home life: "If I couldn't get out of the house, I stayed in my room," Mom says. "I knew nothing about the world outside."

Her only refuge was the home of her best friend, Suzie Glantz. "They really treated me like family," she says. That's where my father saw her, for the first time in several years, almost immediately after he returned from California.

She could be part of the plan.

Go to medical school. Get married. Birds? Just a hobby.

He swept her off her feet. He was five years older. He'd traveled. He lived in Greenwich Village. He played a fairly competent jazz saxophone (a skill I picked up as a teenager, using Dad's old horn). Mom had just entered college. She spent a semester in upstate New York at Syracuse University; it was the farthest she'd ever been from home, and she quickly returned to complete her freshman year at Queens College, where she majored in English. Having trouble with a mandatory science class—Dad's pre-birding obsession, astronomy—Mom remembers sitting at her parents' kitchen table while Richard explained the arrangement of the solar system using a bowl of fruit. "I'll never forget it," Mom says. "He showed me the universe with apples and oranges. I was spellbound. He was brilliant."

Dad showed his younger girlfriend things she never knew existed: jazz clubs, museums, poetry readings in Manhattan. He also introduced her to marijuana—drugs would become a bigger and bigger part of both their lives from that point on—and birds: "We went to Jamaica Bay on dates sometimes," Mom recalls. "It was this beautiful, outdoor place, so near to where I lived. It was such a surprise to me."

Some things Mom found curious: "What struck me about his bird watching was the list—I never understood that. It seemed like he didn't appreciate their beauty." But she loved his intellect: "I thought," she says, "he knew everything."

EIGHTEEN MONTHS AFTER THEY BEGAN DATING, Richard and Rosalind married. It was fast, but the pressure they felt from their parents was intense: "My sister had already married a doctor, and my father wanted to make sure I did the same thing," Mom recalls. Dad, too, felt that his parents were pushing him toward what they saw as a stabilizing life change. On June 23, 1960, they gathered at Leonard's of Great Neck—a fancy-functions palace that operated as bar mitzvah headquarters for most of my friends when I was a teenager*—and exchanged vows. It was a nice affair, well-catered, with Mom in a beautiful dress and her father, Murray, congratulating himself, bragging that he'd married off both his daughters to medical men. My mother is beaming in the wedding pictures; my father looks mostly relieved. Sometimes I look at those pictures

---

*Leonard's had moved between the time of my parents' marriage and my own teenage years; the original Leonard's—later the Long Island branch of Manhattan's famous Old Homestead Steak House—no longer exists; it stood about a mile west of the new facility, which remains a crystalline palace of absolutely manic kitsch.

and wonder if my parents ever really loved each other. With my mother, I guess it's pretty simple: She looks happy, but she says that "I felt like it was so much the wrong thing—but I couldn't say it. I didn't know how." My father is more complicated. Like the jazz he loved, his melody is complex, more discordant. "Everyone I knew was getting married," Dad says. "And I understood that if I didn't do what I needed to do, I'd be a total failure—somebody who screwed up everything." It was a happy day, Dad remembers, "but I can't really say *we* were happy."

But nearly forty-five years after that day, and thirty-five years after the divorce, Dad still talks about her.

Does he do it because it was a great and tragic love, one that can never be put aside? Or because his failure at marriage placed his heart in obsession's grip?

After a wedding night at a local "hot-sheets motel," Mom recalls, the Koeppels set out on a six-week road honeymoon across the United States. The prospect thrilled my mother, who had never traveled farther than Syracuse. They bought an early 1950s Hillman Minx, a British import with a convertible top and a crank starter. It was a wildly eccentric automotive investment, especially considering the trip they were about to take, but it was typical of my dad, and to Mom, it was another sign of his Bohemian worldliness. They loaded up a canvas tent and a green Coleman stove and headed west.

Dad's list, as the trip began, was at 357.

And since he was finally doing the right thing, he was determined to add to it. Just as a hobby.

The couple drove into Pennsylvania Dutch Country, stopped in Chicago, crossed Wisconsin, and headed toward the Continental Divide into the Grand Tetons, Yellowstone, and then the Pacific Northwest, through the redwoods, down to San Francisco. They drove south, turned east, and crossed back through the southwest, visiting the Grand Canyon, Utah's arches, New Mexico's Indian ruins, finally crossing Texas and Arkansas before turning north on the Blue Ridge Highway, which led them home.

What kind of honeymoon was it? Depends on who you ask.

"The honeymoon was enjoyable," Dad says. "We saw a lot of the country, and I loved showing your mom new things—the mountains and the California coast, the national parks." And birds? "I knew that once we crossed the Mississippi, there would be new birds all along the way. So when I saw one, we stopped. She didn't mind. She waited in the car."

"It was incredible," my mother recalls, "and your dad showed me things I never knew existed. That was the amazing part. But the birding—I'd wait in the car for him, sometimes for hours. If I tried to go with him, he'd make me walk behind and tell me to be quiet." Those waits, my mother says, were sometimes terrifying: "I was a frightened child, and I'd be all alone in the woods. Or waiting in the car, scared out of my wits. And I was starting to have thoughts that I felt so guilty for, that I wasn't liking the way this was going." Mom pauses a bit, catching her breath. "It was our honeymoon," she says. "I was nineteen."

My mother learned about something else on that trip: Dad's submerged ambitions. "He told me he never wanted to be a doctor, but he had to do what his parents wanted—he was the only surviving child, and he had such reverence for Rose and Morris. He did what he had to do, but even then, I could see the resentment building up."

She didn't know how to help him. She barely had the tools to help herself.

And soon, she'd be pregnant. Dad added sixty-three new birds on the honeymoon—his largest new block of sightings since he was a teenager. That brought his lifetime tally to 420.

SOMETIMES YOU HAVE TO TAKE A BIRD OFF YOUR LIST. In January 1961, Dad spotted a Lesser White-fronted Goose in Islip, Long Island. This is an unusual bird—relatively common in Asia, but seen just three times during the entire twentieth century in the United States. The Peterson guide doesn't even list the bird on the page that contains other geese; instead, it is grouped with more than a dozen other species on a page called "Accidentals from Eurasia."

Can you count an "accidental" bird?

It depends on the accident. The Fieldfare is a bird found mostly in the world's northern reaches—Greenland, Siberia, and Scandinavia; it is possible—though not common—for the bird to have been blown by strong winds toward North America during migratory season. Other accidentals might arrive by following ships. But Peterson cautions against counting most such birds: "Some sightings of European waterfowl are suspect and could be aviary or zoo escapees."

It makes sense: A bird on the lam from a zoo isn't native. The American Birding Association's official rules devote a whole section to the notion: "The bird must have been alive, wild, and unrestrained when encountered." So, in addition to arriving without much human intervention—following a sea vessel is considered an act of will by the bird, so it remains wild even though it has succumbed, anthropomorphically, to temptation—you also can't count an egg, road kill, or a bird in a cage. Escapees do have a chance of making it to legitimate listing: When a large enough breeding population is established—as with the Monk Parakeet, a South American species originally sold in pet stores, which now ranges from Florida through Chicago and even Maine—the ABA can add the species to its accepted list, and listers can tally another tick mark.

So Dad initially counted the goose, but over the next few years, he decided he'd seen an escapee. He didn't encounter the bird again until 1981, in China.

"I was waiting to see it," he says, "because I hated erasing it the first time."

The goose—and the removal of it from his list—was Dad's most exciting birding encounter of 1961. He was in his last year of medical school, and had little time for even the most passing jaunt to Jamaica Bay or the Bronx Gardens. By summer, Mom—still in college—was pregnant. Dad brought his stethoscope home, and on hot summer nights they'd listen to my heartbeat, the heartbeat of their unborn child. Both of them remember the joyous feeling of that summer, but Dad also remembers feeling increasingly anxious. He'd checked wife, career, and, soon, fatherhood off his life list. But he couldn't find meaning in any of it.

"I had no idea what I was doing," he says. "I had no idea of what I wanted."

Everything was in place, but nothing was in order. The apartment was too cramped. Rosalind and Richard were beginning to fight. And Dad's wild friends, the buddies he'd met during his years roaming downtown Manhattan, were still wild. Dad found himself drawn to them, and torn between his role as a father and young doctor-in-training and the Greenwich Village lifestyle he was a borough away from. One evening, Dad had too much to drink and insisted on driving; when a friend took the keys, Mom went home on her own, while Dad roamed the streets, furious. He ended up returning at four in the morning, desperate and angst-filled, wondering and asking, over and over, why his wife had abandoned him.

In November, my parents took another cross-country trip. Once again, Dad was pressing against the entrance to his unfulfilled dreams. He'd chosen to complete his medical internship in California, and the couple traveled up and down the West Coast, Dad interviewing for residency positions at hospitals along the way. They chose the last place they visited: San Diego. It was a gorgeous spot; they decided to live close to the ocean, where there would be seabirds and Balboa Park and a Shakespeare Festival (my mother was building an interest in the theater, a pursuit that would take her far afield in the years to come).

They returned home on December 1. Mom was seven months pregnant. The couple spent Hanukkah with Rose and Morris; that month, from the way Mom describes it, was one of the few periods in their marriage when there was a semblance of normalcy, of anticipation that a future full of the ordinary could be satisfying and peaceful. They sat down for family dinners; they went to the movies; they talked. My grandparents seemed even more content: "They had tremendous expectations for your father," Mom recalls, "and they were finally coming true."

Christmas that year was gray and dry. But it flurried the following week, and by December 31, snow was coming down in greater quantities, stopping and starting throughout the day. As evening fell, Dad and Mom drove into Manhattan, crossing the Triborough Bridge, then heading south toward the Staten Island Ferry. Dad doesn't remember for sure, but since I've taken a dozen boat trips with him and never seen a single exception to this behavior, he almost certainly stepped on deck and looked for birds. (Some current New Yorkers might wonder about the notion of cars on the boat shuttles; they were allowed then. Automotive transport was reduced when the Verrazano-Narrows Bridge, stretching from Brooklyn to Staten Island, opened two years later, and eliminated entirely in 1997.)

When they arrived at their destination, the party was already in full swing. Everyone was dancing. A year earlier, a singer named Chubby Checker had started the biggest dance craze ever to hit the American charts. "The Twist" reached number one on January 8, 1960, and stayed in the Top 40 for nearly five months. A follow-up song, "Let's Twist Again," stayed on the charts for nearly half of 1961; next came "Twistin' USA," and, toward the end of the year, the re-release of the original hit. The second coming of The Twist was as potent as the first. The song reentered the Billboard Top 100 on November 13. On New Year's Eve, it hadn't quite reached number one—it was moving up, but wouldn't displace "The Lion Sleeps Tonight," by the Tokens, until January 13.

And my mother, not yet due for a month, attempting to twist the night away, broke water one hour before midnight.

The question I'm most asked when people learn that I was born on New Year's Day is whether I was the first child to arrive in New York City in 1962. Not a chance—another woman was in labor at Methodist that evening. She'd already given birth four times. "She was a lot faster," Mom laughs. I didn't arrive until early afternoon, January 1, 1962. I was premature and tiny, just about five pounds, but healthy enough that extra measures weren't needed.

"It was a beautiful thing," Mom says, "though I was terrified."

What about Dad? How did he feel about fatherhood?

As usual, a quick answer—"I liked it"—then birds; a road trip to Florida after medical school graduation.

"I saw thirty new species."

When Dad talks about the list, I hear a passion only hinted at when the discussion turns toward moments others might consider more important: Dad gets most excited about a bird that has long since been removed from the official list of countable birds. The Dusky Seaside Sparrow disappeared from Merritt Island, Florida in 1962, vanishing along with marshland cleared for the construction of the Cape Canaveral Space Center. A second colony of sparrows survived, but only briefly: Their habitat was destroyed by the construction of Walt Disney World. By 1980, only seven sparrows were left. A captive breeding program was attempted, but too few birds remained. The last Dusky Seaside Sparrow died in 1987.

The sparrow was one of six new birds he saw that day, bringing his life list to 439. Mom—with me fast asleep beside her—waited in the car.

THE LITTLE HOUSE ON POINT LOMA BOULEVARD is still there, even though it is now surrounded by the sprawling development that has transformed the Southern California coastline from a pleasantly rugged (and bird-filled) place into a land of asphalt and minimalls. But hints of what appealed to Dad are still evident. You can hear waves crashing on rocks, even above the traffic, and there are still spots nearby—the picturesque Sunset Cliffs; the Cabrillo National Monument—where birds, especially during spring and fall migration, can be found in ecstatic quantities.

San Diego offered Dad another reason to feel optimistic: He was finished with his studies, which meant his medical school draft deferment would soon expire, but at twenty-eight, he believed there was little chance he'd be called to military duty. "I thought I'd licked it," he says. We arrived in California in July 1962. The home was pretty bare—in the few photos I've seen of it, there's practically no furniture—but San Diego's charm wasn't indoors. "We'd go to look at the sunset each night," Mom recalls. "You, me, and Dad. That's what our life was about there."

There were, of course, birds overhead, as well. The California sojourn began auspiciously, when Dad spotted an Elegant Tern— the bird is a good illustration of how plastic avian populations are, even in the short term; it was a rare sighting back then, though to- day, I can head to almost any Los Angeles area beach and be fairly sure to see one. That sighting was followed by an even bigger rar- ity, the Yellow-green Vireo. On weekends, Dad made trips, mostly alone, adding to his lifetime tally. For the first time, his major frus- tration was something he welcomed: He was on a quest to see the soon-to-vanish (in the wild) California Condor. He'd not succeed, but the effort was just as much fun. He'd drive up to Sespe Canyon, north of Los Angeles, which was then the bird's last re- maining U.S. habitat. (Seventy captive-bred condors have been released into the wilderness area, but they've had little reproduc- tive success. I could take Dad to see a Sespe condor on one of his infrequent visits to Los Angeles, but he scoffs at the thought. "I never saw it," he says, adding emphatically: "And I won't count one now [because the bird is in captivity, and therefore not ac- ceptable to listers], so there's no point.")

Despite the easygoing atmosphere, the clockwork nature of my parents' relationship began to assert itself. In the fall, the couple decided to try for another child. This time it was easy, and by my first birthday, Mom was preparing for a May delivery. Again, she enjoyed being pregnant, though she had her hands full with one in- fant and my father, who was pushing himself to complete the in- ternship. The drive led to an increase in his compulsiveness, which wore on my mother. "He was a lister in so many ways," she says. "He'd make lists of things I had to do. Sometimes I resented it. But mostly, I just didn't understand it."

LOOKING BACK, I THINK SAN DIEGO WAS A CRITICAL JUNCTURE, precisely because there seemed to be little conflict, little excitement. Dad was working; Mom was pregnant. Life was low on intensity, but easy. Sometimes I wish my parents had chosen to embrace that, to stay there. But they didn't. They couldn't. As his medical training drew to a close, Dad became restless. Again, I'm guessing that deep down, this wasn't what he wanted, and he found it impossible to force himself to believe otherwise, though he'd come close.

What if we'd stayed? Even though it was my brother Jim who was born in California on May 21, 1963, I feel like I've spent most of my adult life trying to answer that question. All my life, I've heard Dad's stories—filled with longing and fantasy—about the West. I started visiting during my college summers. I finally moved to the West Coast for good in 1990.

Three weeks after my brother Jim was born, Mom got on an airplane and flew back to New York, with the new baby and me in tow. A few weeks later, Dad loaded up the car and headed east. This trip netted six new species, mostly in Arizona's Organ Pipe Cactus National Monument. "I didn't believe I could be happy in California," Dad says. When I ask why, he talks about the first half of the drive, which he completed with a buddy who, in addition to having just finished medical school, had a genuine offer from a major-league baseball team. "He didn't know what to do," Dad says. "He was planning to ride his bicycle from Arizona back to San

Diego. He thought the trip would help him figure things out."
What happened to him? "I don't know," Dad says. "I left him in the
desert. Never saw him again."

It isn't really an answer to the question, but I think that, on a
subconscious level, Dad tells the story because he, too, was left in
a desert of his own making: the world of obligation he still felt toward his parents. California was a place of radical self-
reinvention—something Dad might have longed for, but couldn't
accomplish. Staying might have forced him into that personal ref-
ormation. By returning to New York, close to Rose and Morris, he
guaranteed he could never betray his unspoken promise to fulfill
they ambitions they'd set out for him.

Forty-eight hours later, after dropping his friend off, without
having stopped to sleep or to tally another new bird, Dad was
home. California was over, and the decisions my father made—or
didn't make—in the aftermath were no longer in his hands. My
memories, fragmented before, become intact and whole here. And
here's where the trouble starts.

IT WAS AS IF VOLITION, SO LONG AVOIDED, had finally decided to vanish completely from my father's life. There was work. Dad began a
dermatology residency, though he soon quit, mostly because he
didn't want to be tied down with a regular practice. His continued
ambivalence over his career choice was reflected in what he did
choose to do, practicing as a physician in an itinerant fashion: He
freelanced on house calls for a municipal health agency; he toyed
with—then rejected—the idea of an industrial medicine practice;
he worked for the U.S. Selective Service, giving examinations to
young men who'd just entered the armed forces—a fate he believed, at the age of twenty-nine, with a wife and two toddlers, he'd

avoided. In those days, most draftees went, if not enthusiastically, then with a sort of willing resignation and a sense of duty. There was still very little awareness, for most U.S. citizens, of what was beginning to happen in Vietnam. A prelude to the war's eventual escalation came in July 1963, when President Lyndon Johnson ordered that five thousand additional military "advisors" be sent to Southeast Asia. Still, there were just twenty-one thousand Americans fighting overseas.

The buildup that eventually led to full-scale U.S. involvement in Vietnam is usually seen as a gradual thing. But it was just a few days after Johnson sent the advisors that a single event sent the entire, tragic war into its chaotic trajectory, making it a thing that changed not just political currents, but the entire social structure of American life—including my family's. On August 4, 1964, North Vietnamese forces attacked a pair of American destroyers anchored in the waters off Saigon. As retaliatory action was launched, Congress made what many believe to be the most colossal decision (and biggest mistake) of the era: The Gulf of Tonkin Resolution was, essentially, a blank check to President Johnson to prosecute the Vietnam conflict as he wished. By 1968, over five hundred thousand U.S. servicemen would be fighting in Vietnam. The average American death toll was over one hundred soldiers every week. (Viet-

---

°One less-spoken-about effect of the Vietnam conflict was its impact on wildlife. Though the country is a major destination for birders now, with over seven hundred species occurring there, there are at least ninety bird species in Vietnam classified as endangered, many due to lingering effects of the war—especially the use of herbicides as part of a U.S. defoliation strategy—and subsequent development-related deforestation. One encouraging note is the recent finding of a population of the Eastern Antigone Crane, a subspecies of the Sarus Crane, in the Mekong River delta; the bird was thought to be on the verge of extinction, and its reappearance is a sign that the Vietnamese environment may be recovering.

namese losses were far higher.*) The unreserved support for a war that just wasn't workable fomented unprecedented opposition; the peace movement moved in parallel with the era's other cultural changes, unraveling dozens of societal institutions and sending the survivors into their own catastrophic orbits, out of which heartbreak, loneliness, and obsession often grew. By the time all that happened, Dad was opposed to the war. But as 1964 drew to a close, Dad—seeing ten or twenty young soldiers each day—felt as most Americans did: "The government," he says, "knew better than me."

For the next year, Dad worked his various jobs. Mom took employment as a substitute teacher (she was working on her master's degree in English, but never completed her studies) and we all lived near my grandparents' house in a rental property in Kew Gardens Hills (my only memory of which is playing hopscotch on the flagstone tiles that led to our front door). I attended nursery school, and my parents, perhaps aware that they had little to offer each other (and a future that was uncertain in what it would offer them), spent much of their time in activities that didn't involve much one-on-one contact: "We had parties, friends, and we smoked pot and did a lot of completely crazy things," my mom recalls. "But I can't really remember what it was like to be in a room alone together, having a conversation."

In early 1965, Dad's military worries reemerged. More and more medical personnel were needed for the growing conflict. "It was becoming obvious that I hadn't avoided the draft. Nearly every doctor I knew under the age of thirty-five was being called up." It was just a question of when. Dad waited, his anxiety vanishing inside of him, emerging as a form of paralysis: plans to open a medical practice were abandoned, and the house hunting my parents had just begun also halted.

He didn't watch birds.

Nineteen sixty-five was Dad's second year since he'd begun birding that he saw no new species. (The first, during his post-college struggle to find direction in life, was about choices unmade. Now it was about choices that no longer existed, that had dissolved into awful inevitability.)

That submerged, unfulfilled desire exploded in February 1966. The pressure had built unceasingly, and my parents had a huge fight: My mother went home from a party by herself, while Dad roamed the streets, enraged. When he finally returned, a shouting match erupted. I don't really know what happened, what precipitated the fight, or what exactly my brother and I were doing as the screaming wore on (later recollections of their conflicts are filled, for me, with awful details). But I can say that this began what became a secondary pattern: Mom unloaded her frustrations on Jim and me. It was the first time she'd treated her children in a way that—when I think about it—echoed what her own mother had done to her (again, I don't recall this). She says now, when asked: "I freaked out on you kids. You poor things. It was horrible." I began to have nightmares then; they still come back to me, now, on rare occasions, and they're always the same: I'm waiting, somewhere, for Dad—or some surrogate hero—to rescue me. But he never comes.

THE LETTER FROM THE SELECTIVE SERVICE came soon after. Mom remembers it beginning with a typographical error: "Greeting," it read. But the rest of it wasn't funny. Dad had a choice. Standard conscription called for a year stateside and a year in Vietnam. But as a doctor, he had an alternative: an extra year, with the entire term most likely spent in Europe, family included (though nothing was guaranteed, and the prospect of Vietnam always loomed). Dad asked Mom what he should do.

"If I choose Vietnam," he wanted to know, "will you wait for me?"

My mother said she wasn't sure.

My mom's memories of this reflect how conflicted she was. Sometimes, as we spoke, she seemed to say she knew the marriage wouldn't last. Other times, she recalls, as does my dad, that there was a sense of hopefulness that the stay overseas might help things: "The idea of Europe was very exciting," Mom says. "It seemed like an unbelievable adventure."

Today, Dad only recalls that "the prospect of Europe was exciting, bird-wise." I don't know if he understood, somehow, that the relationship was sputtering to an end. I don't know if he believed living abroad would offer us a chance for real adventure—human adventure. What I do know is that Dad doesn't want to go back to that time, because whatever hopes he had then would ebb and flow, but ultimately pass beyond his reach.

THERE WOULD BE LOTS OF BIRDS IN EUROPE. But first, there was Texas. Twelve weeks of basic training. Propelled, perhaps, by excitement over the future, my parents got along. They found a French restaurant they liked in, of all places, downtown San Antonio, just blocks from the Alamo. Dad continued his pattern of solo weekend birding: on March 13, 1966, he saw his five hundredth species at the Santa Ana Wildlife Refuge. It was an ordinary bird, the Olive Sparrow, and there was no celebration. Late during the Texas stint, Dad rented a car and drove to the Rio Grande, bagging thirteen new species. It was his biggest day since being a teenager.

I was four years old—old enough to know how to swim; old

enough to ride a bike; old enough to have birds pointed out to me, and to know that doing so made my father happy, and made me feel proud. Old enough to always remember the Scissor-tailed Flycatcher, to feel—to this day—that it's the best bird. My favorite.

We were scheduled to leave for Europe on June 3, 1966. When he finished basic training, Dad's feelings about Vietnam and the military were fairly unformed. But both my parents sensed the changing of the times. Part of it was the futility of his duties: Dad was being trained, more or less, to be a mess-hall inspector—an essential job, for sure, but not much of a medical practice. And there were harbingers of the social upheaval to come. My mother was becoming curious about the nascent women's movement—especially the sexual freedom it offered. And Dad remembers the moment his counterculture roots—the Bohemian leanings he'd abandoned upon entering medical school—returned. He was driving back from that Rio Grande birding excursion, flipping the radio dial, trying to find something beyond agricultural reports and Spanish *nortenos* that blared from powerful, cross-border transmitters. He paused for a moment, as an odd and unconventionally musical voice sang, twisting words over a simple strummed guitar and breathy harmonica. "I can't really describe what I thought," Dad says, "other than it was so different—even outrageous." Bob Dylan sang: "Everybody must get stoned." To a barely reformed Greenwich Village hipster, those four words were enough to reawaken curiosity.

We left for Europe on June 3, 1966. Dad's life list was at 505.

CHAPTER FIVE

A NEW CONTINENT

" It isn't very often that you see a bird well and are unable to identify it. But that's what happened in May 1968. I went on a Greek island cruise and one of the stops was the island of Crete. That afternoon, I saw a small bird—a passerine, probably a warbler, and clearly a bird with which I was not familiar. It seemed to be about five inches long, with a small body and a very long tail. There was nothing in my European Peterson that resembled it. I made some notes and chalked it up as unidentifiable, at least for the moment. In the back of my mind was the thought that it might have been an Asian or African bird, somehow strayed out of range. In 1982, I was studying for my first organized birding tour, to Kenya. I noticed that the Graceful Prinia occurred and bred in southern Turkey, Lebanon, Israel, and Egypt. It was clearly the bird I saw! It is apparently unrecorded in Crete, but since that island isn't far from the bird's known localities to the northeast, east, and south, it seemed clear it could be found there. So, it went into my list, finally, nearly fifteen years late."

—Graceful Prinia (*Prinia gracilis*),
June 1968, Crete, in the
Mediterranean Sea, #708 if identified
at time of original sighting.

ONE AFTERNOON A FEW YEARS AGO, when I was visiting Dad on Long Island, I borrowed a car and drove west. I bypassed New York City and headed across New Jersey to Pennsylvania. If I'd described my quest to anyone, they might have thought I was a little crazy: I was traveling to Philadelphia to find an ocean liner. Since Pennsylvania doesn't border on any ocean, the initial geography can be hard to conjure, but there is, in fact, a major port there: the Delaware River snakes beneath the New Jersey border, near Atlantic City, and for many years, the dry docks along that waterfront have been the site of major maritime construction.

But for now, I was looking for something not being built, but falling apart.

My memories of the S.S. *United States* are, of course, tied to Dad, so they're tied to birds. The ship was probably the greatest American-flagged passenger vessel ever built: It still holds the record for the fastest-ever Atlantic crossing, making its July 1952 maiden voyage from Norfolk, Virginia to Bishop Rock, England, in three days, ten hours, and forty minutes, averaging over 65 mph. It was the biggest ocean liner ever built in North America, and ran continuously until 1969. Our voyage left New York Harbor on June 3, 1966. We were on our way to Germany, where Dad would be stationed. Normally, draftees and their families didn't get to use luxury liners to report to their postings (besides Dad, Mom, Jim, and me, the passenger manifest for that journey included the Duke of Windsor). But Mom was afraid of flying, and Dad had another reason to provide for her comfort: "I knew there would be birds I might never have a chance to see along the way."

Before I left for Philadelphia, I asked Dad how he'd managed to convince the army to allow this rather unusual request from a young officer with little clout. It wasn't hard, he said: "Everyone told me it would be impossible, but I found out who to make the request to, and wrote letters to them in Washington."

Though Dad's ability to show focused determination has long since ceased to surprise me, I was marveling at how far he was willing to go to confront authority in order to get my mother something she wanted when I arrived at the dry dock. Though I remember specific things that happened aboard the S.S. *United States*, my recollection of her is mostly informed by a single black-and-white picture that has survived the years that followed our trip: a four-year-old boy, not even tall enough to reach his father's waist, holds his father's left hand, and his mother holds the right. The little boy and the father are looking in the same direction— out and up, toward the open ocean. They're both wearing horn-rimmed glasses; the little boy is in a navy suit, bought just for the trip. His facial features—dark eyes, a small nose—duplicate his mother's. She peers in a different direction, maybe toward home. A smaller boy, with pale blond hair, holds her other hand. His gaze follows that of his older brother and father. All of us are wearing life jackets as we cross the deck.

Dad and I spent a lot of time looking in the same direction on our five-day trip, Dad scanning the sky with his binoculars. I was trying to look for birds, but mostly, I was looking at him.

I tried to help. "A sea gull! A sea gull!"

Correction: "A Herring Gull," Dad said, reminding me to refer to a specific species; to this day, I find myself feeling a bit smug when I hear people referring to big white shorebirds using the more generic term. But then, I mostly just wanted to get it right. "A Herring Gull," I repeated, once out loud, then over and over again to myself.

A low warehouse sits at the end of the parking lot in Philadelphia. A few crooked trees grow through cracked patches of asphalt. And beyond the building, almost hidden—as odd as it is to believe that one could keep the presence of an ocean liner a secret—I see a pair of broad, faded crimson streaks, the ship's old smokestacks, just peeking above the artificial horizon.

I have to walk around the warehouse to see the entire vessel.

I'm stunned. That whole boat trip comes rushing back; I remember my grandmother Betty visiting us before we set off from New York Harbor, and admonishing me not to fall overboard; it was an anxiety Mom clearly shared, as she checked the straps on my life jacket a half-dozen times each day. I remember the shuffle-board courts and what were, to me, the magical daily fruit bowls that somehow appeared each morning in our cabin.

The boat towers above me, as tall as a ten-story apartment building. The white paint beneath the main deck is flaked; the portholes below are covered in rust, and some are broken. The black paint below the ship's waterline is cracked and peeling. But the ship's name is still intact; not a single letter is obscured. The words curve around the bow: UNITED STATES. And then, just below, the former home port: NEW YORK. The railing that surrounds the bow is partially destroyed. The missing section is exactly where I stood, with my father, nearly forty years before, admiring him as he peered into the onrushing ocean. Sometimes he'd step away, and I'd feel proud that I was trusted with the post, even for a second. My mother would rush to grab my hand and pull me away from the edge; I remember reflecting, alternately, my dad's feelings of adventure and Mom's anxiety, especially when I let a balloon drift from my hand, over the bow of the ship, and was struck by guilt for having set it free so far from shore.

I wandered around the dock for a while, walking the length of the ship, before returning to the bow. It was nearly noon, and with the sun glaring overhead, I could barely see. I liked the feeling. It made it easier for me to imagine that a small boy was still there, still staring, with his father, into the future.

IN THE PICTURE TAKEN ON THE DECK of the S.S. *United States*, we all look happy, excited. Mom says now that she was forcing a smile—she was just too confused, too worried to be happy—but despite this, I love the photograph. When I imagine a family, this is what I see. I remember tugging away from the pier on Manhattan's West Side; we steamed south, passing the Statue of Liberty, and then turned east, along the south shore of Long Island, overtaking Dad's favorite birding spots: the Rockaways, Jamaica Bay, and Jones Beach. Our journey would take five days; we'd initially dock at Southampton, England, and then continue on to Bremerhaven, a German North Sea port that was built from scratch in 1827 as a city exclusively devoted to then newly born, deep-water maritime commerce. It remains one of the world's leading seaports; if you own a German car, it was shipped out of this city.

Dad didn't expect to see many birds on the trip, since there aren't that many species to spot on the open sea, but the ones he saw were important, tough finds for the average birder. Dad's first nautical lifer was the Manx Shearwater, a desirable oceangoing bird that spends practically its entire life at sea, skimming the water's surface for food—that's where the name comes from. (Later, as a teenager, I'd be with Dad when he made a potentially important shearwater spotting off Long Island. It was one of the first demonstrations I had as an adolescent of his genuine birding skills.)

Over the next few days, Dad added three more species to his life list: Leach's Storm-petrel, Great Skua, and the Fulmar. Dad darted about the boat with his binoculars, while Mom spent most of her time looking after us. When Dad did relax, joining us as we lounged by the pool, he made sure to bring, and study, his newly purchased Peterson's *A Field Guide to the Birds of Britain and Europe*. In the evenings, Dad recalls, we did what most maritime travelers do: "We ate. There were enormous amounts of food." (There was entertainment on board, as well. I remember a piano being played constantly; I later learned that this was a special instrument—the world's only *fireproof* grand piano. In fact, the entire S.S. *United States* exhibited an anti-incendiary obsession, and when the ship was mothballed at the end of its career, it needed to be sailed to Europe, where a specialist could safely dismantle the vessel's asbestos infrastructure.) At the Southampton docks, five British species—the Shag, Rook, Carrion Crow, Swift, and Shellduck—boosted his life list to 515.

In those days, that was a fairly formidable quantity, though the number was small enough to signify dedication, not obsession; birders with higher numbers tended to reach them mostly because birds were their profession, and not a passionate hobby. It was a small and nearly imperceptible overture to what would become a consuming lifetime of global counting; Dad's playing field was expanding, but he hadn't yet set his sights on the world. "I was doing what I always did," he says. "Birding wherever I went. But I didn't really think I'd go much farther."

From England, we traveled overnight, arriving at the German coastline as dawn was breaking. Mom remembers the lights of Bremerhaven growing larger and larger as we approached, and feeling more and more excited about the new world she would experience. (To both my parents, Europe seemed mostly exotic; though Mom had some ambivalent feelings about the Germans left over from World War II, for the most part, they saw the continent of the 1960s in Cold War terms, as a transformed place and partner to America.) Dad changed into his military uniform and we gathered on deck with our luggage (most of our possessions, including a jet-black Chrysler with tailfins and a passenger-door panel stuffed with marijuana, had been shipped earlier). As we watched the dawn break—perfect birding time—Dad scanned the shore with his binoculars. He quickly added another four species: Blackbird, Chaffinch, Eurasian Jay, and Turtle Dove—all common enough European species, but important because they were his first on the continental mainland. My main memory is of hearing people speak German. My grandparents rarely spoke Yiddish at home, so it was my first conscious awareness that other languages existed. I thought it was strange.

We had a nine-hour train ride to Mannheim, the little town near Heidelberg where we'd first be stationed. As we waited on the platform, Dad made check marks in his new Peterson, carefully noting the date and place. The book would soon be nearly full of those records, and with each one, Dad's life would move more toward being focused almost exclusively on those soaring targets.

✿ ✿ ✿

THE BIRDING COMMUNITY DAD CONSORTED WITH in the United States didn't exist in Germany. Though the country's penchant for order might appear to make it a fine candidate for development of a listing culture, it actually exists, along with other non–English-speaking nations, on the second tier of fanatic avian hobbyism. Why are Americans and Brits seemingly more interested in counting birds? Nobody really knows, but my guess is that the activity is an offshoot of a brand of science that, for the most part, is best conducted by empires. In the earliest days of ornithological activity, both countries were aggressively expanding their borders, and at each new outpost, there was plenty of novel fauna to be found and studied (in the British case, global empire led to some of the first scientific encounters with the astonishing biodiversity of the tropics; America's westward expansion also included discovery, but the conquering aspect of Manifest Destiny also doomed many bird populations). Though a few non-English speakers amassed grand collections of global specimens, the travels of Darwin and his lesser-known counterpart, Alfred Russell Wallace—and the conclusions they drew from their travels—were a by-product of Britain's global acquisitiveness. The theory of evolution grew, in a sense, from these inventories of conquest.

Britain developed a birding culture early, and it has never fully merged with the American sport, though the top listers consolidate their tallies. British birding is seen as even more eccentric than our version of the activity, in league with that country's other collecting obsessions, like trainspotting or growing exotic roses, rather than science. In the United States, folks call themselves either bird watchers or birders, and distinguish the two labels with a rather soft boundary, vaguely related to the seriousness of the pursuit and the pursuer. In Britain, hard-core birders are called "Twitchers," a term tinged with more than a bit of derisiveness. The word refers to the way these birders get "twitchy" when a new species is near. The *Oxford English Dictionary* offers this example of real-world usage, from a 1982 London *Times* story: "Twitchers are only interested in spotting rarities to claim they have seen them. Ornithologists are serious students, who despise and distrust twitchers."

British birders are less dependent on field guides than their American counterparts; instead, they rely on a form of networking that involves trading maps, directions, and other tools for finding a specific species on a person-to-person basis. This birding intelligence is known as "Gen," and is derived from the printed information given to Royal Air Force pilots on World War II bombing runs (there's some debate about the origin of the term; it may come from *general information*, or it may be an abbreviation drawn from the word *intelligence*). But even that kind of random data was lacking in the 1950s, when birders planned to build their lists on the continent. Perhaps because Europe's boundaries are more related to language and culture than geography, only a few individual guides to single countries had been published. But in the years following World War II, exploring the continent became easier; there were better roads and trains, and intranational conflicts centered around Cold War borders, not the individual nations of Western Europe. Roger Tory Peterson's European guide was published in 1954, with the same goal as his earlier U.S. edition*—making birding accessible to the masses.

---

*The guide, at least in subtext, also seemed to serve a political purpose—promoting the notion of Europe as a single entity, as opposed to a conglomeration of bickering nations on a geographic pseudo-continent. "The study of the natural history of single countries is insufficient," wrote Julian Huxley, founder of the World Wildlife Fund, in his introduction to the first international Peterson guide. Huxley's ability to imagine utopia ran in the family, though his brother Aldous's vision, as expressed in 1932's *Brave New World*, is significantly darker.

By the time we arrived in Germany in 1966, Dad had thoroughly pored over his Peterson guide, checking off birds he'd already seen that were common to both continents. Of the 452 species Peterson included, Dad arrived in Germany seeking 299.

He had three years.

IF YOU SUDDENLY WOKE UP IN PATRICK HENRY VILLAGE and walked around, wondering where you were and what bird guide you should use, you would almost certainly reach for one of the North American spotting handbooks. Though the town is just outside of Heidelberg, an ancient university city filled with castles and cobblestone streets, it is, without doubt, the most typically suburban place I've ever lived. We had a movie theater with twenty-five-cent Saturday matinees and we lived on streets named after historic American places—our address was 10 Gettysburg Way—and attended on-base schools, where we sang "The Star Spangled Banner" each morning and pledged allegiance twice a day. As unpatriotic as it might sound, I found the whole ritual rather silly; we knew we were Americans, and it felt more like an imposition of military discipline on grade-school kids (another element of this was the constant monitoring of our Beatles-like hair length; I was sent home several times with notes commanding a barber visit) than anything meaningful.

Our family was different. We didn't fit into the military routine. Dad finagled an odd apartment, a Bohemian series of rooms at the top of our barracks that had been used as maid's quarters back when officers stationed in Heidelberg were treated more grandly; for Jim and me, it meant our own bedrooms, plus multiple playrooms—one for toys, the other for our pet hamsters—as well as a room for Dad to practice his saxophone and several that just stood empty.

But the biggest contrast was related to the way Dad whittled down those 299 species. While other military families rarely ventured beyond the confines of the base—one friend of mine who also spent some time as an army brat explained that her folks "just didn't see the point; they had everything they needed, right there"—we were constantly traveling. Dad's first two excursions in Germany were to the Black Forest, where he'd found a hunting shop that could sell him a pair of Carl Zeiss 8x50 binoculars—the best and most coveted birding glass in the world, costing $175— and to Wolfsburg, where he picked up a 1968 Volkswagen Westphalia camper van (price: about $2,700, or about thirty percent more than the standard mid-1960s cost of a VW Beetle in the United States; we had the Chrysler as well). On the way, he saw seven new birds; again, typical European species, nothing truly rare. The van would open up the rest of the continent. A week later, we took our first European field trip: a weekend in Holland. Another seven new birds. Within a month, Dad's continental tally had reached seventy-six.

IT WAS A GIDDY TIME, and not just about birds. My parents, who seemed to be getting along, even enjoyed some explorations together—staying in a four-star hotel in Luxembourg; visiting Amsterdam's Van Gogh Museum; taking a weekend jaunt to Paris. (Jim and I were left with a babysitter. We both remember Frau Ingeborg as truly evil; she didn't have an ounce of warmth in her, and her preferred means of discipline was a soapy mouthwash.) For the first time in their marriage, there was a pattern, a semblance of routine:

Patrick Henry Village during the week, and travel on weekends (sometimes made long by Dad's knack for creative work scheduling, which he'd later take advantage of to the fullest as his list accumulated into the thousands, roaming the world for weeks at a time as he ostensibly held a full-time job). Dad's military duties were fairly nine-to-five; he was working as a public health officer, inspecting mess halls and bomb shelters. On weekends, with my brother and me either along or left at home with a nanny, Rosalind and Richard traveled an ever-widening circle around Heidelberg. Soon, Dad possessed an easy familiarity with the regional bird life, giving him the chance to pursue rarities: On a trip to the Swiss Alps, he saw what he describes as "my first great European bird": the Wallcreeper.

The Wallcreeper's characteristics are emblematic of what birders prize: its physical uniqueness is an environmental adaptation; what makes the bird fun to look at also makes it hard to see. The Wallcreeper is a specialist, built for climbing high-altitude rock faces, with a long, jabbing beak evolved to snatch insects from crevices. The oddball adaptation to life in difficult-to-access places makes the bird quite a rare find (one British field guide describes it as "One of the most spectacular birds in the world . . . a 'Red Letter' bird whenever seen"). Several members of the seven thousand club haven't seen it, and those who have, with the exception of Dad, made the sighting in Asia, where it is marginally more common.

When Dad told me about the Wallcreeper, he seemed genuinely nostalgic. "What a special bird," he said. The moment has become idealized. Those early trips were tiny islands of joy in seas that were otherwise beginning to look ominous.

THE TRAVEL WAS THE ONLY PART OF OUR LIVES that any of us looked forward to. Dad felt ill-used as a doctor—he basically had "nothing to do"—and especially resented that the skills he'd sacrificed for seemed worthless. But he kept his frustration in check around his family; it bubbled out only in isolated incidents—a fight with a German neighbor after an argument took on anti-Semitic overtones; increased experimentation with alcohol, cannabis, and psychedelics. Mostly, Dad found relief in planning our trips, in getting away from army life. But the trips also served another purpose: They soothed my mother's increasing restlessness. "I just wasn't going to be 'an officers' wife,'" she says. "I was completely bored on the base, and felt more and more desperate to get away."

Dad tells me that he didn't count birds so rigorously in Europe. That's true, to an extent: With just a few hundred birds to see, and a lot of time to see them, Dad was able to maintain a more leisurely pace than he would later, when his international trips spanned just a few weeks for a single country or region. But he has committed every bird he saw, every place, every date to memory; he can tell you what he ate for lunch on those days, how he found the particular spot. Most of my European memories center around those camper journeys, as well. Each excursion made us feel like more of a family, if only because we were all confined, together, in one tiny vehicle, with nowhere but the skies as an escape.

Regardless, those trips couldn't make my mother feel happy, or free. She was becoming more and more aware of a central fact: that she'd married for the wrong reasons. And, like my grandmother, she had bigger ideas of what she could be; trapped as a housewife didn't fit in with her sense of wanting to experience—and be experienced by—a bigger, wilder world. She was making new friends, mostly German students and couples, and she got involved in a theater group, based out of the English department of Heidelberg University. She had a bicycle, which Dad had bought for her; he was desperate to help her find "things to do." Riding into town to be with her friends felt more liberating than any of the trips she took with us. "I felt horrible guilt," she says. "I understood that I was supposed to be a mother to two children, and a wife. But I couldn't be with your father. It wasn't his fault. But I knew that if I left, he'd be lost."

HOW MUCH DOES EXTERNAL CIRCUMSTANCE, history, play a part in personal decisions? How much did the brutality of World War II, and my grandparents' reaction to it, lead my dad toward birds? How much did the aftermath of that war lock Dad into a destiny he didn't want? The rigidness of the 1950s endowed him with a sense of duty, even though his instincts, if followed, would have led him elsewhere. Then, the fracturing of that rigidity in the following decade led my mother astray, making my father believe that the compromises he'd made had paid off badly.

Because of the chaos it led to—I'm talking here about my family, rather than the world at large—I've always held a mixed view of the movements of the 1960s. There's no question that the ideals and the concrete advances of that era—civil rights, feminism, the emergence of political philosophies devoted to peace and tolerance—were badly needed to correct an unbalanced American society. But I hate the era's narcissism and drug use, and the way the sexual permissiveness of the age had such a destructive effect on families. (This comes from an essentially liberal guy, but what I believe in, in theory, doesn't change the messiness of what I saw on the ground.) In reality, the good and the bad are probably inseparable, but I saw how much the bad further made the world my father was living in seem all the more unhappy and beyond his control. (Dad, for his part, didn't ever care for the hippie movement and the loose self-indulgence it promoted, especially in my mom and her friends. He sees himself as more influenced by the relatively rigorous intellectualism of the Beat Generation. But he understands that the times—being an independent woman was suddenly not just an option, but an expectation, especially among my mom's crowd—more than Mom's character, doomed their marriage.)

Dad was not conservative by any means. In the summer of 1967, both my parents were thrilled by the release of *Sgt. Pepper's Lonely Hearts Club Band*. They were stunned and elated by growing protests against the Vietnam war, which they joined, despite the fact that we were a military family. For my mother, those movements seemed especially natural. As thousands of young people crowded into San Francisco's Haight-Ashbury that August, Mom joined demonstrations in the Heidelberg town square. European flower children protested the war and sang folk songs in smoke-filled clubs carved into old air-raid shelters. Dad bought Mom a guitar, and sometimes she took us to town with her. I still love thinking about the sound of her soft singing voice; there was a lullaby she'd made up about two sleeping frogs in the moonlight, and sometimes she'd sing Beatles songs, like "Ob-La-Di, Ob-La-Da," from *The Beatles* (the double-record set is more commonly known as *The White Album*).

But more often, she went on her own. She was drifting away, leading a double life: She was both the cute American girl with long black hair and a peasant blouse, singing and cavorting in the medieval streets and the wife of an unhappy army captain, the mother of two little boys.

IF YOU TURN ON YOUR CLASSIC-ROCK STATION and listen long enough, there's a good chance you'll eventually hear "White Bird." (You might not recognize the name of the song, but you'll instantly

recall it when you hear the odd, five-string violin riffs filling in behind the vocals.) You could easily mistake the contrapuntal male-
female harmonies for The Jefferson Airplane, for Grace Slick and
Paul Kantner. In fact, the singers are David and Linda LaFlamme,
a San Francisco–based duo. He was a fairly well-known jazz violin-
ist who'd lately embraced psychedelia; she was a keyboard player
with a soaring, almost eerie voice.

During the summer of 1967, my mother listened to "White
Bird" over and over.

We had birds everywhere in our house: a metal sculpture of a
peacock; a bronze toucan; pictures and Dad's books. It is almost
too much of a cliché to say that Mom saw herself as a possession,
something to be checked off, but she remembers the lyrics of the
LaFlamme song, and she remembers believing them: "White bird
in a golden cage . . . white bird must fly, or she will die." She remembers learning to play the song, and singing it over and over
(she couldn't quite master her other favorite song, the lyrics of
which were equally telling: the Beatles' "Ticket to Ride").

What if she'd been older? What if my parents had tried harder?
What if Dad had allowed himself to be a little bit more of what he
wanted to be? What if the world had been different? Sometimes,
decades later, I feel like these pointlessly hypothetical questions
are the basis of my own obsessions, which manifest mostly as a re-
lentless perfectionism—borne, perhaps, from a sense of wanting to
live in a more controllable world. But if any of them had actually
happened—and none seem all that difficult—everything would
have been different.

Dad's list is a triumph today. But it is a triumph that can't help
but give rise to alternative scenarios, to imagining a life for my father that didn't center around a single, all-consuming interest,

around substituting, year after year, so many thousands of birds for one real person who knew—as 1967 became American history, and millions of people began to seek ways to live their lives outside of convention—that she'd have to fly.

MY BROTHER AND I ARE CURLED into our sleeping bags, suspended above the front seats of the VW van. The rough canvas hammock that holds us is moist, made wet by condensation dripping off the vehicle's sheet-metal roof, above us. The day before, we'd driven south from Heidelberg, moving along France's Mediterranean coastline until we reached the swampy Camargue region, along the delta of the Rhône River, where the sea is kept in check by sandy embankments. We set up camp on the sand. The brackish lagoons and marshes of Camargue fascinated me; what we experienced there was the beginning of my own love of the outdoors. I wrote a report on the area when I was a little older, noting the place's desolate beauty; that it is famous for the resident *gardians*, a sort of Provençal cowboy; and that it is home to some of the world's most aggressive mosquitoes.

The Rhône delta is France's most bird-rich spot. Over 400 species are found there, with another 150 possible as strays and accidentals. When we visited, the area was still unpreserved, with parts as wild and open as in medieval times. My parents had been to the Camargue once earlier, during Dad's first European spring migration, with new birds in prolific quantities; as they'd traveled along the French, Catalan, and Spanish coastline, Dad's life tally had increased by sixty-nine species.

But the trip—like everything my parents did together in Europe, for better or worse—was more than birds. My father still gets excited when he talks about seeing Neanderthal cave paintings in Basque country and watching Spain's top matador, the legendary *El Cordobes*, fight a bull in Seville. For once, the mix of birds and everything else seemed just about right. The couple continued to Gibraltar, where Dad stopped to try for a few new species at Cádiz, near the mouth of the Guadalquivir River. This is another legendary European birding spot, a place where serious listers pick up vagrant African species (easy to spot among the area's most common birds, the thousands of flamingos that feed on the brine shrimp that live in the delta—the pinkish crustaceans are what give the birds their traditional coloration). Dad quickly added the Egyptian Vulture, a bird frequently seen as a carving on sarcophagi (the endangered species is less ennobled by its habit of eating dung, rather than carrion; the culinary behavior turns out to be a way for the bird to consume essential carotenoids, which give the species its orangish color) and the madly colored Purple Gallinule, paint-spattered blue, purple, and green, with a red and yellow bill (combined with its Chaplinesque waddle, you've got a highly memorable species; even Mom recalls it, though she also remembers wishing they'd "stayed a little longer to actually observe it"). Mom's memories of that first trip to southern Europe are pleasant, and she was able to see the true advantage of traveling with a birder: "We didn't stick to the traditional routes," she recalls. "By definition we had to go off the beaten track." They spent days wandering through gypsy towns where old women worshipped black Madonnas, and camping on windswept beaches where wild horses ran. "He'd be out watching," Mom says, "and I'd be out wandering."

The arrangement was acceptable, but I had to ask: Didn't either of them ever think that they could bird together? Birding couples are famous—Sandra Fisher and Michael Lambarth were a British pair who saw over seven thousand birds together; several others have recently joined the six thousand club. Dad says Mom wasn't interested; Mom's view is a little more introspective: "I didn't have my own binoculars," she says, "but I don't fault him for not asking me if I wanted to watch. I just didn't know how to relate to birds, and he didn't know how to relate them to me."

Even so, the trip was successful enough that, a few months later, my parents repeated the journey with Jim and me. By then, both seemed preoccupied with the uncertainty of their future. I'm not sure what role that distraction played in our poor choice of a camping spot, but I remember being awakened—terrified—by pounding on the camper's windshield before dawn.

Thump!

Thump!

I opened my eyes and saw a face pressed against the glass, obscured by the foggy dew that had condensed inside the van overnight. I wiped the mist away from the big, curved windshield and saw that some of the haze was outside; it was as if we were in a cloud bank. Then, suddenly, the face became clearer: an old woman, panicked.

Thump!

La Mer!

La Mer!

I didn't understand what she was talking about; even if I'd known the translation of the word she was saying, I was half-asleep and wouldn't have comprehended. But as I slid down and opened the passenger-side window, she said it again. That's when I noticed that the car was in a half-foot of water. The ocean was rising! By this time, Mom was awake, and she was shouting at Dad. He rose, too, and the old woman repeated her warning. All of a sudden, there was a frenzy of activity. It was high tide, and one of the levees had overflowed. Dad quickly tossed the nearly soaked camping gear into the back; by this time, Jim and I were terrified, and we huddled with Mom as Dad started the engine and turned the van around, and we skidded away.

It was, I think, the first time in my life I remember feeling truly scared, as if the world were beyond the control of my parents. In fact, until then, they'd mostly managed to hide their troubles, maintaining an illusion that their varied interests, as we traveled in our camper, were complementary, that our family somehow functioned. I knew that we were different from other families—I had a Dad who watched birds and a mom who played folk songs—but I didn't know how different. After we escaped the flooded beach, that otherness would assert itself, note by note, in each one of us. It wasn't that the moment introduced danger to our family—we were already in trouble—but it made it, especially to two young boys, suddenly seem real. It shined light on a precipice that had previously been obscure.

IF WE ALL TEND TO IDEALIZE MOMENTS IN OUR CHILDHOOD, then my most perfected recollection is of the last trip we took in Europe, in April 1969. Maybe it's partly because we spent such a long time—nearly a month—traveling through Spain (my parents took us out of school; that alone is enough to fuel a personal legend). But there's also a bigger reason: During that month, Dad became my teacher. It was as close as we'd ever been. He sat with me every day and used his Peterson *Field Guide* to show me the world. (Practically, my most important lesson was how to use an index; I remember being asked to look up different birds, different places, and then find cross-references. Dad showed me how to be thorough—a trait that I carry through to this day, almost to the point of mania; my editors can tell you how much I tend to over-research my writing projects, to the point where all of us play a knowing shell game of deadlines, specially adjusted for me.) I remember looking up the Hoopoe—still my brother's favorite bird—and then staring at it, in wonderment, as it appeared in real life the next afternoon.*

Those gorgeous moments are a flash of white light in my memory. They blot out the rest of that final journey.

My father had, earlier, had a firsthand experience with the way perception skews toward the things we want to see. He and Mom took a trip to Greece, and "we had a great time," Dad recalls. Then he adds: "It was a total illusion." Not long after returning, Dad found out that if Mom seemed happy, it was because she'd become romantically involved with a member of her Heidelberg

---

*The Hoopoe is one of the most mythical Eurasian birds. The species, which has a crown-like crest, is believed by many cultures to be especially wise. The best example of this comes from the poet Farid Ud-Din Attar, a Persian Sufi (the mystical branch of Islam), who wrote *The Conference of the Birds* in the twelfth century. In it, the birds of the world convene to discover which of them is wisest, and who shall rule them (and, by allegory, the entire corporeal world). The Hoopoe—deftly answering each question—proves to be the bird most connected to the spiritual realm. An example of the Hoopoe's Zen-like thinking:

"So long as we do not die ourselves,
and so long as we identify with someone or something,
we shall never be free.
The spiritual way is not for those wrapped up in exterior life.
Good fortune will come to you only as you give.
If you cannot renounce life completely,
you can at least free yourself
from the love of riches and honors."

(Penguin Classics, July 1984 edition. Edited and translated by Afkham Darbandi and Dick Davis.)

theater group. Dad was devastated—and furious. Unable to resolve their differences, Dad tried desperately to convince Mom to want him, to want to stay, and Mom tried with equal fervor to reconcile her desire to be free with her obligations. Neither succeeded.

It is easy to say that the times had much to do with their inability to live for each other. There's no doubt, as Mom says, that they "were part of something bigger happening in society." But there was more to it: These were two people who had never been able to do what they wanted. Mom had never been on her own. Dad's wants were more complex, and he'd revised them so many times—by compromising on college and on medical school, by marrying so quickly. What was filling him with so much grief was that his compromises weren't even working; he didn't get to dedicate his life to birds, and the marriage and career he'd traded that dream for were broken.

They kept trying, mostly by not splitting up; the most important bond they had were Jim and me. Their fights became louder and messier, and—in a sense—their most intimate (if negative) connection. For the first three months of 1969, their troubles so preoccupied Dad that he stopped watching birds, adding only the Common Crane, spotted as a flock passed over a German highway. We were due to leave Europe at the end of May. In late Spring, they began planning our final trip.

I don't remember how angry Dad was, how he tried, over and over, angrier and angrier, to convince my mother that Spain could make everything better. I don't remember my Mom's response, greater and greater self-indulgence, contemplating other romantic partners and envisioning a life that didn't always involve traditional care-giving for her children, persuaded by her own feelings and the changing times that freedom and family and faithfulness were an incompatible trio.

The troubles couldn't have been invisible to a seven-year-old. I just don't remember them; or, perhaps, I haven't allowed myself to remember them.

I just remember Spain. I remember Dad teaching me. I remember the smell and the smooth texture of the color plates in the Peterson guide. I remember the sound of the sea, not far from where we camped, and the way the book wouldn't close flat because sand was lodged in its binding. We took a ferry to the Balearic Islands, avoiding Mallorca, the biggest and best-known of them, and going directly to Ibiza, then a hippie paradise, where clothing was optional and music played constantly. While we were there, Dad got his second new bird of the year, Scop's Owl, as we rounded a curve and it flew in front of us, glancing off the wide, flat front end of the camper. I remember seeing the bird's belly; it was the color of tree bark (that and the bird's small size—it's about seven inches long—allow it to hide in the brush), up against the windshield, brightly illuminated by our headlights. We rushed out of the car and watched as the stunned bird shook off the blow and fluttered away.

On April 14, Dad saw two lifers: Marmora's Warbler (another member of this difficult-to-identify bird family; most notable is the bird's name: Alberto de Marmora was a general who fought under Napoleon; his hobby—conducted about the same time Elliot Coues was collecting bird skins in North America—was collecting biological samples, and his collection is stored today at the University of Turin) and Temmick's Stint (a bird similar to the sandpipers we have on both our Atlantic and Pacific Coasts). I helped him, marking the Peterson guide that was now ours, a least for the moment.

These memories are so blissful and sacred to me that I was shocked to hear the real story of that last trip.

"We went to Ibiza to try to heal our wounds and regroup," Mom says. I think she means that this was the last chance they had to do something with their marriage. I hesitate to say save it because I don't think that was possible. Rather, I think, it was to consider the future: With our upcoming return to the United States, it was a question, maybe, of whether they'd view Europe as a strange, near-nightmare from which they'd return to normalcy, or simply as confirmation that they were never meant to be together. As usual, Dad believed the former, while Mom knew that the marriage was over.

Every morning we sat next to the camper with the bird book. I'd read the descriptions of the birds and match them to the pictures.

"Which do you think that is?"

"Why are they related?"

"Let's turn to another page."

Every night, they'd fight. It wasn't so much that the arguments were about anything specific; rather, each attempted to convince the other to see the opposite point of view. But Dad couldn't get Mom to stay, and Mom couldn't get Dad to let her go. So they battled, with their irreconcilable points of view creating greater and greater tension, then anger.

MOM TOLD DAD SHE WAS LEAVING, that she'd stay in Europe with Jim and me. On our last night in Spain, after a particularly heated argument—another frustrating and circular battle of intransigent desires—Mom drove off in the camper, alone.

Crying, completely distraught, as she came around one of the island's most precipitous turns—the roads are carved out of cliffs that tower above the sea—she drifted into the wrong lane, running a motorcyclist off the road. The rider came inches from tumbling off the edge. He escaped serious injury, but Mom broke down; she was taken by some bystanders to a nearby convent. By the time Dad arrived, the local police had been called. They knew about the American couple who were fighting and causing trouble.

I have only a threadbare recollection of this; having the incident retold to me as I wrote this book brought some of these memories out: uniformed police officers, looking very martial and imposing—this was, after all, Franco's fascist Spain; shouting and attempts to translate; and Jim and me standing outside, staring, before one of Mom's friends led us away.

We were ordered to leave the island immediately.*

Dad drove the camper alone to Zeeland, Holland on May 2, 1969; we'd ship the vehicle home. Again, it was a way of clinging to any thin thread of things we'd done as a family. On the way he saw a Bar-tailed Godwit, an arctic-breeding, sandpiper-like bird that has recently begun to occur along the Atlantic shores of New England. It was new bird member 221, the last he'd see in Europe, and the sighting came almost reflexively: Dad was looking for birds, but he didn't find much escape in them. "There was just too much going on," he says, "for me to find a lot of pleasure in it. My life was coming apart."

We left on May 23, 1969. This time, there was no ocean liner, no sense of adventure or of a new beginning. We crowded onto an army plane at Frankfurt, bound for Gander, Newfoundland, and McGuire Air Force Base in New Jersey. Mom spent the entire trip

---

*Dad says that we were never asked by police to leave the island; Mom says that we were.

with a blanket over her head. Dad tended to Jim and me. I probably picked up on Mom's anxiety, as I remember feeling airsick the
entire trip, and sensing none of the excitement a seven-year-old
normally might over the first plane journey he'd actually be able to
remember (we'd taken another one, from San Diego, when I was
seventeen months old). Dad's Peterson was packed away. He'd
seen 299 of the 452 European species listed in the book. It was
fewer than he'd wanted.

But, coming from so much bad, it was still a little bit of good.

CHAPTER SIX

HOW BIG A LIST?

" The Saw-whet Owl is a regular but uncommon fall migrant and winter-ing bird in the New York area. Despite having birded in the New York re-gion for over twenty years, I had never seen one. Years before, my friend and early birding buddy Michael Fitzgerald had seen one in an evergreen tree in front of his house on 141st Place in Kew Gardens Hills. But by the time I got home, it was gone. When I heard that there was a 'staked out' Saw-whet Owl in Pelham Bay Park in late January 1971, I decided to take my sons, who I was seeing that weekend, to do a little owling. We drove up on a Saturday morning, and immediately saw several birders gathered. Spotting it was easy. Such a tiny owl was fun to see."

—Northern Saw-whet Owl (*Aegolius acadicus*),
January 30, 1971, Pelham Bay Park, New York, #726.

F ROM THE WINDOW OF MY ROOM, I could see Little Neck Bay. On the first floor, directly below, an oversized sunporch offered a spectacular western view: the bridges that crossed Long Island Sound, and marshes, filled with birds. Dad could have set up his telescope there, aiming it toward the water, and we arrived at the perfect time to do it, late August 1969, just as fall migration was peaking.

But there were no birds that autumn. Nothing new for the list, and not even any bird watching.

After we returned from Germany, we lived with Morris and Rose for a few weeks while my parents were house-hunting. Mom had left New York as a girl, and returned as an entirely different person. Dad hoped that being back in the United States would bring her back to that simpler state of mind. All through that summer, they visited neighborhoods—Whitestone, Queens; Brooklyn Heights; and some of the bedroom communities north of New York City, along the Hudson River—keeping appointments with Realtors. I asked Dad why they did this, since divorce, by then, seemed inevitable. He still had hope, he said: "Having a home might help us." It was a desperate move on Dad's part—a gamble, really, considering that he'd almost certainly lose the house. But there was nothing Dad could do, emotionally or personally, so the symbolic act of making a home—something we'd never really had—was his strategy of last resort. Mom was more pragmatic: She had no way of financially supporting herself—she'd received a teaching credential, but wasn't inclined to launch a career in education—and would need a place to live, whether or not it would be with Dad, Jim, or me. (Mom later built a career in the arts, opening a successful stained-glass restoration business.)

They chose an old Victorian in a tiny community on the edge of Northeast Queens, up on a hill, with a wonderful sunset vista.

Douglaston is a quiet place, filled with trees and large houses. (The community—we lived in a section called Douglas Manor, or "The Manor"—remains mostly the same, though it is now a little more crowded. It is best known as the home of tennis star John McEnroe.) Situated on a tiny peninsula that juts into Little Neck Bay, it is surrounded by marshes. My father had visited the spot many times as a boy, though he knew it by another name. This was the eastern side of the Bayside Woods—Dad's "magnificent" teenage birding spot.

Dad stayed in Douglaston with us, sleeping in the guest bedroom, until November. I remember the fighting, the crying, and the moving, which had brought on a sense of isolation and sadness that, in retrospect, seems anything but childlike. I began to withdraw into books and fantasy worlds; even though I was seven years old, I started wetting my bed; and I found it exceptionally difficult to make new friends. I was a tiny kid—a good six or seven inches shorter than my peers, and burdened with thick, horn-rimmed glasses—and not athletic; that I'd just come from a foreign country and had parents who didn't quite fit in to The Manor's conservative culture didn't help matters. (Jim and I, for years, were among just a handful of Jewish kids in all of P.S. 98, the tiny grammar school near the Douglaston train station where I attended grades three through six—a fairly unusual circumstance in the New York City school system; I never really made any close friends in Douglas Manor, and to this day don't feel a lot of affection for the community.)

I remember the first night Dad didn't stay with us. I remember my mother trying to explain it. I was taking a bath, and she came in and sat beside the tub; I played with a toy submarine as she told me that Dad wouldn't be living with us. I can still hear the sound of the water, splashing, as I recall her words. I was unable to meet her gaze. Mom repeated what parents often say to their children during such moments—"It isn't your fault"—and I distinctly recall thinking, as she made the assertion, that she wouldn't be saying such a thing if I *weren't* to blame. Her further accounting, made to a child far too young to understand, that she'd had gotten married and had children too young, only reinforced my sense of guilt. After all that, how could I not have condemned myself for the departure of the one person in the world who I thought *really did* want me?

From that point on, all four of us would be on separate trajectories. My mother would often melt into her own indulgences, taking varying quantities of drugs and bringing a parade of irresponsible and sometimes cruel men into the house and adopting whatever lifestyle they seemed to prefer: Les was deeply drawn to the era's dark psychedelia; Andrew was a gentle, guitar-playing carpenter; Joe was an angry, corrupt police officer. Jim and I would begin to live in our escapist worlds—for me, writing; for him, music. And Dad, though his life was so overturned that he wouldn't see any new birds in 1969 or 1970—he, too, was reeling, at a loss for a genuine calling in medicine or a true role as a husband and father. He would begin to move away from people, into a numeric and geographic wilderness where he'd struggle, and ultimately find, his own purpose.

ON A COLD SATURDAY IN JANUARY 1971, a father and his two sons—both boys wearing the silly snorkel parkas that were in vogue back then; I'd lost a glove, and one hand was stuck in my pocket—walked on what for birders was certainly hallowed ground. Pelham Bay Park is the city's biggest swath of open space—three times the size of Central Park—and was officially sanctified by birders when Ludlow Griscom and the boys of the Bronx Bird Club perfected their aggressive, fast-paced sighting methods there in the 1930s. We were walking toward one of the park's forested areas; we wound past more manicured gardens, mostly barren now, in the midst of winter, and around frozen lakes.

A few weeks earlier, for my ninth birthday, Dad had given me a pair of gifts, both of which I still own: my own paperback copy of the Peterson guide and a pair of Tasco brand binoculars, heavy, solid, and cheap enough for a kid to destroy without too much hand-wringing (I never did, though a chip in the pair's internal prism has left a tiny shard of glass rattling around the interior ever since I dropped them on a stretch of highway near Jones Beach in the mid-1970s).

We'd settled into a routine: weekend visits—Dad would take us to museums and basketball games, to Chinatown and Central Park—that were, for two little boys, just paradise, pure fun, especially compared to the sadness and turmoil Jim and I experienced in Douglaston, at home with Mom. Mom was earning some money as a substitute teacher. She'd met another teacher—a self-absorbed candle-maker from Brooklyn with a bad LSD habit, his trips and parties accompanied, in our living room, by the constant thrum of mind-bending hard rock—and had quickly moved him in with us. (Dad was mystified and infuriated by this: "Didn't she say she wanted to be independent?") She and her new friends would soon open an arts-and-crafts store across from P.S. 98. The Rosetta Stone—and our house—quickly became the neighborhood's favorite hangout for partying twentysomethings, many of whom had younger brothers and sisters in my school. Repeatedly, I'd be taunted by my classmates about Mom's behavior, and there were homes that I simply wasn't allowed to visit, mostly because anybody associated with 20 Ridge Road, where we lived, earned an automatic scarlet letter.

Dad had become director of a drug rehabilitation program in Manhattan, finally finding some satisfaction in his profession. His job was part of the counterculture, and hip, in a way, and he liked the idea that he was genuinely helping people. And he was actively mingling in New York's wild, post-1960s singles scene.

It was all new, for all of us. But that weekend, something familiar returned.

The Saw-whet Owl is a bird that even the most unrepentant wildlife agnostic would find charming. It has gigantic, orange eyes—they look like a cat's—and a pale white face with fluffy, mottled, brownish feathers. But what makes the owl most appealing is its size: It is among the smallest owls on Earth; the bird's dimensions are about the same as your fist. "It is," Dad says, "cute as hell." (That is about as high a compliment as Dad will pay to a bird. He frequently professes that he doesn't really like birds—at least aesthetically—that what he enjoys is finding and counting them. I wonder whether this is true, or whether the statement is some part of his ancient barrier that hides affection and involvement with the natural world. In any case, his stated lack of love for avian individuals conceals, in a way, a greater purpose: the counting and naming that is so much a part of the way humans interact with nature that it borders on the spiritual.)

I thought the bird was cute, too, but what amazed me more was the chase. Our normal weekend routine began with Dad picking us up on Friday night; we'd spend the weekend in Manhattan, usually going to Chinatown for lunch, then driving around the city playing a form of license-plate bingo. (We'd try, each week, to see as many out-of-state automobile tags as we could. The game, naturally, was Dad's idea, and he kept the list of what we'd seen. Our top tally: thirty-one.) On that Saturday, though, we left the city. I remember that Dad was excited. The bird, he told me, was one he'd never seen before, and I proudly carried along my own Peterson guide and my new binoculars. When we got to the park, we joined dozens of other birders, all excited by the idea of adding a new species to their lists.

It was the first time I ever realized that my dad wasn't the only one doing this.

It took us just a few minutes to see the bird. I remember feeling enclosed by the dark green of the trees, staring up at the little bird on a branch. I remember that the bird seemed to look back at me, and I felt like the four of us—Jim, Dad, the owl, and me—were the only beings left on Earth. It was an absolutely gorgeous sensation. In some strange way, it made me feel like we were special. A family again.

In the parking lot, Dad marked the bird off in his guide (he still used the field guide for notation, though he'd also begun keeping his master list as a separate document). We returned to our normal routine on Sunday, stopping at Rose and Morris's house for dinner, and then Dad drove us home. Dad would pull into the gravel driveway, right behind the old camper—it was Mom's car now, shared with the boyfriend she was living with—and said his good-byes. Jim and I trudged up the porch, opened the shabby double doors to the house, and vanished inside. The sounds that always closed our weekends were the starter on Dad's Volkswagen Beetle, the stones under his wheels as he backed away, and the chatter of the little engine accelerating up the hill that led out of the neighborhood. As he headed back toward Manhattan, again passing the Bayside Woods, Dad later told me, he was almost always weeping.

IT WASN'T QUITE TIME FOR THE ERA OF BIG LISTING TO BEGIN, but people were getting ready. Like Dad and so many other Big Listers, James Clements was a New Yorker—he was raised in a Westchester County orphanage—with something to prove. He was about the same age as Dad, and also discovered birds as a preteen. For him, it was during playtime at the wooded farm along the Hudson River that housed twenty-five boys. (In his unpublished autobiography, Clements describes using his knowledge of birds to excel at games like hide-and-seek: "I explained to the boys that I knew exactly where they were hiding by the birds that they disturbed.") His curiosity ignited, Clements found a copy of Peterson's original guide in the local library and was hooked—helped along the way by some typically stringent, rat-a-tat questioning from Dr. Allen Thomas, who was his orphanage guardian and a member of the Bronx County Bird Club.

After World War II, Clements studied biology, then took a cross-country trip, joining the exodus of young men who, inspired by opportunity and the myth of the great American road, felt the strong westward pull of California. "When I saw the Pacific," he

says, completing the thought my dad didn't act on, "I knew I was
going to stay." By the 1960s, he had a thriving printing business
and was becoming active in a group of birders that, in a more
grandiose way, would become as important to the Big Listers as the
Bronx boys were to general hobbyists: Clements and his colleagues
at the Los Angeles Audubon Society—they'd formed a subgroup
called the Small Birding Club—were having big ideas. At a 1969
meeting, Clements, Stuart Keith—the British birder who'd broken
Peterson's single-year record had resettled in Southern California—
and Arnold Small—who gave a lecture series at UCLA called "Birding Planet Earth"—decided that they were each going to try to
reach four thousand species.

Clements and Small were mostly hobbyists, though Small was a
true birding evangelist: He was known for his readiness to go to
the slide projector and enthrall even non-birders with his passionate and animated accounts of birding adventures in places such as
Africa and the South Pacific that, especially then, were truly exotic.

Keith was the most competitive of the group. He wasn't nearly
as well known as Roger Tory Peterson, but he was a celebrity in
birding circles. In 1968, Keith proposed that bird-watchers send
their lists to a central authority for comparison and validation; the
lists were published in a magazine that later came to be called
Birding, whose readership morphed, by 1970, into the American
Birding Association—the amateur group that keeps most birders'
official counts (though no birder is "required" to submit a list, and
several major Listers—including my father—don't send their records to the ABA). Keith was the group's first president; Small followed him into office.

It was in the pages of *Birding* that Keith and Small began to lay
out the boundaries of what would become a highly competitive,
ritualized sport. Some of the articles that Keith and Small wrote

are both astounding in their numeric precision and hilarious, in a sort of dry, "they can't be serious" kind of way. In an article named after Small's "Birding Planet Earth" slide show, Keith wrote: "Let us start with the first question: How many [birds] are there. For the past 20 years or so the generally accepted figure . . . has been 8,600. Recently, because of the number of birds that have been 'lumped,' there has been some concern that that perhaps the figure is too optimistic. However, in talking to my scientific colleagues, I find the view is that this figure is still substantially correct, according to the formula $1 = S + N$, where 1 is the number of birds lumped, s is the number of birds split, and n is the number of new species discovered or described."

Keith, like most birders of the day, thought that seeing half the species on Earth would be a stellar and difficult-to-equal achievement; in 1974, he became the first person to do so, hitting the 4,300 mark (based on his formula). Small—it was a friendly rivalry—wanted to go further, replying in 1976 with a story, also in *Birding*, called "The White-headed Piping Guan, or, How I Found My 4,000th Life Bird in Surinam." Small's piece is an entertaining travelogue, but it started with a raising of the bar: "While 4,000 might seem like a lot of birds, it is still less than half of all the species occurring on planet Earth. Although some of my friends have already passed 'half' (about 4,500 species), and at least one person has gone 'over the top' with 5,000+, I remain more determined than ever to meet in life as many of the other 5,000 'strangers' as I can."

Small's notion that seeing *every* bird might be possible was entirely new. So were his numbers: Just two years after Keith reached "Half," Small's manifesto seemed to be raising the bar for just about everything—how many species one could see, and how many species there actually were. The primary issue in birding seemed not to be logistics, but inflation. Keith was the one who'd just reached five thousand, and according to Small, his rival was *still* at 'Half,' even though he'd added over seven hundred new birds!

What was happening?

The same thing—but magnified—that occurred during Elliot Coues's era: Splitters were battling Lumpers. Since the early 1950s, Lumpers had held the upper hand in birding; there were more species consolidations than expansions. But now, the Splitters were beginning to gain control, owing mostly to emerging understandings of how birds differentiated themselves, especially in the tropics.

But the increased numbers meant nothing without somebody to count them—and that was where the third member of the early troika of Listers came in.

Jim Clements had just returned from a trip to Africa, and he was vexed. He'd added five birds to his list—not well known, since there was no standardization of species names during that period—by asking local scientists and checking wildlife surveys; upon returning home, he looked up the Latin names for the birds and found that they were all one species. That took four off his list, and he was already behind Small and Keith (Clements finally passed his friends in the early 1990s; currently, his list is at about 7,200— virtually tied with my dad). In fact, the entire birding world was a confused mess of common names, and birders, unlike ornithologists, found going to scientific nomenclature distasteful, too unwieldy, and lacking in romance.

The basic problem, as Clements states is this: "How could you keep a list if you didn't know what to list?"

For any birder trying to reach stratospheric numbers, the lack of a single, unified tally of every bird on Earth made the task less of a challenge, and "more of a nightmare," Clements says.

So Clements attempted what was considered to be impossible.

In preparation for *seeing* every bird on Earth, Clements decided he'd have to make a list of every bird on Earth.

The American Museum of Natural History in New York had kept a list of scientific bird names, but that was—by comparison—simpler, since each bird had only one such appellation. The only "list" ever published with a similar scope was the *Checklist of Birds of the World*, edited by J. L. Peters and published by the Harvard Museum of Comparative Zoology. Peters had begun his opus in 1934 and had issued a new volume approximately every three years, finishing in 1962 with the sixteenth volume. It is an impressive collection, serving as a sort of nomenclatural thesaurus and attempting to list nearly every common and local name for the birds it tallies—but it is hardly hobbyist-friendly.

The Clements project would be different: It would be aimed specifically at bird-watchers, it would be a single volume, and it would contain space for check marks and notes. Clements began working on the list in 1970, using the American Museum's Latin names list and the Peters books (he'd trudge, nearly every day, to the Los Angeles County Museum, where the area's only full set of the Peters volumes were housed). Clements moved quickly; he knew that the procedure would be potentially error-filled, so he consulted ornithologists and stuck mostly to reputable, published references. Accuracy was important, of course, but equally key was that the book "serve a good purpose for bird-watchers."

It was a huge challenge: Nobody had ever before considered that a book listing every bird on Earth would serve any purpose for birders, other than to fill out library space. The reason was simple: It seemed impossible to try to see all those birds, unless you had the toughness of a Dean Fisher—the early 1960s round-the-world birder—or the built-in scientific wherewithal of a Peterson or Stuart Keith. But when the first volume of *Birds of the World: A Checklist* came out in 1974, numbering 524 pages and costing less than twenty dollars, it signaled a change: From then on, seeing everything would be a pursuit limited only by desire. If you wanted to do it, if you were compelled to do it, Jim Clements had provided a road map.

ONE PERSON WHO BUILT THOSE EARLY LISTS was Dad's old college roommate, Joel Abramson. Dad had last seen Abramson in 1956. They'd met on the Cornell campus—both of them were birders— and had pledged the same fraternity.

After graduation, Abramson went immediately to medical school, while Dad wandered. Abramson visited him for what he describes as "a little birding, and a little pep talk." They drove out to Montauk, and Abramson encouraged him to go to medical school. "Your father was drifting," Joel tells me. "He was talking about being a real-estate mogul, about a lot of things. His parents wanted him to be a doctor, and I tried to persuade him that it would be a good profession—because it could provide him with both the time and the money to do a lot of bird-watching."

Abramson finally helped convince Dad to become a doctor. But the move seemed to drain, at least temporarily, Dad's birding ambitions. It would be many years before Dad was able to take advantage of the profession the way Abramson did almost immediately: By 1960, Joel had come up with a plan that paralleled the ambitions expressed by Clements and his buddies. "I wanted to see four thousand birds," Abramson says.

During the 1960s, while he practiced medicine in Florida, Abramson built up his list. He lagged behind Keith, Clements, and Small; in fact, he knew little about them, since Big Lists were so rare that they weren't reported, and it was unheard of for a pure hobbyist like Abramson to amass such numbers. And it wasn't easy. Keith was able to see the birds he wanted by handily arranging an expedition to the place in question—or a second trip, if he missed the target bird the first time. ("It was his edge," Clements says; Keith went to Africa so much, in fact, that he was able to write the first definitive guide to the birds of that continent.) This was an advantage Abramson didn't have.

But Abramson had an idea.

"Birding was costing me an incredible amount of money," Abramson said, "and sometimes, I just couldn't get the opportunities, the access to remote places, to actually find the birds that the other guys had because I wasn't part of the ornithological world." But by the late 1960s, Abramson had noticed that more and more people were becoming interested in seeing exotic birds. World travel was becoming more practical, and Keith and Small were beginning to publish *Birding*, which often featured stories listing various numeric accomplishments, along with rudimentary world rankings. Abramson took out his first advertisement in the magazine in 1969, offering a "birding expedition" to the Caribbean. (Dad says that Abramson's decision to start a birding tour company was a way to get over one of the more difficult parts of the game: the expense. "He found a way to get his own birding trips paid for," Dad says. "It was very sharp," he laughs.) Abramson didn't lead the trips; he organized them, and hired top ornithologists—the people who knew where the birds were—as guides. In doing so, he helped create the template that nearly every major bird tour company follows today.

Other outfitters had offered "bird-watching" trips in the past, but they were hardly conducive to generating huge sighting quantities. "A lot of them," Abramson says proudly, "were not as mania-

cal. They weren't birding endurance tests." Abramson's Bird Bonanzas soon began adding more trips—to Mexico, Africa, East
Asia, and South America. For Abramson, that meant traveling virtually free on the profits from the trips.

In 1973, Stuart Keith took a pair of Bird Bonanzas trips to
Southeast Asia and India. (The trips were led by Ben King, who'd
go on to found his own tour company. A King trip is considered to
be the most hard-core of all birding expeditions. Bird with King,
Dad says, and "expect nothing but birds, birds, birds—and total ex-
haustion." This is said in a gleeful tone that assures the listener that
this is considered a very, very good thing.) In all the frenzy, Keith's
best sighting demonstrated the kind of serendipity most birders
live for. He was waiting in his hotel garden for the rest of the group
to arrive, and began playing back a taped recording of a local
species of cuckoo (audio playback is a key method birders use to
attract their quarry; the right song can bring out dozens of curious
species, looking to see what's invading their territory). Almost instantly, a small bird—a Gray Hornbill—appeared in a nearby tree.
It took a moment for Keith to realize that this was, in fact, his
4,300th species—he'd reached the mythical halfway point, and it
had taken him twenty-seven years. "I'll say this for Bird Bonanzas,"
Keith wrote in the *Birding* article chronicling the sighting, "they
deliver. They don't deliver leisurely breakfasts or relaxed cocktail
hours; they deliver birds. This is hard-core birding, from dawn to
dusk every day, no let-ups." Keith recognized that organized tours
could vastly increase both the speed and the total number of birds
a Big Lister could see; it had taken him twenty-six years since his
first sighting to reach 4,300, and he imagined a prodigy birder
reaching even higher numbers faster. But Keith also disagreed with
his friend Small, saying that a birder—even a prodigy—would be
"doomed to disappointment if he hopes to see every bird in the

world." So what was a reasonable number? "Seven thousand," Keith decided, "is just within the capabilities of an ordinary mortal." For himself, though, Keith knew that he didn't have enough time to reach that goal. "I can just make it to six thousand," Keith wrote, "though I may be in a wheelchair when I do it." (Stuart Keith died on February 13, 2003; he succumbed to a stroke on Chuuk Island, in Micronesia. A day earlier, he'd seen the Caroline Islands Ground-Dove. It was his 6,600th life bird.)

All of the earliest Big Listers went on Abramson's tours. Abramson himself was approaching four thousand, and finally reaching that number in 1976 on a trip to Venezuela. He tried to convince his old roommate to pick up the gauntlet, as well: "Your dad," he told me, "is a phenomenal birder." But being talented wasn't what led my dad toward the numbers. The Saw-whet Owl we saw in 1971 was exciting for him, but he had a new career and was enjoying at least part of being single: Dad was in the thick of the partying and permissiveness that characterized that era, though my brother and I didn't know Dad was dating again until we were introduced to Nancy, one of his first true post-divorce girlfriends. (Jim and I loved her; when we talked about her recently, both of us recalled how badly we'd wanted Dad to marry her. But the burden he carried—the love he still felt for my mother—wasn't only pushing him into obsession and the list; it was also pushing him away from love.)

Still, things felt relatively calm for Dad. A little birding. Fun on weekends. And the need to see birds? He saw nothing new in 1970; just the Saw-whet Owl in 1971; and none in 1972. The Cornell alumnus who became a doctor and avoided studying birds, only to see thousands of them, was Joel Abramson, not Dad. "As for me," Dad says, "I was still a normal person then." It was as if Dad lived in two worlds: the heartbreaking one he'd recently left—birding, it seemed, resided there, perhaps as an antidote, but also as something that could entirely be pushed away—and the other world—his job, his girlfriends, his fun. The latter was one he could navigate more comfortably, and without, at least for the moment, being affected by the gravitational pull of the darker existence he was trying to forget about.

CHAPTER SEVEN

MINUS ONE

❝ *In March 1973, I was booked as a speaker on a cruise that left from Jamaica for Cartagena, Colombia, the San Blas Islands, Panama, Honduras, Guatemala, Cozumel, and Grand Cayman Island. This was to be my first neotropical birding experience, but was hampered by the fact that there was no good field guide for any area south of Mexico. I planned to first spend four days in Jamaica, and the* Field Guide to the Birds of the West Indies, *by James Bond, was quite good. In Jamaica I saw many widespread West Indian species, and all but six of the Jamaican endemics. So my first neotropical species—with thousands more to come— was the Jamaican Oriole, seen in a park in Kingston.*❞

—Jamaican Oriole (*Icterus leucopteryx*),
March 14, 1973, Kingston, Jamaica, #727.

LIKE A BIRD HIDING IN THICK FOREST, Dad's avian desires emerged for brief periods throughout his life, offering a seductive glimpse, then vanishing, leaving nothing but the faint and fading rustle of feathers; it was a siren, promising to add meaning to his life, but never solidly enough for him to truly embrace—though with each departure, it left stronger and stronger longings. After his divorce, Dad's birding self barely surfaced; it was as if his two sides had chosen to live entirely separate lives, and if they passed each other as they made their way to their destinations—the sighting of a rare duck on the way out to a singles house Dad shared in the Hamptons—they were scarcely acknowledged.

In fact, there was very little birding at all. Dad lived just a block from Central Park, and sometimes he'd quit work early and scan the meadows and glades with his binoculars. Nothing new. His New York list was full enough that adding something novel to it was less a matter of chance than attentiveness, as with the Saw-whet Owl, which he'd been told about, then sought.

There were other distractions. Though Dad had an active

dossier of singles-bar encounters, he also had two children to support, the still-fresh wounds of divorce to tend to, and pressing financial needs. When I asked Dad if the split might have led to an embrace of opportunity, the chance to rededicate his life to birds, he said, "I was almost broke, and I had to concentrate on getting my life started." Once again, Dad chose normalcy, responsibility, and—at that point—the best facsimile of the life his parents had wanted for him over whatever personal ambitions he might have harbored.

The free-spirited pleasures of that era seemed to take the edge off Dad's loneliness and heartbreak. But on the rare occasions on which birds did reveal themselves to him, Dad was faced with his own deeper identity. Those moments exposed his true frustrations because they were more than just gratifying—they were gorgeous; they were transcendent; they were fleeting glimpses of a different, secret self. But I think Dad knew that to embrace birding completely would mean a life of far greater solitude. He was compelled to bird, but less obsessed with it, at least at that point in his life. And as more and more of his friends got divorced and joined the same permissive scene he was part of, the oddity and heartbreak of his broken family seemed less shameful, less anomalous. In other words, the definition of a "normal" life had caught up with the events that had, not so much earlier, made him feel completely isolated. Being divorced in Manhattan wasn't what he'd originally wanted, but it was fun, and he was no longer alone at it. The space the birding filled in him had, because of circumstance, briefly shrunk.

NUMERIC LANDMARKS—the five hundredth species, or checking off every bird known to occur in your state—are the key snapshots of birding progress. But there are also more organic thresholds, places where a birder graduates to a higher level of the activity. Often, moving up that notch plants the seeds that ultimately bloom into competitive birding, into the need to see everything. For nearly every Big Lister I've met, the most important of these soft boundaries, the one that lights the spark of competitiveness and obsession, is a first-time visit to the tropics. The reason is simple: more birds.

There are about eight hundred bird species found in the United States. Seeing them all is a huge goal, and one that many listers spend years trying to achieve; there's a subgroup of competitive birders who try to see as many of these species as they can in a single year. (Field-guide author Kenn Kaufman shattered the "Big Year" record in 1973, seeing 671 species; he was nineteen years old and broke, and undertook the adventure with little more than the clothes on his back, a pair of binoculars, and an uncanny ability to hitch rides almost anywhere.) But even for these breakneck birders, a first visit to the world's equatorial regions is an exercise in ornithological ecstasy. Such an excursion can yield hundreds of new species; a moderately experienced U.S. birder might double a list he or she had taken years to build in just the first few days of a trip to Brazil or Peru.

Even less-formidable tropical destinations, like the Caribbean, are riotously rich in avifauna, and often act as triggers for birders who have had deeply buried grand ambitions.

IF IT WAS A "WHIM," as Dad says, it was an impromptu moment a long time in the making. After two years of what Dad characterizes as "infrequent and nonproductive" birding—no new species—in early 1973, he set off on his own brief adventure. He'd been scheduled as a drug lecturer on an educational cruise for doctors, but arrived at the ship's originating port in Montego Bay, Jamaica, three days early. He rented a car and drove into the mountains above Kingston.

It was a magnificent afternoon, sunny and tranquil. He spotted fifteen new birds, and fun ones, in quick succession. It felt nearly intoxicating. The other appeal of the tropics is that the avifauna are much more distinctive there than in temperate zones (more species, evolved to fill more niches, some biologists believe). The next day, he drove into a misty valley called Hardwar Gap; he'd been told about it by some of the New York birders with whom he kept in touch. It was Dad's first experience in true jungle: dark, wet woods, birds everywhere, but the thick vegetation made it truly challenging to see them. Dad added three to his list, though he missed the difficult-to-spot Jamaican Blackbird. "The Blue Mountains were just fascinating," Dad says. "I was completely amazed at how dense and beautiful they were." (Nearly every other birder I've spoken to describes a similar fascination with an inaugural tropical visit; as an outdoors writer, I experienced this myself on my first trip to such a climate, when I biked to the steamy bottom of Mexico's Copper Canyon. Between the wild macaws and papayas growing from trees, I decided that I'd found paradise; I've since visited the spot on eight separate occasions, and I can't wait to go back.)

The day before the cruise began, Dad visited one of this hemisphere's most lush birding spots. The Rocklands Hummingbird Sanctuary sits a mile up a muddy dirt road, but the journey—then and today—remains one of the Caribbean's most worthwhile and lovely nature pilgrimages. The tiniest birds on earth flit above a roughly manicured garden, usually as a few hardy tourists gawk. The refuge was the domain of an early ornithological eccentric: Lisa Salmon—known to the locals as "Miss Lisa"—served in the

Women's Royal Air Force during World War II; upon cessation of hostilities, she built a small home in the hills and thereafter spent most of her time scolding and charming anyone in a position to advance bird conservation. By the 1950s, her hummingbird feedings, held at precisely 3:15 every afternoon, became a mandatory stopover for birders looking to see hard-to-find species like the dark purple Jamaican Mango and the outlandish Red-billed Streamertail, with its multicolored beak and a pair of banner-like tail feathers that stretch back up to twelve inches. Salmon showed both species to my dad, who was by then in a minor overture to the listing frenzy that would fully overtake him a few years later. He nearly missed the cruise ship, boarding just before it departed Montego Bay, thrilled to have expanded his life list by thirty-eight birds—his biggest single haul since he was teenager.

ON THE BOAT TRIP, Dad veered between his post-divorce distractions and his reawakened interest in counting birds. He hooked up with the cruise ship's Swedish hostess;* the fling, he says, was light entertainment, though there was one moment, in his recollection, that was subtly telling, that speaks of the sense of isolation always

---

*The girl's name was a sexually suggestive double entendre, similar to the "Pussy Galore" character found in the James Bond movie *Goldfinger*. I found this amusing, in an obscure way, since it hints at the genuine connection the British spy hero has with birding. Novelist Ian Fleming was an avid lister and lived in Jamaica on an estate called "Goldeneye" (named after a species of duck). When he was trying to name the hero of his soon-to-be-famous series of thrillers, his eye wandered to his own bookshelf, where he saw the same bird guide Dad used for his Jamaican trip. Finding the author's name to be suitably "dull and anonymous," he appropriated it for secret agent 007; in Dad's later birding career, his frequent absences prompted some local speculation that he was himself a spy, a perception Dad, if not encouraging it, found amusing.

so close to him, yet always keeping so much at bay. Dad had become friends with another lecturer, a psychologist who'd found his own hostess girlfriend onboard. One evening, as the ship cruised toward port in Cartagena, Colombia, the two men stood on deck—Dad had his binoculars, of course—and celebrated their good fortune.

"Richard," the psychologist said, with a quick intimacy that hinted at the long friendship that would follow, "I'm in love."*

"You're not in love," Dad replied curtly. "You've been smoking too much dope." (The drug lecturers took a position that was common in those days—that marijuana was generally not harmful, and certainly less of a danger than alcohol.)

"Yes, I am," said the psychologist.

"No," said Dad, ever rational. "You've just taken all your needs and desires and projected them onto this woman."

The shrink stared toward the lights of the South American city they were approaching. "Isn't that what love is?" he replied.

Dad didn't have an answer; his needs and desires, his love wasn't about a relationship. At least, not with a person.

I ALSO FELT ALONE. I was eleven years old and was just entering junior high school. My father was mostly absent, and my mother, who was present, didn't seem to want to be there. I spent most of my time by myself; I'd pedal my bike to the edge of Little Neck Bay, and I'd sit there, looking at the birds, but also at the bridges and cars, at the boats, and especially at the airplanes (we were in

---

*Their friendship was ended by Arthur's untimely suicide in the early 1990s. That—and the early loss of another close friend—gave Dad, as he says, "even less to do at home," and more reasons to go out birding.

the flight path of LaGuardia Airport) taking off for distant places. The anger and tension that had overwhelmed my parents' marriage hadn't vanished—Mom and Dad were still fighting, post-divorce, usually over money—and it made me feel like a surrogate for Dad on Ridge Road, which was becoming a more and more bizarre place to live: Our house was always overloaded with people, sounds, and smells. I felt completely ignored and sometimes threatened by Mom's friends. My biggest relationships were with the equally alienated children of my mother's other few divorced friends, but even seeing them was rare.

Like Dad when he was my age, I needed to escape. Also like him, I got on my bike and pedaled to the marshes. But I never saw a Brown Thrasher. Nothing that was outside of me caught my interest and transported me to emotional safety, or, as my mother invited a parade of strangers—some of whom decided they had the right to discipline Jim and me as they saw fit—into our home, to physical safety. I ultimately found my refuge: I dwelled more and more in fantasy, located somewhere between a tropical paradise under the North Pole (as in one of my favorite books of that time, Edgar Rice Burroughs's *At the Earth's Core*) and a perfect future, where misfit teens were bestowed with commissions aboard the starship *Enterprise*.

Unlike my father's, my obsessions didn't involve soaring, but vanishing into those worlds. In order to encourage my reading, Dad came up with what we called "The Deal": Anytime I'd finish a book, he'd buy me another. I collected authors serially, reading all ninety-six of Lester Dent's "Doc Savage" pulp novels, in order; the entire twenty-six volume Tarzan series; all of Kurt Vonnegut's published work (at the time, seven books) in chronological order; and both *The Iliad* and *The Odyssey*. I was an avid comic-book collector—it was my own form of listing, and each of my titles was as perfectly logged, categorized, and cross-referenced as any bird on Dad's tally. I had to buy every single comic that hit the newsstand on Tuesdays, when the new shipments would arrive. It didn't matter whether it was *Spider-Man*, *Casper the Friendly Ghost*, or some romance cartoon aimed at girls. My goal as a collector was completeness, and order. Dad encouraged this minor duplication of his own personality; when the Scholastic Book Club issued its quarterly catalog for student purchases, he'd allow me to order every single one, as long as I promised to read them all. I'd arrange the new volumes in alphabetical order and plow through them, one at a time, never varying, and I finished each and every one—even if I didn't like the book.

WHEN THE CRUISE SHIP DOCKED AT CARTAGENA, Dad took a quick break along the shoreline. Today, bird scientists have traipsed to every end of South America, producing elaborate field guides that list most of the continent's more than four thousand species. But then, the author of one the very first of those guides—Steve Hilty, whose *A Guide to the Birds of Colombia* was published in 1986—had only just arrived in that country as a twenty-two-year-old Peace Corps volunteer. Over the next decade, Hilty and his collaborator, William Brown, would catalog the birds they encountered, sending their descriptions back to Guy Tudor—an American bird artist whose style is reminiscent of Peterson's, though slightly more lush and painterly—and ultimately producing over 1,700 listings for that reference. But no such book existed in the early 1970s. Whether hobbyist or professional, visitors to places with lots of birds arrived with little information on what—or where—they were. So, departing the boat, Dad took a simple approach. He hailed a cab and told the driver to take him "to the nearest swamp."

Fifteen minutes later, eleven new birds were on his list—including the Wattled Jacana, a tallish bird with elongated toes that, similar to a daddy longlegs, have evolved to allow it to walk gracefully on floating vegetation. The next day, the boat headed through the Panama Canal, with another brief stop.

Dad had gotten directions to a birding location from a friend in New York, but was unable to locate the exact area. It didn't matter. "There were birds everywhere," Dad says. "It felt so good to be alone, enjoying myself, with nothing to worry about." It was as if he were in an over-humid version of Flushing Meadows, living the life he'd put off for so long. In a single afternoon, he matched his three-day Jamaican total. The thirty-eight species he added made the Panama stopover his biggest day ever.

The boat continued on to St. Andrew Islands, Guatemala, and finally to Cozumel, Mexico. He added a dozen more new birds, for a life list total of 834. This was a birder who was beginning to become well-traveled. An idea was forming: "It was very exciting to go someplace and be surrounded by nothing but new birds." On the flight home, he began to think about other places that had lots of new birds: Trinidad. Kenya. Brazil. How many birds were there to see? An answer, for Dad, was beginning to form.

All of them.

I LOVED THE WAY BIRDS MADE DAD an expert in something. His ability to identify what was floating overhead from just a quick glance seemed like a superpower, on par with the skills my comic-book idols possessed. But I didn't really like birds myself. I tried. I had my binoculars and my field guide; I had the Bayside Woods within throwing distance of my house. But I just didn't think they were interesting, and I was getting past the age—about ten or eleven—

where most kids get hooked on birds. I'd already found my refuge. I think the difference was that Dad's birding grew as an escape from a place that was cold, from the Spartan and serious environment that Rose and Morris created. My refuge needed to take me from a far hotter place; escaping the chaos of living in Douglaston required distant fantasy worlds, places I never really had to depart, and which could never be destroyed.

But the one time Dad's birding did rub off on me made me feel so proud of him and of being his son. The autumn after Dad's cruise, an elderly man visited P.S. 98, the tiny elementary school near the Douglaston train station, to talk to us about nature, and about birds in particular. He had two methods of inciting interest in kids who were probably more interested in sports or watching television: First, he carried with him an impressively huge, taxidermied barn owl; second, he had a game to play.

"Who thinks they know a lot about birds?" Will Astle asked.

Hands shot up, but mine wasn't among them. Astle refined his question: "Can any of you name ten different kinds of bird?"

Again, a few hands shot up, and the visitor called on them one by one.

Robin . . . bluebird . . . cardinal . . . chicken?

The next kid added "sea gull."

I knew *sea gull* was a generic term, and therefore wrong, and that chicken—well, that just didn't count because they were talking about the kind your grandmother made into soup, and it was beneath mentioning. Still, I hadn't raised my hand. I was too scared to speak. Mr. Astle asked again, and again.

Finally, I knew I had to volunteer. I could tell by the look on his face that he expected me to falter, as the other boys did.

It wasn't easy. I wasn't used to being under pressure, and I kept drawing blanks. Cardinal. Robin. Starling. Bald eagle.

Those were obvious ones.

Barn swallow.

I paused, but Astle gave me time.

Herring gull.

He raised his eyebrows.

Osprey. Saw-whet Owl.

All birds Dad had shown me.

One more. Again, I drew a blank—and then, of course, it was there. How could I forget the two most important birds? Jim's favorite, and mine.

Hoopoe. Scissor-tailed Flycatcher.

Mr. Astle's eyes lit up. I had named one bird that wasn't even found on the continent, and another one that was only seen in Texas. My teacher, Mrs. Quinn, applauded, and the rest of the class was duly impressed. But Astle was the happiest. Birding, as I've said, appeals especially to young boys—maybe because it adds a very rational, linear structure to adventure. Astle's purpose in going to schools, I later learned, wasn't just to get a bunch of blasé kids slightly pumped up about nature; it was to find young potential birders and steer them onto the right path.

Will Astle believed he'd found one that day.

"What's your name?" he asked.

"Danny," I replied. "Danny Koeppel."

He smiled. "Ahh," he said, "you must be Richard's son."

It turned out that, in his early teens, Dad had seen the very same stuffed owl; Will Astle was one of the founders of the Queens County Bird Club. After class, Mr. Astle asked me if I knew any other kids who liked birds. I didn't, and he was slightly disappointed that he hadn't found an untouched prodigy (since it was assumed that my birding education was in good hands). Still, he was relieved to assume—though it wouldn't turn out to be true, either for Jim or for me—that P.S. 98 would be well represented by at least one junior avian enthusiast.

THERE'S AN IRONY TO LISTING: The more birds you count, the more you leave the world of flesh and feather and enter a universe of abstractions, of human-imposed taxonomic decisions that can change your tally, even if you're just sitting at home. At the end of 1973, the American Ornithologists' Union announced the lumping of the Blue Goose with the Snow Goose, and the Eurasian and Green-Winged Teal. There was also a split between the Willow and Alder Flycatchers. Most birders never experience (or at least aren't terribly aware of) such technical fluctuations in their list, and though Dad's net loss was just a single bird, it would be the beginning of a decade of huge changes in the way birds were defined (and counted), ultimately leading to a statistical end to most lumping, and an explosion in the number of split species. Dad found the reduction of his total, tiny as it was, disconcerting: "I can't say why," says Dad, "but it felt strange." My guess is that it violated the sense of order that his birding most indulged. A seemingly inexplicable and surprising change in his list added uncertainty to the thing that had always been his rock. (He'd later come to fully embrace those uncertainties, especially after he saw how they could be studied and exploited to build his numbers, and therefore his ultimate sense of control.)

CHAPTER EIGHT

HOW MANY BIRDS CAN THERE BE?

❝ The Andean Coot was split from the American Coot in the 1990s; until then, the two birds—geographically far apart—were considered the same. I first saw the American Coot way, way back, in the very beginning, in my first year of birding. I was told about the split on a trip to Peru, so I went back to my list and found my sighting of the South American version of the bird. So it was almost thirty-five years between seeing the two birds, and nearly ten more before I got the split and was able to add it to my list.”

—Andean Coot (*Fulica ardesiaca*), October 22, 1984,
Cochabamba National Park, Bolivia, #2585;
American Coot (*Fulica americana*), October 1948,
Flushing, New York, #80.

IT SEEMS OBVIOUS, but you can't count a lot of birds if there aren't a lot of birds. What makes that an interesting thought is that the number of birds on Earth has been growing—rapidly. When Dad first started birding, there were believed to be about 8,600 known species. Today, there are closer to ten thousand—and in a decade or two, some ornithologists believe that number could double, or even triple. It isn't that brand-new birds are being discovered in the jungles and forests of the world. What's happening is that a specialized (and scientifically based) form of list mania is sweeping across the landscape of serious ornithology. But what's even more fascinating is that, despite continued ambivalence on the part of professional bird scientists about pure hobbyists—a phenomenon that has existed since the earliest days of avian study—there's little doubt that counting birds for fun, and naming birds for science, are complementary and intersecting arts.

Let's jump ahead here for a brief lesson in science, semantics, and taxonomy. We already know that naming birds is the most important part of counting them because you need to have something to check off on your list, some way to keep track. But the science behind the way birds are named—especially in modern times—is what's really important to the bigger questions birding and ornithology raise, questions about how we define and differentiate life on Earth.

THE BATTLE BETWEEN SPLITTERS AND LUMPERS is as old as ornithology itself. It has taken many different forms over the past 150 years; the earliest battles—once again, spearheaded by the fiery Elliot Coues—were tied to how bird species would be scientifically named. American ornithologists, especially, favored "trinomial nomenclature," in which a third Latin designator would be used to define a subspecies; European scientists opposed this, but the American school—the Splitters—began to win out, mostly because there were so many new species to be found in the New World. But the ebb and flow between the two forces quickly asserted itself, and by the turn of the century, as Mark V. Barrow, Jr. writes in *A Passion for Birds*, his excellent history of American ornithology, "American ornithologists continued to create new subspecies based on smaller and smaller distinctions and to discover prior names for previously accepted forms. By the turn of the century, even several proponents of trinomialism began to question whether its practitioners had gone too far."

The early battles over species consolidation had an academic— nearly a linguistic—air to them, though they occasionally broke into whimsy. (A poem published in 1889's *Ornithologist and Oologist* magazine tried to make light of the topic: "Kind reader, we call to your careful attention, This wonderful growth of a modern invention. Lord knows where we'll end if this craze increases, Such a trotting out yearly of created SUBSPECIES.") That bit of doggerel would be roughly topical today, except in one essential aspect: Scientists like Bret Whitney—who guided Dad to his seven thousandth sighting—are now exploring the definition of life itself. Their splits are intimately tied to the species concept, which is a fundamental credo of evolution. And for the first time, laboratory techniques are emerging to help confirm debates that were once decided exclusively by the whims of the academy (for listers like Dad, this is a good thing—as is anything that extends the game or adds new twists to it).

FOR MANY BIG LISTERS, the person who most epitomizes the intersection between numbering and naming is Whitney. Over the past twenty years, nobody has described more new species than Whitney. And there's no ornithologist working today who is more influential, visionary, or strangely gifted. Understand what Whitney does, and you understand not just the chase that my dad and his competitors engage in, you understand why it actually means something concrete, why it actually helps us understand the nuts-and-bolts nature of life on Earth.

First, you have to understand Whitney's talent. The best thing to do would be to see it firsthand—you'd find it astonishing. But because Whitney spends nearly all his time deep in the forests of South America, and because the few ornithological field trips he leads are excruciatingly lister-heavy (three weeks, nonstop counting; unless you're truly serious about birding and don't mind missing *everything else,* forget it) you'll have to rely on my description: Bret was the leader who took Dad into listing history, but what amazed me most about him happened much earlier in that excursion.

Our group stepped off a tiny boat onto a nameless island in the heart of the Brazilian Amazonia. All twelve of us were carrying binoculars, but as we searched for birds amid the thick vegetation, our precision optics seemed less than useful. But with Whitney along, that was no problem. For Whitney—and this is key to the species explosion—ears are more important than eyes. A pair of tape recorders was strapped across Whitney's shoulders, and pouches on his belt were stuffed with audio cassettes and digital tape recordings. A directional microphone, half as long as my arm, hung at Whitney's side.

We'd set out that morning to find something very specific: a small, red-brown bird that hugs tree trunks inside the dark, swampy locale. Until recently, Zimmer's Woodcreeper was an utter mystery, listed in guidebooks as "unknown in life," meaning that it had been spotted and recorded decades earlier, but hadn't been seen since. It was a real bird, but at that point, only in theory.

At least, to everyone but Whitney.

The bird's call is distinctive: a short, descending trill that fades away at the end. I couldn't hear it. The rest of our group strained. Whitney and Mario Cohn-Haft, our co-leader and head ornithologist at the Brazilian National Institute for Amazonian Research, signaled each other and we started to walk—softly, but fast, off the main trail, nearly bushwhacking. But as suddenly as we started, we stopped. Not a word. Whitney gently pushed the PLAY button on his cassette recorder. A crisp, clear sound echoed from the speaker.

Challenged, agitated, the little bird zipped in to defend its territory. It peeked at us a couple of times, and then popped into view. Now, with binoculars up, we became the first people in over five decades to actually see this bird, which is now *known* to science, and to my dad, who marked it off on his list: 6,995.

❀   ❀   ❀

BRET WHITNEY IS AT THE VANGUARD OF A MOVEMENT that, more and more, looks at song—the official term is *vocalization*—as an important key to defining what birds are. By analyzing vocalizations, and the differences between them, Whitney and his colleagues are emerging as a new kind of Splitter, basing their findings on real, measurable, biological differences rather than on points of taxonomic philosophy, as their earlier counterparts did. The result of their work is a species explosion that seems, once and for all, to have put Lumpers into permanent retreat.

Species splitting is especially powerful in South America, where hundreds of different birds can be found in relatively compressed geographic zones. The new Splitters are increasingly showing— by determining differences in song and backing up that evidence with information about plumage, habitat, and, ultimately, genetic analysis—that birds previously thought to be one are two, three, four, or more. Vocalization-based ornithology has been a growing force for the past two decades; more and more proposed splits are gaining wider acceptance in the scientific community, including the influential American Ornithologists' Union, a group that officially maintains a list of birds occurring in the New World. (Vocalization is controversial in hobbyist birding, as well, but for different reasons: Tape playback is a highly effective tool for drawing birds out into the open, but some birders and land managers believe that using recorded songs is less than sporting, and have banned it.)

Some ornithologists believe that the twenty-five thousand figure is an overestimate. "I think ultimately, that's too high," says Nigel Collar, a biologist with Cambridge University and an avifauna-specific conservation group called Bird Life International. Collar, one of the scientists who helps maintain "the red book," an official listing of endangered avian species, says that the rest of the world may be different than South America. "We can't make the same assumptions," says Collar. "I don't think there will be a wholesale unlumping that results in those kinds of numbers," he says, adding that he expects that there are probably thirty thousand subspecies, and twelve to thirteen thousand species (so, even Collar, who is considered more a Lumper than a Splitter, sees an increase in the total world species count by as much as 50 percent).

It is true, that, as Whitney says, "the birds don't care." And the notion of what species is is as much a question for philosophers as for scientists. But Whitney's work moves the debate onto the ground and into our backyards; by sharpening the definition of what species is, scientists gain a greater understanding of evolution. Those findings are crucial in determining how ecosystems function, what makes them unique, and which may be most important to preserve. That work is becoming more and more critical as habitat is lost. "There's a race now," Whitney says, "and it isn't simply to tick off new species. We're working on a puzzle that's been produced over the last twenty-five million years. That puzzle is almost done, and during our brief view of the world, we've got to work backwards to find out how it was completed. We've got to do it before many of the pieces vanish forever."

TRAVEL WITH BRET WHITNEY, and you'll see hear—and see—astonishing things. In Brazil, with Dad, Whitney took us to a remote observation tower, high above the Amazonian canopy. We climbed the creaky stairs at dawn—it was already beyond sweltering—and as light splashed across the trees, there were birds everywhere, probably over fifty different species, tearing through the sky amid leaves, vines, and branches, chattering in an airborne feeding frenzy (for breakfast: insects, leaf-crawling beetles, flies, and thousands of other species, many of which are uncataloged by science). Whitney called off bird names like an auctioneer: Racket-tailed Coquette! Short-billed Honeycreeper! Olive-green Tyrannulet! Crimson Fruit-crow! We swung our binoculars from side to side, trying to keep up. That evening, moving downstream on a triple-decker house-boat, Whitney recapped the day's sightings, as the listers—ranging in lifetime tallies from under two thousand to over seven thousand—followed along. Whitney may be the planet's most productive discoverer of unknown birds. He's averaged at least one new-to-science species, described in academic journals, every year since the mid-1990s. And Whitney gives hope to hobbyists everywhere: He's self-taught, with no advanced degrees and no significant time in the lab or classroom. He earns his living mostly by leading bird-watchers to South America. Whitney's lack of advanced academic credentials has long since ceased to matter in scientific officialdom, says Van Remsen, curator of birds at Louisiana State University's Museum of Natural Science, in Baton Rouge: "Bret is a superstar. He's a reservoir of information and ideas unparalleled in the ornithological world."

WHITNEY'S LIFE SOMETIMES REMINDS ME—in both the hard details and as the fulfillment of a fantasy—of the life Dad might have had. Whitney traipses through the jungle, searching for birds, and it seems lonely, but when I watch him chat up young women in a honky-tonk near his stateside home in Austin, Texas (or with equal ease at a tiny outdoor bar on Fernando de Noronha, the biggest island in a Galapagos-like chain one hundred miles off the Bahia coast), I see Dad as he wanted to be: an ornithological buccaneer.

Whitney started out like Dad, too; the bird obsession hit early. Growing up in rural Indiana, Whitney was interested in nature even as a toddler, says his father, Chuck Whitney. At age four, Bret was stricken with both measles and mumps. Stuck in bed, his grandmother gave him a set of flash cards, 150 of them, each with a different bird on the front, and a description on the reverse. "I fell in love with~~really loved~~ those cards," Whitney says. Chuck Whitney made a game ~~if~~ of it, and in less than a week, his son had memorized each card: "He got so good at it that I could cover nearly all of the card, and he'd still know the bird."

Though Whitney couldn't read, he found the text on the back of each card more fascinating than the standard bedtime stories. Whitney told me this as we sat in an Austin coffee shop, eating pancakes. He put down his fork, and began to recite: "This bright little bird, with yellow and orange stripes . . ." The bird on the card was a Yellow Warbler; a few months later, Whitney was catching frogs by a creek when he heard something over his shoulder. He turned, and was "astonished to see that it was the bird on the card! It was real!"

By the time he was six, Whitney had learned how to slip silently and patiently through vegetation to sneak up on birds for a better look (it would be a couple of years before he became aware of the existence of binoculars). Whitney even recalls his first notion of species: He saw an a semi-familiar bird in his yard; it looked like a yellow-billed Cuckoo, but it had a black bill. "I knew it was a cuckoo, but I knew it wasn't the Yellow-billed from the cards," he says. When Whitney received his first printed Peterson's a few years later, one of the first things he did was look for that "different" cuckoo. There it was: a Black-billed Cuckoo. "It was a tremendous validation," he says.

Whitney wanted to know more about birds, but at that point, he was still primarily a bird-watcher—albeit one who didn't care much about keeping a list, and who didn't mind spending weeks in Arizona or Mexico hunting down particular species. He wasn't sure about his next move. Chuck Whitney confesses that his son had him a little worried: "I told him to get real. He wasn't good enough to play pro baseball, and I didn't think anyone could make a living looking at birds." Whitney had been accepted to graduate school, but he was hesitant; he didn't want to leave the field.

As it turned out, he didn't have to. In 1978, Whitney got a job with a fledgling company called Victor Emanuel Nature Tours. Emanuel, the company's cofounder and principal owner, was one of the first to realize that birders wanted—and would pay for—the opportunity to travel to remote parts of the world in order to see big numbers of new species—*lifers*, in birders' jargon. Whitney worked in Emanuel's office and slept in his living room, answering the phone, booking reservations in faraway places, confirming flights. It was about a year before he received an urgent call from his boss, in Peru: Emanuel was short a leader, the trip was happening, and Whitney—who'd never been to South America and had never studied Peruvian birds—was invited. "He crammed on the plane," says Rose Ann Rowlett, who also worked for Emanuel. By the time he'd returned from Peru, Whitney knew what he'd be doing for the rest of his life.

Whitney, Rowlett, and several others formed their own bird tour company in 1985; his outfit and Emanuel's would end up showing Dad over 70 percent of the birds he'd see between his one thousandth and seven thousandth. In that sense, Whitney was less a lister than a list-enabler, but his fascination, unconstrained, did flourish into real scientific discovery. Whitney was on his way to becoming the world's best field ornithologist: somebody who discovered species for others to count.

Perhaps Whitney's most kindred spirit was the late Ted Parker, another self-taught ornithologist, whose biggest contribution to Dad's list was on a trip to Peru, in 1992, when he predicted to that Dad the Andean Coot would soon be split from the American Coot.* Like Whitney, Parker had an astonishing ear, and was prolific at recording Neotropical birds; Parker had been taping since 1974, and had contributed more than fifteen thousand sound samples to the Macaulay Library of Natural Sounds at Cornell. Parker was both an inspiration and a role model for Whitney and many other field ornithologists. On August 3, 1993, Parker and some colleagues were surveying a remote part of southwestern Ecuador when their small plane smashed into a mountain; whether you're going to count exotic birds or study them, the game can get dangerous in remote areas, so it is no coincidence that both the top list creator, Parker, and the top lister, Phoebe Snetsinger, both died in the pursuit.

Whitney probably would have started doing more influential work whether or not Parker lived, but it's clear that his colleague's passing affected him deeply. By the mid-1990s, Whitney had effectively picked up the torch Parker had left behind: "If Ted was the godfather of the movement to make sure we have all this biodiversity cataloged and analyzed," Van Remsen told me, "Bret is the current spiritual leader."

---

*A further adjustment later renamed the Andean version of the bird as the Slate-colored Coot; this was so birders wouldn't confuse it with the Giant Coot, a coot found in the Andes, twice as big as the other coots, which was often called the Giant Andean Coot.

❖   ❖   ❖

THAT WONDERFUL MELODY YOU HEAR IN YOUR GARDEN is not just one of nature's best-loved hits. Most people identify birds by sight: the red breast of a robin; the brilliant azure of a Mountain Bluebird. So it can be hard to understand that hearing—not seeing—is closer to believing in ornithology. But the notion that the ear is bird identification's primary tool makes sense, and not only because bird songs are so distinctive. It also has to do with the way humans are built, says Remsen: "If you think about it, hearing is more reliable. Our ears play far fewer tricks on us than our eyes." (Here's a good example of this principle: You might not recognize Paul McCartney if you saw him walking down the street, forty feet away from you, but you can *definitely* pick out "Yesterday" from the song's very first three syllabic notes).

Whitney's work has helped cement that notion that the *birds themselves* also find songs more important for identification. Though controversy will always rage about the definition of species, the majority, including Whitney, subscribes to the "biological species concept." (Think back to high school: The species are populations actually or potentially found in the same habitat—for example, Herring and Laughing Gulls on a New Jersey beach—that still won't breed with each other.) Though birds sing to warn, navigate in flocks, or communicate with offspring, the most important vocalizations—and the ones humans find prettiest—are used to attract mates: "In the forest, birds can't see each other most of the time. And one's not going to fly up to another to get a look and find out whether it's the same species," Whitney says.

There are dozens of similar birds, many once thought to be the same species, many which look virtually identical. But they're not the same. Whitney is trying to find out exactly how different they are. Which are separate species, and how do we find them? Such debates don't just rage in the tropics. If you live in the Pacific Northwest, you've probably encountered a greenish-gray bird once called Traill's Flycatcher. Recently, the bird split into two species: Alder and Willow Flycatchers. They look so similar that many field guides print a single picture for the two of them, but their songs are entirely different. Another difficult bird family to identify visually are warblers: There are over fifty species in the United States, and many of them look alike—especially females and young warblers in fall plumage (to be good at distinguishing warblers is a valuable skill, birders who possess such talents are often sought after for team counting events).

As a concept, splitting and lumping has moved beyond birds. In Utrecht, Netherlands, a publication called *International Code of Nomenclature for Cultivated Plants* holds authority over the naming, renaming, and dividing of horticultural species, and avid gardeners (most of them British) follow the changes with both a religious fervor and a sense of vexation; the most recent shifts involve chrysanthemums, which have been the subject of endless taxonomic revisions. Splits and lumps are occurring in spiders—over thirty thousand known species, and growing—and coniferous trees—six hundred species, up from half that several decades ago. The splitting even extends to humanity: One of the oldest evolutionary debates is whether Neanderthals were a separate species from *Homo sapiens*, or a subspecies (the most recent evidence splits the two). And geneticist Luigi Luca Cavalli-Sforza has used the splitting/lumping concept to help trace the evolution of biological traits and language in human populations (though he isn't saying that different *races* of people—a meaningless term,

genetically—are separate species; he's speaking in a more concep-
tual sense about regional differences between various populations
and communities).

Birds have led the way in splitting and lumping, and have also
been at the forefront of determining what criteria need to be used
to prove differentiation—a process that requires a combination of
intuition, science, and detective work. Whitney recently encountered a sample of a bird called the Bahia Antwren, found on the
coast of central Brazil. The specimen had been sitting in a Berlin
museum for 170 years, having been collected in 1830 by a German
explorer named Friedrich Sellow. (Sellow was one of the most prolific collectors ever to visit the tropics. From 1814 until 1831, when
he drowned in the Rio Doce, Sellow gathered over 125,000 biological samples—nearly all from a narrow strip along Bahia's shoreline.) It had already been proven that another bird—the
Black-capped Antwren, which lived in areas adjacent to the original Bahia variety—was a distinct species. Whitney believed there
might be a third.

The first problem was confirming which of the three possible
antwrens the specimen actually was. Many biological samples
gathered during the collecting frenzy of the nineteenth century
are now useless, mostly because of poor labeling or lost records.
Sellow's bird was marked with a date and a place name: "Bahia."
Too general. But Whitney and his colleagues discovered a report,
prepared by a German geographer in the 1940s, that reconstructed
Sellow's exact itinerary. By matching that report to the date on the
bird, the scientists were able to establish the bird's likely point of
origin—right in the center of the Bahia Antwren's range.

The next step was to establish differences between the birds in
question. Many different attributes—size, beak length, color—are
used as defining criteria in the hunt for new birds. But for Whitney,

song is critical. Whitney traveled through Bahia, recording sample vocalizations. In the United States, two of his partners—Morton and Phyllis Isler, amateur ornithologists whose hobby has transformed them into the world's leading authorities on antbird songs—began analyzing the recordings (the Islers have collected over twenty-five thousand individual antbird vocalization samples, stored digitally; Whitney, Morton Isler says, gathered over seven thousand of those). The antbird family is huge: It contains at least 207 species, of which Dad has seen 157; there's also a similar family—formicariidae—which encompasses antthrushes and antpittas; 62 birds are included, of which Dad has seen 22. All of these birds live low to the ground in dense, tropical brush, making them among the most difficult (and satisfying, when it finally happens) birds to see.

No two birds sound exactly the same, even if they're the same species, but Whitney and the Islers were able to synthesize enough data to come up with a baseline of differentiation. This was done by measuring the differences between gathered songs and searching them for established identifying characteristics. The results were clear: A third species—now named the Caatinga Antwren—is found mostly in northern Bahia, living alongside the Black-capped Antwren, and further separated from Sellow's original species.

Dad has seen many of the antwrens Whitney has split, and when I informed him of the changes, I got an e-mail that provides an interesting insight into the complicated tracking process the phenomenon has led birders to undergo: "The situation with these antwrens is very confusing," Dad wrote. "I have seen Black-capped in Bolivia in 1984, and in Northeast Brazil in 1993 at de Baturité and Juazeiro do Norte. I have seen Bahia or Caatinga or Pileated in Northeast Brazil in 1993; at three different locations on that trip: Juazeiro do Norte, Petrolina or Jeremalbu, and Jeqiuie (Boa Nova).

My notes do not distinguish, but list them all as H. pileatus." A few minutes later, Dad sent a follow-up e-mail, intended to clarify: "I have counted two so far," he wrote: "Black-capped, and H. pileatus, which may turn out to be more than one."

I was as lost as you probably are right now, yet somehow relieved to know that the laws of physics appeared to be superseded by the laws of splitting—which stated what is absolutely true as an equation, but somehow bizarre, in the context of bird identification: "Two . . . may turn out to be more than one." Topography turns out to be a key to species evolution. Whitney has found that birds separated by even the slightest of barriers—a shady slope, a patch of open space—can turn out to be different. An excellent example of this can be found in the antbirds; Whitney has studied antwrens and antpittas species which, dwelling just yards from each other, have evolved to fill their own particular niches—sometimes as many as *forty* different species in a single area, each demonstrating its own survival strategy. For example, the Caatinga and Bahia antwrens were once considered the same. The former species is found only at the middle and upper tree levels of woodland and scrub forest, while the Bahia species inhabits adjacent coastal areas with different vegetation types. The birds can best be distinguished by song.

"Some birds won't even cross a river," Whitney says. That such small barriers can lead to biologic distinctiveness isn't just a theoretical notion: "What it proves is that there's still so much exploring to do—there are tons and tons of things out there that nobody has ever encountered."

EXPLORING IS THE MOST IMPORTANT thing to Whitney, but to listers like Dad, what's more crucial—and what's a more fun part of the game—is the counting, the constant shuffling of lists as splits and lumps are accepted, modified, and occasionally rescinded. This is the most soft-focus part of the Big Listers' game. Many top birders prepare for potential splits years in advance—they know a scholarly paper might be coming out, so they'll make sure to see the soon-to-be-split species in all the areas where it occurs. (For example, if you know that a hypothetical bird, called the New York Tern, may be split into Bronx, Brooklyn, Queens, Manhattan, and Staten Island varieties, you'll make it your business to see one in each borough because when the split arrives, you can only add the ones you've actually seen.) Birds awaiting splits appear on lists as shadows—species that don't yet count, but which hover above, waiting to come in for a landing.

When I asked Dad to explain his birding career to me in terms of splits, he sent me six pages of single-spaced chronology, with dozens of species changing, dividing, and renaming.

"It can get confusing," Dad says, "especially now, since there's a profusion of bird books and it appears that everyone simply expresses their own personal opinions on the splits. But with DNA work and new concepts of species, it is clear that lumping is pretty much over."

Every Big Lister has sources that they trust—and ones they don't trust. Dad often listens to Whitney, but some splits, it seems to him, come because "a scientist today might realize that coming up with a split is the best way to get published."

A birder with a list numbering over six thousand can probably attribute several hundred of his species to splits. But he probably won't gain a big advantage over his rivals, since they're playing the same game. "The rules seem to change as far as what species is," Dad says, "but we all play pretty much by the same rules."

That's Dad, talking today. But in 1979, just as Bret Whitney was beginning to lead bird tours, as he was making the transition from prodigy to professional, Dad hardly knew what a split or a lump was. "I was vaguely aware of it," he says, "and I'd recorded several over the years. But the big-time listing—and the splitting and lumping that went with it—was just about to begin."

CHAPTER NINE

INTO THE THOUSANDS

❝ *What's memorable about this bird is not so much the bird, but the incredible setting in which I saw it. In 1981 I went on my first Earthwatch expedition. It was to Tasmania, and the purpose was to explore the biologically unknown northwest portion of the island. The area was known to be a migration stop-off point for the endangered Orange-bellied Parrot, and was thought to be the most likely area to find the apparently extinct Thylacene, or Tasmanian Tiger, which had occasionally been 'sighted' nearby. Once at the research site, I was assigned to a sea-watch, to identify and estimate numbers of passing seabirds. And there were many: albatrosses, shearwaters, gannets, pelicans, gulls, terns, and cormorants were common. One afternoon I had some time off and I decided to walk south along the coast. The area got wilder and wilder, with magnificent cliffs coming down to a wide sandy beach, and small watercourses coming out of the hills to become small deltas running into the sea. I could see the aforementioned seabirds offshore, and scattered shorebirds along the beach. Wedge-tailed Eagles soared overhead. Suddenly, a huge and magnificent White-bellied Sea Eagle appeared overhead. It was a life bird, buts it was the setting that left me breathless.*"

—White-bellied Sea Eagle (*Haliaeetus leucogaster*),
March 5, 1981, Tasmania, #1077.

FIVE THOUSAND BIRDS STILL SEEMED like a number an ordinary birder, even in the grips of obsession, could barely contemplate. By the late 1970s, only Stuart Keith had reached that mark. Roger Tory Peterson was still trying to reach forty-five hundred, and nobody had seen six thousand. And the birders who did reach the big numbers were able to do so because they were superstars. Peterson and Keith were famous; their notoriety allowed them to devote themselves full-time to the chase, and they were accepted as true ornithologists. The mantle provided cover. It made seeking the big numbers seem a little less crazy.

But an ordinary person? How could somebody with family, career, and convention see that many birds?

Impossible.

To do it, lives had to change. Birds would have to become everything. A potential Big Lister had to *allow* birds to consume him.

The moment had to be right.

The first step was to see it as possible. For Dad, that logistical notion began in a tiny way, with the simple awareness of the numbers themselves. The arrival of Jim Clements's master checklist had suddenly given concrete form to the act of counting—soon, there'd be competing avian directories, as well—but something else was missing. If Clements was, in a way, the Peterson of world tallying, coming up with an easy means of telling watchers what they needed to look for (though he didn't provide a method for identification), then Peter Alden and John Gooders were the Allan Cruickshanks of the movement. Alden was a Boston-based birder who'd spent most of his youth searching the wilds of Mexico for birds, and had a reputation as one of North America's best sources of species location information; Gooders, who was British, had a similar reputation for African species. In 1980, they published *Finding Birds Around the World*. It was a global version of Cruickshank's New York guide, the book that had captivated Dad and contained his earliest lists as a teenager. Alden and Gooders's plain-spoken, "anyone can do it" assortment of sighting lists, how-to instructions, and hand-drawn maps cataloged over 111 world-wide birding "hot spots" where dozens of rare species could be seen.

Dad got the Clements and Alden/Gooders books at around the same time, and was fascinated by them. But he didn't know what to do with that interest. He was beginning to understand the mechanics, but the counting? That desire was buried. Something would have to make it come out.

OLD WOUNDS REVERBERATE. They're passed on. So, when I look for the reasons Dad finally decided to re-create the world according to his own desires, I see the world that created me. My parents divorced in 1970, but the marriage didn't end then: It transformed into an exhausting, brutal series of tortured skirmishes. Those battles left Jim and me feeling utterly insecure and caught in the middle. But I think the fights were even harder on Dad.

Dad's obsession didn't emerge gradually. It built itself, hidden, before appearing as a fully formed, consuming force, a final and almost desperate means of eliminating unpredictability from a world that seemed to have always conspired to bring Dad to his knees. My mother was angry for much of the decade following the breakup of her marriage. There were good reasons for her to feel that way, and bad ones, but in either case, her rage seemed uncontrollable and terrifying to me: The more she realized that divorce hadn't automatically granted her the freedom she'd fantasized about, the more furious she got. She and Dad spent most of the 1970s in court, in that same dance of stubborn will that had killed their marriage. Dad still wanted her to be the one who made his compromised dreams worthwhile, and Mom wanted the innocence she thought had been stolen from her returned—or at least compensated for.

In between court battles, Mom hopped from relationship to relationship. Each new boyfriend seemed to push Dad's heart further into recession, and he went from having girlfriends to having encounters. (I don't know if either Mom or Dad would agree with my tying their separate romantic lives together in this cause-and-effect way, but I truly believe it, and my brother and I were the only ones to witness both sides.) I spent most of my time wishing Dad would rescue me—from Mom's boyfriends, some of whom were shady and violent, and from my own sense of loneliness, of feeling as unseen as Dad must have when he was a teenager. I wanted Dad to see how terrible Douglaston was for me, but I kept silent; I wanted him to see me in the crosshairs of his telescope, to know what was going on.

I'm not sure why I didn't develop an interest in birds, as Dad did. I tried. I'd ride my bike to the bays and beaches and stare out at the ducks and gulls. But it was the journey to those places that enthralled me; I'd spend hours on my bike, traversing much of Long Island and Queens, and as I pedaled I'd conjure science-fiction stories, or lyrics to songs, and—when I was on especially lonely roads—imagine a different family, a father who'd rescue me, somebody who could take me away from everything. By the time I was in high school, I was spending entire parts of every summer on my bike, taking long-distance tours to Pennsylvania, Vermont, and eastern Canada. (I'd joined a sort of whole-wheat bike collective in Lower Manhattan, and the trips I took were sponsored and led by that group; the collective was part of the huge boom in bicycle touring that swept much of the United States in the mid-1970s, culminating in a 1976 cross-country ride called "Bikecentennial.")

I finally got away in 1979. I was seventeen, and Dad drove me up to college in New England. I unloaded a few things from his Volkswagen Beetle—including my binoculars and my Peterson guide, which I've carried everywhere I've lived to this day, even if they've remained mostly untouched—and waved good-bye. I'd never felt so lonely. There was so much that had never been spoken about, so many secrets, that I didn't feel anything—not relief at leaving home, nor longing for what I was putting behind me. (My lack of feeling wasn't helped by the oversized partying habit I'd developed during my last two years of high school; I'd cut most of my classes as a senior, instead spending hours listening to Led Zeppelin at the house of a friend we'd nicknamed "H.R." [as in the kid's character, H. R. Pufnstuf; it was widely rumored that the initials stood for "Hand-Rolled"].)

It was a haze that seemed impossible to break, and it was becoming more and more permanent. The single time it was penetrated was not long after I started school. I was a shy teenager, and it wasn't until my second year of college that I began dating; when my first serious relationship ended badly (I got the news in a phone call while I was home for Christmas break), I slipped into the most private part of Dad's house—his bird-book room—and lay on the sofa. I remember the way the blue woolen slipcover felt: itchy against my wet face. It was as if every moment of heartbreak I'd felt as a child had suddenly manifested and was pouring out. Dad came in and put his arm on my shoulder; I could hear his friends laughing in the living room. I felt embarrassed, but I couldn't stop crying, and Dad stayed. I wish I could have told him, then, how my heart felt permanently broken, and had for so long, but I didn't know it myself. Dad whispered to me, his voice cracking in frustration, "I don't know what to do." But his presence, his touch, meant so much to me; it made me feel as if he finally cared enough to love me.

It would take a long time for us to be that close again. Over the two decades that followed, that room would become too crowded; the books and maps and lists would push out the sofa, and soon, except for some pictures propped above the desk, there'd be little room for anyone else—happy or sad, loved or hated.

THE FALL I LEFT FOR COLLEGE was also a milestone in Dad's birding. When he got home from the trip north, he found the Clements checklist waiting for him and began to pore over it. It was then that he learned a lesson all true Big Listers have to learn: that to really tally every bird, you have to add species not just in your yard, your country, or the most remote parts of the world—you have to add them in your living room.

Getting a copy of Clements was just part of a vague plan—even Dad wasn't totally sure what he was aiming for—that had begun earlier that year. He gave up his Manhattan apartment and moved to Long Island full-time. His days as a swinging single were over. He also quit the job he'd started at the rehab clinic in Manhattan a few years earlier. Instead, he began to take temporary positions—a stint as a substitute physician on a Montana Indian reservation; a month at a migrant laborers' clinic in California's San Joaquin Valley. These jobs allowed him to search for new species in new places, but they also gave him time at home to start to organize his lifetime tallies, which were recorded (at that time) in a series of notebooks and tattered field guides. Dad says that he hadn't quite been gripped by the birding obsession yet, but he was getting close: When he took a rare vacation, signing up for a week at a Mexican Club Med, he quickly tired of the partying-and-pleasure routine and escaped to the mountains surrounding the resort, where—alone—he added forty new species to his list.

Dad gathered his lists of sightings and compared them, bird by bird, to the species tally assembled by Clements. Starting with his earliest check marks in Cruickshank and working right up to his penciled-in sighting records on the cardstock lists issued by the American Ornithologists' Union, Dad ordered, consolidated, and put the work he'd done over the previous thirty-five years into context. After four weeks of work, it was done—and to his dismay, Dad ended up losing nineteen species. The Lumpers, in 1979, were having a final gasp, and Dad had to subtract the Great White Heron, which had been combined with the Great Blue Heron; the Bullocks and Baltimore Orioles, which had merged into the single Northern Oriole species; and the Yellow-green and Red-eyed Vireo. (All of these birds have since been re-split; the list giveth and taketh, and that lovely Oriole with the orange-wing bars at your bird feeder doesn't seem to notice that people are arguing over his name.) One more measure of Dad's increasing seriousness: He scrubbed a few more birds from his list, ones that, after studying Clements, he determined were escapees. The revisions, which are designated in his notes under the oversized heading SPECIES LOST IN TRANSCRIBING CLEMENTS, left him with a life total of 907. It was a number that indicated serious birding, since it exceeded the total found on the North American continent, but as a contending Big List, it was only a statement of possibility. "I got ideas," Dad recalls. "There were seven thousand birds left for me to see."

ONE OF THE PROBLEMS YOU FACE WHEN YOU'RE CONTEMPLATING a run at a Big List is money. Many of Dad's competitors were independently wealthy. The expense involved in seeing six, seven, or eight thousand birds can be fairly astronomical, and the price of admission rises as your list gets bigger. The term birders use for this is CPB, or cost per bird. It was Dad's explanation of this concept—we were standing in his bird room, and he quickly went to his trip records, which contained all of his sighting lists, expense reports, receipts, and reference materials—back in the early 1990s, when I innocently asked him how much he'd spent (his guess is over $300,000) to get his list to 6,500, that gave me the first clue that the birding world was intensely arcane, fascinating, and absurd.

Here's how it works: In order to see a lot of birds, you have to travel. You have to travel to remote places—places that are expensive to reach. You could do this on your own, as Dean Fisher did in the 1960s, or as Peter Alden proposed in his book, but you'd pretty much have to have no other obligations, and plenty of time. Because of these difficult logistics, none of the Big Listers in Dad's generation were able to take that approach. Instead, most of them built their lists into the low thousands on their own, and then began taking the private tours offered by the birding specialty companies that began to emerge in the 1980s.

Those trips are expensive. My excursion to the Amazon with Dad, for example, cost nearly $6,000 for three weeks, not including airfare. I'm accustomed to traveling to remote places on my own; I can make a thousand dollars last at least a month just about anywhere, and yet I was shocked by the expense, since the accommodations are often rustic, and the actual costs involved are low. But you're paying for the expertise of the guide, as well, who prepares carefully for each trip; each birder receives a crib sheet of expected species in advance, and the guide's major job—the only job he has that truly matters—is to deliver each and every bird to each and every guest, no matter how much time it takes. (This can be truly frustrating if some of the trip attendees are unskilled, the pure counters; the guide wants them to get a real look at the bird, but the guest often can't see or distinguish it. In the evening, as the day's sighting list is revisited, the guest usually checks it off regardless of whether he got the kind of look that might lead to independent recognition of the same species later on.)

If you want to see a lot of birds, you initially start with a fairly low cost per bird. Let's start with Dad's first trip with a bird-specific travel outfitter, in 1982, to Kenya. For the sake of math, I'll round the trip's total price—not including airfare—to $5,000. On that two-week trip, Dad saw 517 of the nation's approximately 1,200 species. Cost per bird is a relatively modest $9.67.

There are lots of countries you haven't visited at this point, and you can keep building your list by going to new places.

"But to be a Big Lister," Dad says, "you have to double back."

So you return to Kenya. There are 650 species left to bag. They're rarer, of course, so you see fewer—Dad saw a hundred—

but your trip cost remains the same. CPB: $50—a 500 percent increase!

But wait. To be a really Big Lister, you may even have to triple back—or more: Jim Clements has just nine birds left to see in Peru. He's been back there over twenty times. (Birding slang for a visit designed to close out a country's list is "cleaning up," as in, "He's out cleaning up Argentina right now.") On some of his trips, Clements hasn't seen a single new species. CPB: infinite.

Dad estimated that his total birding expenditures turns out to be a low sum compared to other Big Listers: Once you're in the cleanup phase, you often have to book private trips, each of which can cost tens of thousands of dollars. (Phoebe Snetsinger estimated that she spent nearly two million dollars to reach her world record of eighty-five hundred birds—with a weight portion of that expenditure paying for her final five hundred species.)

As a doctor, Dad could certainly have earned the money he needed to chase birds, but the fights with my mother had led him to limit his income; their complex divorce agreement tied the dollars she received to Dad's salary, and he felt she was disinclined to spend it on her children (though the truth was more complicated than that; the struggle over cash was, to me, just an extension of the stubborn fight over unquenched desires both of them started in Europe).

Dad never wanted to be a high-volume kind of doctor in a private practice. Instead, he chose positions that were more oriented toward public service, often with relatively low salaries. Still, he'd always been incredibly thrifty, so he had the funds to get started, if he kept working. The problem was that work meant time, and he needed a job that he could bend, much as he'd done with the army regulations when we were traveling in Europe, in order to accommodate the list.

The answer? Change his specialty to emergency medicine and take a position in the urgent-care department of a tiny hospital in the resort community of Greenport, Long Island. In the summer, the ER was busy, and Dad kept more or less regular hours, which was fine, since he could sit by his pool in June, July, and August and scan the skies for species to add to his yard list. But the facility slowed to a crawl in the winter, with fewer than a dozen cases per day. The routine was perfect for somebody who needed large blocks of free time: Dad would work an eighty-hour shift, sleeping in a cottage on the hospital grounds. When a patient was coming, he'd be notified by radio and be ready when the ambulance arrived. One long shift meant two or three weeks off—just the right amount of time for a birding excursion.

Of course, to make the schedule work, Dad had to exercise control over it, so he quickly worked his way up to running the emergency room. Many of his birding plans involved the precise allotment of time over the winter; the shifts he worked and the trips that contained the birds he needed had to be perfectly synchronized. Ultimately, this meant that Dad had a very good idea of where his list might go well in advance. He had five birding outings scheduled the year he reached seven thousand, and his prediction—that he'd see that bird sometime during his second week in Brazil, on trip number four of that year—was just about perfect; he told me this a year in advance, though I had to cajole him just a little. I finally realized that he was superstitious about jinxing himself.

What place does superstition have in what is fundamentally a scientific pursuit? When you're in such a long-term chase, you feel like you can't afford to leave anything to chance, but whether you get those final few reclusive birds hidden in impenetrable jungle, in Peru or Brazil, after the schedule is made and the money is spent, comes down to luck.

❀   ❀   ❀

DAD HAD TAKEN BIRDING TRIPS ON HIS OWN, and he'd gone offshore on bird-watching boats, but the idea of leaving the country for a week or more just to look at birds was completely new and exciting to him. And he had an idea of where he wanted to go: For years, he'd heard about a bird-rich oasis in Trinidad called the Asa Wright Nature Centre. The facility was—and remains—a required stop and an excellent, close-to-home launching point for any serious avifaunal enthusiast contemplating birding by volume. Of the more than one hundred species endemic to the rain-forest facility, Dad saw ninety-six—his largest single-day total in years, including one of the weirdest birds in this hemisphere: the Oilbird, or Guacharo, the world's only nocturnal, fruit-eating avian species. To see one anywhere else in the Caribbean or South America requires some serious good fortune and nighttime foraging—never easy— but the breeding colony at the nature center's Dunston Cave now numbers nearly two hundred Oilbirds. (The name comes from the fatness of the birds' chicks, which gain so much weight after hatching that they often weigh considerably more than their parents; they're so corpulent that they were often captured and rendered for fuel by Trinidadian natives.)

Dad was lucky to get onto the Trinidad excursion; only a few visitors are allowed at the Asa Wright center at a time, and initially he'd been told that the trip was full. But a birding club from Pennsylvania had a last-minute cancellation, and Dad's travel agent found out about it. He suddenly found himself part of a community of birders. It was pleasant enough, but the pattern he'd establish throughout most of his future bird-finding trips began to emerge: As a line of binocular-carrying enthusiasts snaked through dense forest, Dad would drop back to the end of the line, where he could smoke cigarettes without disturbing anyone and see a few extra birds without being disturbed. "The group would flush up new species as they passed, and I'd be far enough behind to catch them as I arrived," he says. Alone in the woods was how he started birding, and that escape would continue throughout his birding life.

It was on one of these lonely walks that Dad saw the Blue-crowned Motmot. It is a fun and spectacular bird for anyone—enthusiast or not—to see: eighteen inches long, with a green and red body and a head streaked in multiple shades of blue, some so bright they seem painted on. The bird is found around the edges of forests, and is fairly tame. Dad was able to get a close look, approaching to within a few inches. They stared at each other for a few moments.

It was bird number 1,000.

THINGS WERE CHANGING SOCIALLY, too, rearranging themselves for a person who wanted to put birds, more than people, at the center of his life. The wild lifestyles that both my parents enjoyed during the 1970s were coming to an end. Mom was settling down, and Dad was finding his ability to meet women more and more limited; a series of health scares—first the herpes epidemic, and later AIDS—made casual encounters risky. (Other factors, ranging from increased penalties for drunk driving to the introduction of VCRs and the early fitness craze, in Dad's analysis, "destroyed the scene.")

So, in 1980, just after returning from Trinidad, Dad did what he hadn't done in nearly a decade: He got a girlfriend. I wasn't really sure how I felt about Judith. I was eighteen years old, and no longer experienced the longing for a stable mother figure that had made me love Dad's earliest girlfriends so much. I was beginning to become aware that the wounds inflicted by the divorce were still active in Dad; that maybe he was still in love with the girl he'd met as a teenager; that the heartbreak bubbling beneath the surface prevented him from engaging with the women he'd later be involved with, driving him further into isolation. That isolation led him toward more birding in another way, as well: I think extended periods of togetherness became more and more difficult for him. I didn't sense any true closeness in Dad's relationship with Judith, and when I asked him, once, if he ever thought they'd get married, he completely scoffed at the idea. "No way," he said, without a second's hesitation.

I knew, then, that Dad would never allow himself to fall in love again, at least not with a human. I knew—and he knew—that his soul would have to gain satisfaction from something else.

In Trinidad, Dad heard of a group called Earthwatch. The company offered "science vacations," on which interested laypeople could pay to be included on a genuine research team; they'd help the trip leaders complete important projects in biology and ecology, and get a tax deduction and a working vacation as a bonus. Dad booked himself on a trip to Tasmania, and even on the way, there were signs of his growing obsession. He got into the habit of looking for birds from airplane windows as his flights left and arrived on the tarmac at Fiji, Australia, and New Zealand (he even has a sublist, these days, of birds sighted that way). "I got five life birds in the Auckland transit lounge," he says; he arrived for that trip with a total of eight new species, ahead of the game. But in addition to all that counting, Dad expanded his interest in birds to a place he'd only dreamed about: He did real science, working with the ornithologists to survey local species, catch them in mist nets, and collect specimens. Dad's inherent skills as a birder were re-warded when one of the trip leaders gave him an assignment: to do a species count of passing seabirds. Dad spent days sitting on the rocks, staring out to sea, surveying hundreds of thousands of birds—shearwaters, gulls, albatrosses, and terns. "It was really, re-ally fun," he says. "I totally enjoyed it."

Over the next two weeks, Dad camped with his fellow re-searchers, adding sixty-three birds, including the rare White-bellied Sea Eagle. And he began to bookend his birding. Instead of going straight home, he spent an extra day in Sydney, Australia, with the express purpose of seeing birds in Royal National Park. He drove there, slept in his rental car, and in the morning was re-warded with a sighting of a Tawny Frogmouth, an utterly bizarre-looking bird that resembles a stubby owl, though it is more related to the nightjar. (The nightjar is a species found in the United States. I often see them on mountain-bike rides at dusk; the little birds seem to squat on open trail. If I'm riding with headlights, their eyes flash, and they fly off only after I get very, very close. Birders use a similar technique, shining a high-intensity light into the brush, to spot other nocturnal species.) The Frogmouth was his last lifer for the trip, one of fifteen he saw on his own in Australia.

Dad returned from that trip with 103 new birds. It was his first triple-digit excursion. But the obsession was growing in a different way, now, as Dad was making time for birding, and just birding. Still, he says, there was balance. He had a relationship. Both his kids were in college. He was enjoying being a doctor; the hours and the action of the emergency room suited him. And birding? Well, it was, on one level, a rich hobby; the numbers were a fun game, but he was getting to do some real studying as well. But to me, it looked like more than just a pastime. I knew Dad wanted—and probably needed—birds to be something more; I even asked him about it several times, wondering why he hadn't become an ornithologist. His quick dismissal of the idea indicated that it occupied a large—but shut-off—part of his psyche. But whatever he was about to become had always been waiting to happen. I knew that even if he didn't, though I wasn't always happy about it, birds—regardless of how much Dad indulged his need to see them—always seemed more important to him than anything else.

Dad was in his late forties. He had 1,116 check marks in his Clements guide.

CHAPTER TEN

HOW TO COUNT BIRDS

❝ *The oddest birds on my yard list are ones I've spotted on my swimming-pool cover. The swimming-pool cover is solid and, unless pumped, pools of rainwater will accumulate atop it. Such was the case on September 30, 1992. I stepped out of my rear kitchen door to see a female Wood Duck sitting in a small pool of water on the swimming-pool cover. It immediately took off. Apparently it had mistaken the green and wet cover for a natural wet spot, and, when flying over, stopped there to feed or rest. Wood Duck is an uncommon, but regular, migrant in my area, and I did expect to see some flying over my property at some point, although I had lived here for seventeen years without seeing one. That's not the reason I got the pool, but it definitely gave me something to do with it during the cold season.*❞

—Wood Duck (*Aix sponsa*), September 30, 1992,
East Hampton, New York, Yard-list bird #179.

DURING THE SUMMER, DAD SITS BY THE POOL. He reclines in a lounge chair, his binoculars resting on his chest. He's looking up. Something flies overhead, and he identifies it with a shout: *Osprey! Common Tern! Prairie Warbler!* Some visit every day. Others return in spring or fall, but Dad keeps searching for them, calling their names. Visitors—Arthur, the psychologist he befriended on his first Caribbean trip; Al, a financial advisor who he met at a group house on Long Island in the 1970s; or Charlie, his closest remaining friend from childhood—stop in. They talk. With Arthur, it's about women; with Al, the stock market; and with Charlie, motorcycles (the two scraped together money in the 1950s and jointly bought one from a young actor named Steve McQueen). But Dad's reminiscences end when something passes overhead.

All of them regard Dad's skills with a combination of bemusement and teasing skepticism. It seems impossible that anyone could identify a bird hundreds of feet overhead.

"You don't really know what they are, Richard," one of Dad's friends used to say. "You're just making it up."

Dad, knowing that wing shape and flight style are reliable long-distance field markings, never replies. I think he finds the ribbing a little disrespectful, though he'd never let on (birders tend to over-compensate for the rather tender perception their hobby often conjures; Dad played junior football, and Bret Whitney was a star baseball player).

I know he knows what he's seeing. But for most of my life, I really didn't understand why he was spending all that time out there with his birds. I knew, on one level, that it was what he was meant to be doing, but I can't say I really liked it all that much; I'd have much preferred to be spending time with Dad at the movies, or wandering New York's Chinatown, rather than exploring lonely marshes and shorelines. It didn't seem like a father/son activity; every time Dad looked through his binoculars, he seemed to be looking away from me.

THE BACKYARD IS GROUND ZERO for birders, whether Big Listers or ordinary folk watching chickadees flutter around a feeder. The "yard list" is the most common kind of tally birders keep, and adding a new species to that list is exciting. It's not an exotic experience, as it was in Brazil's Jaú National Park, where Dad and I become the fourth and fifth people on earth to see the newly described Yapacana Antbird. Rather, increasing your yard list is more like eating a slice of homemade apple pie. A birder's backyard is a comfortable and well-ordered place, with strategically chosen fauna, feeders, and sources of water. Why shouldn't the lords of these cul-de-sac Edens census their domains?

An online search for the term *yard list* yields over ten thousand different Web pages. Some of these personal tallies are rudimentary, with just text and numbers, while others offer photos, life histories, and counts of individual species (some birders see a bird once and eliminate it from their visual targeting; others want to know exactly how many Red-tailed Hawks have flown over their yards during a lifetime).

That so many yard listers feel compelled to share their tallies with the rest of the world is one of the more curious aspects of the practice. You can't compare one at-home tally to another, since no two yards are alike. And yard listing is unmoderated—there are no ornithologist tour leaders, guides, or fellow birders to check your accuracy. This is in direct opposition to Big Listing, where the right to interpret—assuming a split that hasn't been "officially" recognized—becomes implicit only after you've worked up toward the highest reaches of the tallying hierarchy.

That said, most yard listers probably, at some point, gain awareness of the "rules." The basics are pretty much the same as with any type of bird count. You should be sure of what you're seeing. Pretty sure, maybe, and possibly don't count, though many yard listers tend to their tally of "possible birds" that might be identified later. (For example, if a "maybe" bird is a rare one, and a birder gets an unsatisfactory glimpse in his yard, he might grant himself the check mark if he gets a more assured view down the street a few hours later—though technically, most yard listers limit themselves to birds they've seen or heard on or directly above their property, though some will include birds seen from their property, even if not directly overhead.) Once again, the yard lister reigns over his domain: "This is a list of all the birds I have seen on or from my property. I know that may be stretching the rules for a backyard list, but it's *my* list and *I'm* making the rules," writes a Portland, Maine, birder in an online report of his sixty-four sightings. (A yard list of sixty-four isn't very large, really, but you'll find even smaller ones on the Internet. Why post such a small tally? I think about all the tiny castles in the tiny hill towns of Italy; even the most threadbare palace was still someplace that somebody once was absolute ruler of.)

The keeping of a home tally is an increasingly popular activity. The National Audubon Society estimates that more than 60 million Americans do it. The extension of this trend has been a proliferation of products aimed at the casual lister, many sold at "birding shops," which often smell like potpourri or pine needles: identification handbooks aimed at dummies and idiots; feeders and seed; avifaunal tchotchkes, such as plush and statuary bird likenesses; and the popular "Singing Bird Clock," where a dozen different species—House Finch, American Robin, Northern Mockingbird, Blue Jay, House Wren, Tufted Titmouse, Northern Oriole, Mourning Dove, Black-capped Chickadee, Northern Cardinal, White-throated Sparrow, and White-breasted Nuthatch—mark the hours with their particular songs. Despite the grating effect of the timepiece, the songs are authentic, having come from Cornell University's Macaulay Library of Natural Sounds, to which Bret Whitney has contributed over five thousand audio samples. (Dad has spotted all twelve of the clock birds at home. I once tried to stump Dad by e-mailing him the names of the dozen species on the timepiece,* asking him what the relationship between them was. He got the answer in about half a minute.)

Yard listing is intimate, and patient. It isn't just the hours and

---

*The clock is the most popular birding-related item ever manufactured, not including books. There is also a sequel—the Singing Bird Clock II—which corrects the original product's Eastern bias; three of the dozen birds on the follow-up clock are Western species. The new dozen are: Red-tailed Hawk, Acorn Woodpecker, Eastern Towhee, Scarlet Tanager, Steller's Jay, Eastern Screech-Owl, Yellow-bellied Sapsucker, Indigo Bunting, Rose-breasted Grosbeak, Whip-poor-will, Limpkin, and the Common Loon.

years spent gazing overhead. A pair of catbirds has been returning to Dad's yard for years; so have several robins and jays. Dad says that he doesn't feel sentimental about the returnees, though he's quite quick to trap any wild mammals that might act as predators toward his on-site flock (he catches them in a humane trap and then sets them free in a state park up the road). A yard list also provides some interesting lessons in human interaction with the natural world. Dad's pool is not just for watery recreation, but watery re-creation: It is a vinyl-sided wetland, a minor attractant for migrating shorebirds. Some land on the pool's waterlogged cover during the winter; others skim insects from the surface of the water on autumn nights. Figuring out ways to get birds to come to your property is another way in which yard listers make their own rules.

A yard list ages with you, slowing with time. When he moved in to his very modest, slightly ramshackle house in East Hampton (he lives at the end of a road that, until recently, was filled mostly with fisherman's shacks; his own home originally had two small bedrooms, though an addition—which served as a beauty parlor before he bought the place—provides a third; the most attractive thing about the property is the large plot of land, which includes a small wood and well over an acre of open space) twenty-five years ago, Dad's guess was that he'd reach two hundred birds in his lifetime on the property. In the first twelve months he lived in the house, he saw over sixty species. Over the past decade, he's added just eighteen birds to that tally, with some years completely bereft. His total as of this writing is 198. (As I was making final revisions to this chapter, he came close to adding one more, hearing what he thought was a White-eyed Vireo—a bird that is becoming less common on Long Island—in his backyard. But there was something slightly off about the song, and he wasn't able to actually spot the bird. It occupied the list in pencil for five days before Dad finally—and with some regret—erased it. It was a rare moment of wishful uncertainty for an advanced birder.)

THE YARD LIST NATURALLY EXTENDS into a county or city tally. If that excites you, you'll probably want to start keeping a state list. At some point, you become a lister as much as a birder. The demarcation is different for most because the two activities are pretty much inseparable; most folks find it hard, once they've started listing, to stop, though the transition from keeping a list to competitive, sport-like tallying is more rare.

At various times, Dad has kept several of those list types, as well as tallies of birds he's seen in specific places—at certain wildlife refuges or habitats. He lists by trip, country, and continent. Some birders also count genera or taxonomic family; others chase only specific species. (Antbirds are a favorite; so are raptors. One couple, Morton and Phyllis Isler, of Virginia, have become so expert on antbirds and their songs that they spend most of their time analyzing new recordings of that species' vocalization; they explain that it is the detail of sorting through so many similar species that absorbs them, perhaps in the way that some people like to do jigsaw puzzles with no images printed on the pieces. Raptor-watchers tend to enjoy the action of watching birds on the hunt a little more; when I witnessed a Prairie Falcon in a 100 mph "stoop," or dive, over Idaho's Snake River, I understood why the other birders in my boat, all accomplished observers of birds of prey, could view similar scenes again and again without a hint of boredom. Field-guide author Kenn Kaufmann theorizes that we choose the birds "whose energy is most like our own." If that's true, the restlessness of the global lister reflects a sense of wandering—almost homelessness—but also a conquer-it-all majesty.)

You can invent your own kind of whimsical, noncountable tallies as well: for instance, birds seen in zoos or pet stores. When Dad was ill and couldn't get out, the sighting of a Red-tailed Hawk on *Xena: Warrior Princess* led him to consider my suggestion of a count of birds seen on television. (Ultimately, he decided against it. "You don't count birds that don't count," Dad said. Though that never stops him from shouting out the names of the species he sees on his favorite programs.)

The most hotly contested "small" list is the lifetime tally for our continent. Over the years, this count has steadily grown. The current leader is Florida's Dan Canterbury, with 1,731 species seen in the American Birding Association's officially defined "North American Region," which has little to do with the Atlantic, Pacific, and everything in-between. "The North American Region," the ABA states, "includes all of the Aleutian Islands, and is divided from Eurasia by a line in the Bering Sea running midway between Attu, St. Matthew, St. Lawrence, and Little Diomede islands on the North American side, and Medny (in the Commander Islands), the Siberian coast, and Diomede Island on the Eurasian side. The North American Region includes Greenland; other related islands within 200 nautical miles of the Pacific and Atlantic coasts; the Bahamas; all of the cays and islands lying between Nicaragua and Jamaica; and all of the Greater and Lesser Antilles south to and including Grenada and Barbados (but excluding Trinidad and Tobago and the other Caribbean islands specifically included in the South American Region). The North American Region includes all of Panama, and extends across the Caribbean Sea halfway to South America and its related islands." Similar descriptions exist for the other four "official" continental regions and the three ocean zones recognized by the ABA and affiliated organizations.

The boundaries make biological sense, though the ABA's published criteria for determining an official region sounds more concerned with procedure than with scientific rigor: A region is defined as including all interior seas; "related" islands that lie generally within two hundred nautical miles of the continent; and a "pelagic belt" extending seaward another two hundred nautical miles from the coastline and/or related islands, or half the distance to another continent or islands in an ocean region—whichever appears first. Birds beyond these pelagic belts are the world's most difficult to see, even for the Big Listers: There are several dozen such species that are excellent candidates for the world's most impossible to spot. (One contender is found only on a tiny atoll 1,755 miles east of Cape Town and 2,200 miles due north of Antarctica. The bird takes its name from the island it occupies: the Inaccessible Island Flightless Rail. The first three words of the bird's name provide a clue as to exactly how great those distances are; there's no place this bird could seriously get to from here. Evolutionary adaptation has taken away the physical means for the rail to even attempt a journey to oblivion.)

FIGURING OUT WHERE TO COUNT IS EASIER than learning how. A bird list is anything but a simple progression of numbers; birding officialdom has a way it *likes* tallies to be handled, and then there are the ways Big Listers modify the game in the field. The American Birding Association first attempted to outline exactly what constituted a bird sighting in 1983, and amended those regulations—to great controversy—in 1992. There are only five official commandments when it comes to allowing a check mark, but within them is encompassed every scientific, competitive, and debatable issue avifaunal observers encounter.

ABA Rule Number One is this: "The bird must have been within the prescribed area and time period when encountered." This rule is followed by a definition of exactly what "within" means. I first came to understand this bit of counting esoterica while competing in an event called The Great Texas Birding Classic, where teams of birders compete in a five-day, nonstop marathon to see the most species along the Gulf Coast of Texas. I was standing on the northern bank of the Rio Grande River; our team had wandered into a marshy, humid area and was pushing along a dirt path, around barbed-wire fences and bougainvillea plants. As we stood before the absolutely still waterway, my teammates counted a Spotted Sandpiper, a Great-tailed Grackle, and a pair of Mourning Doves. Then, on the opposite bank, I made my own sighting: a shorebird, some kind of tern. "There," I shouted. "Tern."

"Caspian Tern," said one of my teammates. But he didn't tally it. The Texas Classic follows ABA rules, and a bird that's flitting about on the other side of a national border can't make *your* country list, no matter where *you* happen to be standing.

I stood there, trying to will the bird to undertake the fabled crossing. But the tern headed further south. As we hiked back to our vehicle, I decided that the ABA regulation was silly and capricious. But in the time since, I've come to understand it. Of course it is arbitrary, as made-up as bird names or national borders. But we can't manifest our impulses to count if we don't, on some level, relish our role as arbiters.

Besides, the rules don't completely forbid me from counting the bird, stating: "Within means that the bird must be within the prescribed area when observed, although *the observer need not be* [italics mine]."

The Caspian Tern is now one of my Mexico sightings. (I'm hesitant to call it a list, since I don't really make much out of it. It's more part of my recollection, though even as a memory, I'll still follow the ABA commandments and say that it was a south-of-the-border encounter, just in case anyone should ask me.)

The ABA's second rule is the one that has the most to do with science, and it borders on tinkering with the definition of life itself (though it leaves the heavy lifting in that regard to higher authorities, like the American Ornithologists' Union). This by-law is also the one with the most codicils; there are six main parts and four subparts. The rule concerns the task that is at the center of all of birding and ornithology—the definition of species—and it starts with a statement that sounds simple, but under which lies a labyrinth: "The taxonomic status of a bird as a full species, and thus its countability, is determined by the standard for the list on which the bird is to be counted." Since different lists use different standards for different areas—the ABA is its own authority for North America; it only uses the Clements or AOU checklists for areas beyond its home zone—it is possible, as the ABA rules continue, "that two birds seen in the Continental USA would be counted as one species on state and ABA area lists, and two species on a world list, or vice versa." (This can lead to some level of temptation for the various keepers of the lists. Jim Clements recalls understanding that the Black-billed Magpie wasn't the same as the bird's European version; most birders who've seen both know the species look identical, but sing differently. Many birders who kept world lists chose to consider the bird two species, but the American Ornithological Union—and the ABA—didn't actually split the bird into the American and the Eurasian Magpie until 2001, which was when Clements added the split to his list. "I was tempted, but I decided to wait until the Ivory Tower boys got around to it," he jokes. At that point he put it in the checklist and officially increased his personal species tally.)

We're still not finished with Rule Number Two. Other sections have to do with introduced species and reintroduced species, usually birds that have tottered so close to extinction that scientists have begun to breed them in captivity, hoping to create populations stable enough to return to the wild. A reintroduced bird can't be counted until it has become an autonomous, successful breeding population, so the California Condor—decidedly *not* on Dad's list—won't tally because it hasn't had great reproductive success. The Peregrine Falcon, on the other hand, was near extinction after the DDT crisis of the 1960s and 1970s, but is now ubiquitous, with many of today's birds not descended from ones bred at the World Center for Birds of Prey near Boise, Idaho. Whether you see a Peregrine above remote Hell's Canyon, north of there, or dive-bombing for pigeons from a Manhattan skyscraper ledge, you can count it.

The third ABA law is about the state in which seen birds can be tallied: "The bird must have been alive, wild, and unrestrained when encountered." The first requirement—that the bird not be dead—seems somewhat obvious, though non-birders nearly always ask if dead birds count. You also can't see a bird and then intentionally kill it—that's in opposition to the separate ABA Code of Birding Ethics, which requires that birders "promote the welfare of birds and their environment." The no-kill rule harkens back to the collecting days, when killing birds was pretty much the only way *to* list them; Spencer Fullerton Baird—Elliot Coues's mentor—kept, as his primary tally, an inventory of skins, not a list of sightings. However, there's a gray area: If you accidentally hit a bird with your car and it dies, it is probably countable. I remembered hitting the Scop's Owl in Spain—that bird survived—and asked Dad if he'd ever seen a life bird that subsequently perished. "They all died after I saw them," he said, making a dry wisecrack about the relatively short lifespan of most bird species. Joke or not, when I pointed out that some species of parrot he's seen can live for over fifty years, and are likely still roaming the jungles with their mates, he exclaimed, "That's true!" sounding almost delighted, and giving as much of a hint as he's capable of that he really does like birds, that he really does connect with nature—perhaps because nature, unlike most of the other things in his life, is the ultimate earthly exemplar of longevity.

The final requirement of Rule Number Three also makes sense: Birds at the zoo don't count. But the middle one is a bit more subjective. How wild are birds that always appear at a feeder? Some individual populations have become so dependent on human support that they've changed their migratory habits, appearing where they "shouldn't," failing to go south for the winter. But these birds usually count; there's no percentage in destroying at-home birding, especially since it is the way most casual watchers build their lists.

The fourth rule is the one that leaves non-birders incredulous, and it's the one that has created the most controversy within the birding community. It concerns what constitutes an acceptable sighting: "Diagnostic field marks, sufficient to identify the species, must have been seen and/or heard, and/or documented by the recorder at the time of the encounter." People nearly always wonder how birders can be sure of what they've seen—like Dad's backyard skeptics—and the abilities birders have to quickly spot and identify from great distances can be baffling to nonbelievers.

That part has to be taken on faith. The section of Rule Number

Four that most inflames birders is the one that allows them to check off species they've heard and not seen. (This was the 1992 addition.) It is true that sound can be more reliable than sight when it comes to bird identification, for both birds and people. And if you go to the tropics, you're going to be using sound, for sure. Imagine the Peruvian rain forest. You've just taken your first birding walk around the Explorer's Inn, one of the most popular spots for world birding. (The facility, which operates as both hotel and research station, sits in the center of the southeastern Peru Tabopata National Reserve. It possesses the world's largest yard list: over 600 recorded species of birds, along with 1,200 butterfly species, and onward; if your passion is to count dragonflies, you'll find over 175 species in the immediate vicinity.) In rain-forest density, identifying by vocalization makes sense. That's the way birds do it; it is safer and more efficient to discover a chosen paramour by hearing than by flying in close for a look.

If birds use sound to identify themselves, the argument goes, humans should be allowed to do the same thing. The rule change speaks to the same phenomenon Bret Whitney is leading on the scientific side. (Though Whitney himself doesn't offer an opinion on what birders should count. "I leave that to the customers," he says. "I point out what they're seeing and hearing.")

Despite this, many birders refuse to allow heard birds onto their lists. Dad doesn't. Neither did Phoebe Snetsinger, who so disagreed with the 1992 rule that she stopped submitting her list to the ABA. (The disagreement is a possible violation of the fifth commandment, which instructs that birders obey the previous four.) Today's most prolific lister, Peter Kaestner, also refuses to count heard birds: "We believe there is just too much room for misidentification of sounds in the forest, and for people to count species pointed out to them when they had no idea what the call of the species was," he says. "After all, we are bird-watchers, not bird-listeners."

HOW TO SEE. HOW TO COUNT. This is what nearly everybody asks when you talk about birds, bird-watching, and bird-counting: "But how do you know people are being honest? How do you *prove* you've seen that many birds?" It's a question serious birders occasionally whisper about, but there's really no satisfactory answer for those who ask most persistently. The way outsiders see it, most of birding operates on the honor system. Birders frequently pursue their hobby on their own, and even those who go out with groups are going to see a large number of birds on solo outings.

It would be easy enough to say that birders are simply the most honorable and upstanding folks on earth. But that might not be totally true.

A few things keep birders in check.

First, if you're a Big Lister, you probably have to go on birding trips. So, some of the world's best ornithologists—and your competition—are watching you all the time. Second, if you fudge, there's a good chance you'll get the science wrong. A birder—I can't use his name because what few whispers there are about him are unproven, and for the most part, his name has been erased from the annals of Big Listing for his alleged indiscretion—once claimed to be approaching eight thousand; he'd done much of his birding solo, before the major tour companies arrived in many areas. The problem was that he reported birds that even the experts hadn't seen, or, in some cases, even knew existed. As this birder surpassed a claimed eight thousand, the rumors got louder: He was making things up.

The result?

Immediate ostracism. This fellow is now unmentionable, excommunicated.

There's also a more subtle vetting process that resembles the one used in the Texas Birding Classic.

At the end of our four days, we reported to the Holiday Inn in Port Aransas, a Gulf Coast town a bit south of the Louisiana border (best known as the home of Janis Joplin; there's a statue of her on Main Street). We had to turn our lists in to the judges, though we first ran into an incredulous biker, who asked what all of us were doing wearing binoculars. When I explained, he frowned and said: "Seriously? Counting birds?" He paused for a moment, leaning against the hotel's front desk. "You mean, like vultures and shit?"

Well, yes. All birding contests—global, regional, or time-delimited—have official checklists. Three hundred sixty species, including two kinds of vultures, appear on the Texas tally. The birds that appear on it are the common ones, the species participants are fairly likely to see. The trickier birds occupy a secondary list of 123 Texas Review Species. When teams report one of these birds, they're required to submit a report form for rare species. Birds not on either list require additional documentation—usually pictures. The judges can reject a sighting if they don't find a team's evidence convincing (not an uncommon event; nearly every team loses a bird or two in the final count).

If you choose to submit your Big List to the ABA, you can expect a similar type of scrutiny, though there's no official panel of judges—just thousands of interested ABA members and their fine-toothed curiosity. Birds that everyone can see are usually not questioned, but the rarer a bird is, the more scrutiny you can expect.

Some birds are just impossible in certain places, though there are always a few birders who claim to have seen them.

Insistent misidentifications are a bigger problem than is outright fraud. Even bird scientists makes mistakes. One of the most famous in recent years occurred in April 1999, when a Louisiana State University ornithology graduate student reported seeing a pair of Ivory-billed Woodpeckers near Louisiana's Pearl River. The spectacular bird is something of an ornithological holy grail: They were thought to be extinct through much of the early twentieth century, were rediscovered in the 1950s, and then vanished again. (One nickname for the two-foot-long, red-crested bird with a huge, hammering bill is the "Lord God Bird" because, as the legend goes, that's what people say when they see one.) Scientists from Cornell and LSU began a project to find the birds, and on January 17, 2002, a dozen freestanding remote sound recorders were placed deep in the bayou. The plan was to let them listen for a month.

On January 27, something happened. At 3:30 PM, after gathering more than four thousand hours of audio, the researchers—stationed in a nearby bunkhouse—were astonished to hear a loud, echoing pair of beats—*TOK! TOK!*—that sounded, to some of them, like an old recording of the Ivory-billed Woodpecker. The news traveled quickly, and even the *New York Times* reported that the quest may have yielded spectacular results. The audio samples were sent to Cornell for analysis. They also went to several ornithologists, including Bret Whitney.

The effort to rediscover the Lord God Bird was monumental. Two universities and one binocular-maker had invested heavily in it. New technologies were developed. The search captured the public's imagination, as well, with national newspaper stories and reports on radio and television. But several ornithologists—including Whitney—didn't believe it.

"People really wanted it to be," says Whitney. "I wanted it to be."

But it wasn't. As soon as Whitney heard the tape, he knew it. He recognized the distant, reverberating pops. He could understand how they'd be mistaken for the lost woodpecker's distinct double rap, a sound unlike any made by other North American woodpeckers. There was a fairly credible layman's case to be made, but Whitney had grown up hunting. "It was gunfire," Whitney says. "Automatic gunfire, in the distance."

Nobody has ever determined who was firing the guns, or why. The young ornithologist who'd made the first report truly believed he'd seen what he'd seen. But no lister could ever have claimed the Ivory-billed Woodpecker, since it remained officially extinct throughout the search (though a few living birders actually saw one when the bird was still around). A compacted version of the same process holds true with listers who submit to the ABA. You'll likely have some species chucked, or at least questioned; you'll need to provide a defense, though it's unlikely any major expeditions will be mounted to vet your most rare sightings.

Fundamentally, birding is a self-disciplining activity. There are too many complexities and variations to get away with lying for too long; you'll be tripped up by your fellow birders and guides. (They may not be able to check your specific claims, but they'll know very quickly if you're the real thing or not; if you're not, the word will spread, and you'll be finished.)

Of course, you don't have to be sure of every bird you see in order to get a Big List. One of the top listers—Harvey Gilston, a British birder who was approaching eight thousand before his retirement—was known for spending a fortune on birding trips and hardly knowing a single bird. He'd head out with the ornithologists and groups, and when a mixed-species flock was swirling around a tree, in a frenzy, he'd listen as the guide called out the names of what was there, and check them off. It was unlikely Gilston could identify even a quarter of the birds he'd seen in some of remote areas he traveled, but that didn't matter. He'd seen them, and for him, it was all about the numbers. (Gilston also counted aircraft registration numbers.)

"He saw the birds," Bret Whitney, who'd taken Gilston on many birding expeditions, told me. "Even if he didn't know what they were."

THE LIST TAKES DIFFERENT FORMS. Dad's basic tally is kept in his hardback Clements guide; each time there's a new revision, Dad painstakingly reenters his check marks, with increasing adjustments for the splits (and a few lumps). But the backbone of his count are notebooks—reports on each trip or place—that he's kept throughout his life. Before each trip, Dad gathers the field guides he'll need and makes a list of "target birds" for each trip. The list might include a few lines covering specific identifying characteristics of each bird. For group trips, a key element of constructing this list are trip reports previous groups have generated—that's one of the best indicators of birds he's likely to see, and especially which *new* birds are likely. The sources for this information were, until the past decade, almost always printed volumes—oversized books that listed the birds of the world in great detail. In recent years, the Internet has made finding compact information about bird species easy, both in terms of knowing which birds are where, as travelers publish their personal regional lists, and in terms of knowing what those birds look like, through enormous collections of field accounts, photography, and, most recently, recorded vocalizations and video.

Phoebe Snetsinger's system was more complex. She made similar preparations, building a notebook for every trip. But her list's primary manifestation was a paper filing system that included color-coded index cards, marked with each species, variants, and (ultimately) sighting information; and grid paper, used to reconcile the Clements checklist with alternate world bird lists.

None of these first-generation Big Listers had computers. Listing software has made keeping track of numbers, splits, and lumps much easier; software is also now available to make the handmade mini-guides both Dad and his peers created. Every birding trip Peter Kaestner makes, for example, is accompanied by a concise, electronically generated list of birds he might see, all of which are coded by typeface or identifying symbol into category: must-see birds, desirable birds, unlikely-but-possible birds, already-seen birds, new-to-a-country (but not to a life list) birds, and more.

Dad's world birding took a pause while I was writing this book—his health prevented him from traveling—but he still managed to add nearly one hundred birds through splitting. One bird tour guide is keeping Phoebe Snetsinger's list alive now, five years after her death, as a tribute. The point isn't just sentimentality. That's the greatness of the Big List—the birder may slow down, or stop, or even die, but the list lives on. It isn't just life's work, it's the work of life.

CHAPTER ELEVEN

MORE
AND MORE

" *In the spring of 1984 I led a group for Earthwatch to the Zha Lung Crane reserve in central Manchuria. On May 5, 1984, I saw a small passerine feeding on the ground. It had brownish upperparts, a whitish belly, and a rufous tint to the wings and tail. At first I thought it was a thrush, perhaps a chat or a redstart. Then I noticed that it had a whitish, horizontal throat patch and, on either side of the patch, a small blue spot. This was unlike any bird in* A Field Guide to the Birds of Japan, *which was, at the time, the only guide applicable to northeastern China. So the bird was a mystery. Later that year two books were published on the birds of China. Neither had very good illustrations. Nevertheless, a little reading revealed that the mystery bird was either a female Fujian or Rufous-bellied Niltava, both forest flycatchers of southern China and southern Asia! The bird was over a thousand miles north of its normal range. Spring overshoots are a well-known phenomenon with Asian migrants, best illustrated by the many records of Asian birds at Attu in the Aleutians, where these lost birds also occur well out of their usual habitat and far north of their usual range.*"

—Fujian Niltava (*Niltava davidi*), May 5, 1984, Zha Lung Wildlife Reserve, China, #2375.

"**I** WAS BECOMING A LISTER," DAD SAYS. After his solo trips to the Caribbean, Dad began to think about other places he could search for birds. He'd participated in a few Earthwatch trips. They weren't bird-specific, but as a volunteer assisting scientists performing biological surveys in Tasmania and Belize, Dad was able to boost his list by nearly two hundred species. The mania had definitely arrived. He didn't just add birds during the "official" parts of the trip, but also through airplane and departure-lounge windows along the way. Stopovers in Fiji, Auckland, Melbourne, and Sydney tacked another dozen onto his count.

But it was Kenya that at last seemed to promise a life closer to his dreams than he'd dared to get before.

I spent most of the summer of 1982 in East Hampton, working as a reporter on a local newspaper and getting ready for my last year of college (though Dad was hitting the books—ornithological texts—much harder than I ever did). Nearly every afternoon, he'd sit at his kitchen table, surrounded by oversized avifaunal references. These books were far too large to carry along on birding excursions, and there was no readily available Kenyan field guide, so Dad made his own, drawing in a spiral notebook crude images of birds he expected to see, coloring them with bright pencils. Dad describes the result as "absolutely moronic," but I think they're lovely. They're functional enough, and you can feel the anticipation each tiny avian image represents.

Dad left for Kenya on October 22, 1982. It was his first trip with a true ornithologist as a guide, and he instantly understood the advantage of having somebody show you birds hidden deep in the jungle. Will Russell, Dad recalls, "was the first super birder I'd ever met. He knew the songs, knew the field marks, and knew the birds. I'd been with other birders who I thought were really good, but they weren't in the same class." Russell still leads tours; like Bret Whitney, he's part of a group of about fifty elite ornithologists who make their living supplying birds to listers.

From the start, Kenya was staggering. On his first day, Dad saw sixty-two new species. The complexities of world birding—the gamesmanship involved in sorting through competing checklists and guides, evaluating splits and lumps—asserted themselves quickly. The Clements listings suggested differing taxonomy from that in the African references Dad had used for his homemade field guide. The East Africa Natural History Society also had its own distinct tally of native species. Big Listers sometimes choose to stick to a single source, but other times, they play the field. That doesn't necessarily mean cherry-picking the taxonomic directories to yield the highest quantities; rather, the goal is to find the one for a particular area that best matches your judgment of what you actually saw on the ground. Of those first sixty-two birds, Dad chose on his own to add the Black-shouldered Kite. The American Birding Association's world list at that time declared that this was the same species as our own White-tailed Kite. (The bird is fun to watch—it hovers, nearly perfectly still, above its prey, then dives in for a precise kill.)

When Dad saw the Kenyan bird, he concluded that "there was no way it was the same species. I decided to list it separately." It was the first split Dad ever determined on his own. Today, every major listing authority, including the ABA, recognizes the kites as two species.

All of this happened within twenty-four hours of arriving in Africa. There were still three weeks to go. The small group continued to Nairobi, then Nyeri, where they could see snow-covered Mt. Kenya in the distance. In Meru National Park—site of Joy Adamson's *Born Free*, which has made it one of the world's most popular destinations for all kinds of wildlife watching—Dad added over one hundred new species. Over and over, he noted differences between the Clements list and the check-mark guide provided by the East Africa Natural History Society. It wasn't that he found one more authoritative than the other; rather, it was the opposite. He loved the differences of opinion, the labyrinth of counting, the latitude it gave him to apply the expertise he was gaining as he studied; the more complex it got, the more he enjoyed it—especially since the fuel for his explorations were real-life adventures, measurable by his ever-increasing numbers.

TODAY, ORGANIZED BIRDING TRIPS ARE FAIRLY POPULAR—even less serious birders enjoy the easy access to spectacular scenery and unusual avifauna. But in the early 1980s, nearly every trip was its own breeding ground for Big Listers. Over the next few years, Dad would travel with nearly all of his equally obsessed rivals in the chase to see seven thousand or more species. On that initial voyage to Kenya, Dad met a British couple, Michael Lambarth and Sandra Fisher. They'd gotten into the chase just a few months earlier, on a birding vacation to Suriname. More than Dad, Lambarth and Fisher were pure listers, with numbers outweighing birds as their primary interest. Dad noticed this immediately, and found it rather odd, but also appealing: "Sandra was good at *finding* birds," he says, "but neither always knew what it was they were finding." The couple's listing also was romantic: If both didn't see a bird, it didn't go on their list.*

Dad's count was more solitary. He liked it that way. He preferred to trail behind the group, usually smoking a cigarette, finding as many birds as he could on his own. The last few days in Kenya were spent in the Sokoke Forest, which remains East Africa's largest surviving expanse of dry, coastal woodland. As a habitat, it is distinct from the rest of Kenya, and contains birds that can't be seen anywhere else. Dad missed the tough-to-spot Sokoke Scops Owl and the Sokoke Pipit. They're both birds a Big Lister would like to have on his list, but they're traditionally higher-cost birds, requiring revisits. But Dad wasn't thinking about that: For the moment, the 517 new species he added on the trip were more than enough. On the plane back to New York, he kept going over his trip list and his homemade notebook, counting and recounting. He couldn't wait to get back home and add the check marks to his Clements guide. "I was mind-boggled," he recalls.

---

*I wish I could add more about Lambarth and Fisher. But Fisher has reportedly died, and Lambarth completely dropped out of birding; I attempted to contact him several times, but his silence—the only response I got—leads me to believe that the birding chapter of his life is permanently and tragically closed. This, in a way, is the most telling thing about them and the general obsession for birding: An all-consuming pursuit, by nature, leaves almost nothing in its wake, and when it ends, it can become a nearly annihilating force.

"The excitement, the numbers: I felt like I was doing something completely new."

It was the world, being offered at last.

THE CASCADE OF EVENTS THAT FOLLOWED DAD'S RETURN from Kenya were certainly not planned, but there was a certain synchronicity to them, as if fate were giving Dad a signal that he could now safely dedicate his life to birds. I was about to turn twenty-one and was planning to graduate from college that January. Jim was nineteen and also in school. Though Dad was paying for both of us to attend private universities, and still sending monthly alimony to Mom, an end of those financial burdens was in sight. Mom was involved in a serious—and for a change, healthy—relationship. Dad asked me if I thought Mom would remarry, which would free him from having to send her a monthly check, and I said yes (and she did, a few years later). I know the thought hurt him, but he suddenly found a reason to be happy about it: The woman he probably still loved would become more irrevocably unavailable, but he'd gain funds for a pursuit that occupied his heart in a way a romantic relationship never could. Dad was also dating. His bond with Judith was serious in that they seemed to spend a lot of time together, but Dad told me on several occasions that he wasn't in love with Judith, and never would be. I think part of his pleasure on those early birding expeditions was that he could get away from those conflicted feelings, which were mixed with a sense that he was finally being offered a chance to do the things he wanted, as well as with some guilt over not wanting the relationship with Judith to advance and the lingering, still incomprehensible feelings he felt over having done the right thing with Mom and failing anyway. There was fear, too—of being lured by a relationship and the promise of a "normal" life, just as he was getting to the point where he could pursue birds exclusively and not disappoint anyone. It wasn't that the list could replace all these things, but it could absorb the feelings around them, obscuring them.

Around Thanksgiving, another of the things from Dad's past that had held him back fell away. After his father died in the mid-1970s, Dad had moved Rose from the house on 141st Place to a garden apartment a few blocks away. She lived across the street from her sister, Leonie, and the two elderly women took care of each other. (They never stopped hoping that Dad would remarry, and they never understood why Mom had left him.) Dad would never say this, but I think his mother was beginning to feel like a burden. His resentment toward her began to bubble out. She was losing her hearing, but Dad often seemed sharp with her on the phone; at one point, I mentioned it to him, and he told me to mind my own business and then stormed out to the backyard with his binoculars. I don't think Dad ever realized that he was allowed to be angry at the way he had allowed his sense of obligation and his parents' desires for him to eclipse his own, that such anger wouldn't negate compassion or love—or even forgiveness.

Now, those feelings were brought up, urgently: Rose—she'd just turned eighty-five—had fallen in her apartment. She was in the hospital with a fractured hip. I was in California, spending the holiday with a friend; I flew home, and by the time I arrived at Booth Memorial Hospital—right on Main Street, built where Dad had done much of his woodland birding as a teenager—she was on life-support and barely conscious. While in the hospital, she'd had a stroke.

Dad and I visited together the next day. I saw his stoicism as heroic. (And tragic, when I learned the true circumstances of Rose's death, which Dad revealed to me as I researched this book. Upon entering the hospital, she'd received a vascular catheterization—an unnecessary procedure, Dad believes. The tube was initially inserted in an artery, not a vein. The stroke was instantaneous. When Dad got the news, he arrived at the hospital, baffled, and accepted the doctor's explanation that the stroke had been a coincidence, one of those systemic failures that happens when an elderly person is stricken. It was only after a nurse inadvertently mentioned the catheter procedure that Dad examined his mother's neck, finding the telltale puncture wounds. "I really believe they killed her," he says. In the weeks following her death, Dad consulted a malpractice attorney, but couldn't find one willing to take the case: "They told me a little old lady's life wasn't worth making a case over," he says. "And it wasn't going to bring her back.")

Against this backdrop of grief and guilt, of relief and confusion, Dad arranged his mother's funeral. I never saw him cry, though I know his sadness was real. He might have been angry over the way his parents had frustrated his dreams, but you don't give up so much for people whom you don't truly love. As his eulogy ended, Leonie stood next to me and whispered, telling me something I'd never overtly known, but which has become, since then, central to my understanding of my father: "He can seem hard sometimes," Leonie said to me, "but your father has a heart of gold." She took my hand. "Remember that."

DECEMBER, THEN, BROUGHT A PAIR OF INTERTWINED PROJECTS: Dad was laying Rose to rest, and preparing to begin his real life. He simultaneously got his mother's affairs in order and worked on reconciling his life lists, comparing the birds he'd recorded in his ABA/AOU tally to the Clements guide he was now using. He was orienting himself toward quantities of birds, and that required a new level of accuracy: "I didn't mind losing a few birds," he says, "because it was more important that I get things right." Big Listing is such a technically maddening task that the honor system asserts itself at the earliest stages of the pursuit. You don't have to be told the rules when you understand, inherently, that following them is the only way to navigate the game. He subtracted ten birds Clements lumped, added five splits, and corrected a pair of misidentifications, for a net loss of six birds.

By New Year's Day—my twenty-first birthday—he was ready to venture out. "I felt a desperate need to do something," he says. He called Victor Emanuel and asked the bird tour leader what the next available opening was. There was a trip heading to Panama in a few weeks and he signed up. He also booked a second tour, in Mexico, and an Earthwatch trip to Manchuria.

I graduated from college on January 18, 1983. I had a job lined up in New York, working as an editor on a video-game magazine. I had an apartment and a girlfriend. Jim and I would room together in Manhattan, and we both seemed to be on track. I didn't tell Dad how confused I was, how meaningless my job future seemed, how I wished he'd have some advice for me. He was going to Panama, and his life list was at 1,760 birds. That was where his focus was; it had always seemed to be there, from my point of view, but for the first time, it was overt.

"I'd finally become something," Dad says, inadvertently denying the importance of having been a son, a doctor, a husband, a father. "I was a lister."

LISTING IS NOT ORNITHOLOGY. Dad knows; the bird guides know; the British scientists who deride Twitchers know. But Dad is more than a lister, at least in terms of his skills and knowledge. I asked him if the urge to approach birds more seriously ever occurred to him during those early days, when he had the opportunity, at least, to do whatever he wanted. He replied by telling me about his visits to Manchuria. I remember his preparations for that. As with Kenya, he spent hours drawing his own field guide. This wasn't an ornithologist-led counting tour; rather, the Manchuria trip was a scientific expedition, but unlike previous Earthwatch ventures Dad had participated in, this one was about birds—a single species. It was a chance for Dad to do real science.

Panama had been successful; 186 new birds brought his life list to 1,946. The Chinese refuge where Dad would be working might yield only forty species, but Dad worked hard on the trip's fringes to add more. He wanted to hit two thousand on the trip. He got one new bird from his hotel in Beijing, and on the train ride to the preserve added twelve more.

Dad was working with George Archibald, who represents an entirely different kind of obsessed birder: focused on a single avian family. As a boy in Nova Scotia, Archibald crawled after ducks and geese on his farm. In college, he became fascinated by cranes and ended up writing his doctoral thesis on how crane vocalization affected speciation. For the next decade, he traveled the world, setting up crane refuges in Japan, Korea, and Thailand. Dad met him when he was beginning similar projects at the Zhalong Nature Reserve in northwest China, and in Jiangxi Province, for the Siberian Crane, one of the world's rarest birds. (You might have heard about Archibald; he's known for breeding a human-imprinted Whooping Crane. The female crane, named Tex, had no mate, and wouldn't lay eggs. Archibald decided that the crane needed stimulation, so he moved in with the bird and regularly performed his version of the male crane's mating dance. It took five years, but the bird finally began laying eggs again, which were then artificially inseminated. Archibald had proved that cranes—endangered in many parts of the world—could be bred in captivity.)

Archibald was just the kind of dedicated oddball Dad liked, and the crane expert was impressed enough with Dad that, a year later, he'd ask Dad to lead a second Earthwatch trip to the refuge. But Dad also found that the Chinese sanctuary was a good spot for new birds. The tiny marsh where the cranes were housed was surrounded by more developed areas, making it a "migration trap"— the only place within miles for passing species to stop. Dad's two thousandth bird, on June 7, was the Oriental Stork; the accomplishment was privately noted, but not celebrated or announced to his companions in China or to his friends and family back home.

You need time and money to be a Big Lister—and Dad had both—but you also need a plan. Back home, Dad looked at the next two years. He made an initial decision to do a pair of birding trips annually, coinciding with spring and fall migrations, and adding minor excursions when he could. But he soon found he was less interested in the kinds of trips he'd been doing, where he'd add birding to a journey intended for a different purpose. Arriving five days early to a medical meeting in Puerto Rico, Dad added sixteen species, including the now nearly extinct Puerto Rican° Parrot, but was restless at the conference itself, and even more so at the end of

---

°The Puerto Rican Parrot is one of the more tragic stories in the recent history of attempts at species preservation. Deforestation led to the initial decline of the bird, which was down to a population of just thirteen in the mid-1970s. A conservation program tripled those numbers, but half were lost in September 1989, when Hurricane Hugo hit the island. Today, about forty parrots can be found in the wild, and another hundred or so are in captivity. The first five breeding pairs from that population were released in May 2004; the goal is to allow two hundred more to go free over the next few years. Whether the program will be successful or not won't be known for at least two decades.

the trip, when Judith joined him at a beach resort for a mini-vacation. "I wanted to be birding," he says.

He was also beginning to become aware of the competition. On an Ecuadorian trip in early 1984, Dad met Harvey Gilston. Dad added 292 species, but was astonished at Gilston, who—content to have the guides do all the identifying, as long as he got the check mark—vowed to become the first to reach seven thousand. Gilston saw listing purely as a race, and one that he *had* to win. (Gilston went on several trips run by Dad's old college roommate, Joel Abramson, who also had a list numbering into the thousands. "Harvey was convinced that I had several hundred secret birds," Abramson says, "that I'd seen, but not reported, kept in reserve so I could pass him if he suddenly gained a big lead.")

"I'd never seen anyone like him," Dad says. But he liked Gilston, and didn't feel—as some other birders have expressed—that Gilston was sullying the activity by making it about counting. "That was the way he wanted to play," Dad says.

Dad's scorekeeping wasn't about surpassing anyone else. He was measuring his chase for the long term. Still, the twice-a-year schedule soon dissolved; he increased his pace to three trips, then four, then five. His pursuit was never as oddly pure as Gilston's; Dad knew what part of his pursuit science served, paying closest attention to splits, lumps, and identification skills that could boost his numbers. Dad's first ambition—to be an ornithologist—was nearly gone, and finally, that was fine by him. His final flirtation with the pure science came on his second trip to China, which he led for Earthwatch. He enjoyed the work, and was especially happy for the thirty-three new birds China yielded (and the fourteen more he got on the grounds of the Tokyo airport hotel). But upon his return home, he was disappointed to learn that some of the Earthwatch guests had complained. "They said I was too obsessed with birds," he says, pausing. "I thought that was the point of the trip." The criticism hurt, but it told him something, as well: These science-oriented journeys weren't helping. "They were pulling me away from my goal," he says. "I wanted more birds."

DAD'S FIRST YEARS OF LISTING were a time during which I had a desperate and conscious need for him. Growing up in Douglaston, I idealized Dad—wanting him, almost literally, to turn into a superhero—but I didn't outwardly know how badly I wished for his presence. I was unable to talk to him about how unhappy I was in my mother's house. But in 1984, it was different. I hated my job in New York; I hated my entire life. I was taking writing classes downtown, but for the most part, I felt stuck and hopeless. I wanted Dad to notice; I wanted to feel like he cared. Every time I'd ask him for advice—on my career, on money, on getting along as a young man—he'd quickly change the subject. He was always in his own world, and it was making me more and more angry. Why did he always seem to reject any attempts I made to be close to him? I had no idea if he was interested in me at all, and if I imagined he was, he was so incapable of demonstrating it that I'd get even angrier. I felt like I didn't have a father.

I'd become friends with one of my writing teachers. Robert Phelps was one of the best-known translators of Colette, and an inspiring teacher who encouraged his students to generate prose that was detailed, emotional, and intense. I took his short-story writing workshop at The New School for two years. Phelps shared a brownstone with his wife in Greenwich Village, and after class, I'd drop by and listen to him tell stories of Paris in the 1920s. The tales would usually to include some famous names: Hemingway, Stein, Camus (it was my own French poetry period, thirty years after

Dad's). The idea of Europe began to intrigue me, especially be-cause I had so many memories of living there. I had some money saved, so in January 1984, I quit my job and bought a one-way ticket to Paris. I'm not sure what I wanted out of that foreign so-journ. I was just as at a loss for what my future might be as Dad had been at my age.

I SPENT EIGHT MONTHS WANDERING. I went to the Camargue, where the flood had nearly swept us away, and to Ibiza, where Dad and Mom had begun the final battle of their marriage. The island, by then, had turned into a sweaty morass of discos and alcohol-soaked resorts. I felt lonely, but I kept moving, which helped. So did increasing quantities of drugs. But things felt under control un-til I got to Heidelberg, where I looked up one of Mom's old friends, mostly because I was running low on money and needed a free place to stay. During my visit, I found out—for the first time—the logistics of Mom's misery. I found out she'd had an af-fair. I grew pale as my host told me how Dad's time spent birding provided a convenient cover for Mom's getaways.* I was unable to ask for specifics, though; just the information that Mom had strayed sent me reeling.

"You didn't know?" he asked. (How could I? I'd been six years old.)

I left the next morning, stunned. I headed toward a small village on the border of Germany and Holland. A Dutch friend lived there in a squatted house. I can't recall much of the next two months, just flashes, moments when the spiral suddenly paused. I

---

*Dad says that this isn't quite right, since most of his birding was done on trips out-side of Heidelberg.

spent most of my time in a intoxicant-fueled stupor, rarely eating or leaving the squat. I lost nearly thirty pounds during those few months. There were moments, when I was alone, that I'd try to call Dad, collect. But he was always off birding.

Just as Dad had spent part of his early twenties in an angry state of dissipation, so did I. So I turned to the same solution he'd hoped would work for him: I decided that if I found the right woman, everything would be fine. When I first arrived in Europe, I'd met an American girl in Paris. It was a scene straight out of *Á bout de souffle*; she was working on the *International Herald Tribune*, and I was (as she put it) "a rock-and-roller." (As a teenager, I'd taken up saxophone—using Dad's old alto horn—and ended up making pocket money by playing on the streets wherever I went in Europe, none of which should indicate that I was a very good musician, especially compared to my brother, who is a virtuoso guitarist.)

I called and told her I'd be on the next train to Paris. An hour after I arrived, we locked the door. We stayed in bed for three days.

I hid my feelings until the very end. But I couldn't hold back; a lifetime of longing poured out on one idealized girl. Needless to say, it was not the best way to end a fling in the City of Light. "You have to go," she said, and showed me the door; I was in shock, walking through the streets of Paris with my backpack and saxophone, nearly in tears, and feeling not even remotely romantic about the whole turn of events. It wasn't just this rejection, it was all the rejections; every part of my isolated self was feeling, for the first time, outward heartbreak.

I had my ticket back to Holland, but something told me not to return there. I truly don't think I'd have survived. Instead, I headed to Switzerland, where a couple I'd met on my first visit to Paris had invited me, months earlier. When I arrived in Zurich, they saw the kind of shape I was in, and let me stay. For eight weeks, I slept on the floor. I spent most of my days wrapped underneath a set of headphones or riding the old trolley lines to the city's lakefront beaches.

In August, I tried calling Dad again. This time, he was home, and he had news. Before I'd left, I applied to the graduate film program at New York University. (I had no real desire to do this, except that it seemed a way to make a better living as a writer than struggling as a magazine editor or newspaper reporter, and a few of my close friends were entering the movie industry.) Dad told me that my application had been accepted, and I needed to decide right away; the fall semester was beginning in a few weeks.

I honestly didn't want to go, but I knew I couldn't stay in Europe. The weight of the past—mine and my parents', which now all seemed to be mixing together, leaving me in a precarious and grief-ridden state—was too crushing, too dark.

"What should I do?" I asked. I wanted Dad to offer me something—maybe just comfort—and I didn't understand why he couldn't. I wasn't able to understand that, having arrived at his own destiny only recently, and only through such heartbreaking detours, he was barely standing on his own two feet, barely in a position to offer life-affirming advice.

I CAME HOME. Mom met me at the airport. When I got off the plane, she saw how thin and unhealthy I looked, and started to cry. Going back to school didn't make things better; I hated it. The teachers seemed like burned-out refugees who'd been destroyed by what minor success they'd achieved in Hollywood, and who were determined to make things as hard on their students—especially those whom they perceived as weak—as the "business" had made it on them. Whatever else had happened to me in Europe, I'd developed a more gentle creative sensibility, and the phony trial-by-fire NYU offered seemed sadistic and ugly. I quickly joined up with a group of fellow students who felt the same way; by December, we were all ready to quit, though Dad made it clear that this was my only shot at graduate school as far as his contributions were concerned. (I understood, and I knew that he wanted to earmark the money for birds. Paying for my studies at all was a nice thing for him to do, though I kept wondering what he might have done if his parents had been similarly rigid over his multiple excursions into postgraduate study.)

What does Dad remember about December 1985? That he was paying attention to reports of a Gyrfalcon at Jones Beach. The species isn't all that uncommon, but Dad hadn't seen one. It had become a nemesis bird—a species a birder should have seen, but through sheer bad luck, has managed to miss. Twice, he rushed to his car and drove to his childhood birding haunt, to no avail. Finally, on the third try, he saw it. It wasn't hard: Two dozen other birders were also there, surrounding the two-hundred-foot tower—the beach's major landmark, modeled after the Campanile in Venice, Italy—where the bird was perched.

Dad didn't know what I was doing, or feeling, and I'd decided he didn't care. To me, his "heart of gold" wasn't just hidden, it was receding into a world of numbers and a quest to conquer the ethereal which, however profound it might have been for him, struck me as, if not a waste of time, then at least a way of using time that didn't really allow for another soul, whether it was a son or a girlfriend (he and Judith split up for good in 1985, as well), for even a moment.

He was jetting around the world and returning with check marks on a list that was for him, and him only. I resented it. I resented having to give up any idea of continuing my studies; I resented feeling so alone. Why wasn't Dad looking out for me? Why had he never, really, been there?

CHAPTER TWELVE

THE BEST
BIG LISTER

❝ *In 1987 I went on a Field Guides tour to New Guinea, and took a pre-tour extension to the Sepik River area. Though I didn't add big numbers of birds, I saw some I'd never have gotten the chance to get otherwise. Our whole group had seen the Victoria Crowned Pigeon from a boat as we cruised the river. I was frustrated because I missed the Cassowary—I was at the back of the boat, smoking. On our last day, we departed a tributary of the Sepik and joined the Sepik itself. There was a fallen tree leaning into the water on the boat's starboard side. As we passed, I saw what initially looked like a short, cutoff branch. I put my binoculars on it and realized it was a Forest Bittern! This is an exceptionally rare bird, seen very infrequently—it was rumored that even the author of* Birds of New Guinea *hadn't seen it. I yelled out: 'FOREST BITTERN!' and we slowed the boat, turned around, and slowly cruised back. The Bittern—amazingly—stayed put. Everyone got fabulous looks and many got excellent photographs."*

—Forest Bittern (*Zonerodius heliosylus*),
July 23, 1987, New Guinea, #4218.

THERE ARE BIG LISTERS, and then there's Phoebe Snetsinger. Dad first met Snetsinger on a trip to South Africa in 1985. She was already legendary. She'd reached four thousand species a year earlier (Dad was a thousand birds behind) and was on track to become the first woman to see five thousand species. What was even more important than that, though, was that Snetsinger wasn't a professional ornithologist—she was the first true Big Lister to reach that mark, beating her closest rivals, Harvey Gilston and Joel Abramson, by at least a year.

Like most birders, Dad was astonished by Phoebe's drive—though it made sense, once he heard her story. If Dad's obsession grew, almost darkly, out of a lifetime of repressed desire, then Snetsinger's mania, conducted at higher speeds and with more intensity, burst from a single event. Birding was just a hobby—albeit a passionate one—for the St. Louis housewife until 1981, when she was diagnosed with the deadliest form of skin cancer.

"Consultations with three independent oncologists gave me the same shattering prognosis," Snetsinger wrote in her autobiography.

"Three months of good health, then inevitable, rapid decline . . . and death within a year."

Snetsinger wasn't yet fifty years old, and she was facing a precipitous end to her life—the end to an idyllic, if outwardly typical, existence as a suburban housewife with a husband and three children. (The truth about Snetsinger was far more powerful. She'd always been a restless intellect, and was the heiress to a fortune left to her by her father, legendary Chicago advertising executive Leo Burnett, who'd created the Marlboro Man.) Snetsinger underwent basic treatment, but decided to refuse more serious, experimental therapies. She had her own plan: to go to Alaska and look for birds. "If I still had a period of good health remaining," she recalled, "there was nothing I'd rather do."

She returned home feeling healthy, with a life list that had just topped two thousand.

She decided to keep going, and fast, because she didn't know how much time she had.

I'm proud that Dad is one of the world's best birders—by the numbers, and by his lifetime of dedication. But alongside Snetsinger? Nobody measures up. Not Tom Gullick, today's top lister (about 8,200 birds); not even Peter Kaestner, who is likely to catch and pass Gullick sometime in the next two years (Kaestner is almost two decades younger than his rival). "Phoebe," Kaestner told me, "was as good as anyone could get."

Her race against time—which lasted over twenty years, through three recurrences and subsequent remissions of her cancer—moved her as close to perfection as any birder could ever hope to be. Snetsinger's preparation for a trip was as tightly woven as a military campaign. She prepared a special notebook for each excursion, complete with a handwritten paragraph on each target bird's key identifying features. She was a stickler for scientific accuracy, making sure that she knew both the English and Latin names for each species, as well as whatever it might be called in local languages. During the trip, Snetsinger recorded details of the birds she'd seen in the notebook, then transferred that information onto individual species cards when she returned home. She insisted on copying each sighting, word-for-word, sometimes twice, as a way of reinforcing and remembering what she'd seen. She did this for *every single one of the 8,500 birds* she encountered, not just for new ones or favorites. This paid off in 1990, when ornithologists Charles Sibley and Burt Monroe published *Distribution and Taxonomy of Birds of the World*. Snetsinger was able to use her cards to reference over five hundred potential splits declared in the new bird guide. (The Sibley and Monroe book adhered to a significantly different taxonomic order for birds, and was controversial; the authors came out with their own checklist—a rival to Clements's—in 1993. The debate over competing lists and naming conventions was cut short in 1994, when Burt Monroe died of cancer, and the project was abandoned. Still, the Sibley and Monroe guide remains a major reference for world birders.)

All those lists and names make Big Listing a daunting task for birders considering moving into the thousands, but Snetsinger reveled in it. In her autobiography, she spends nearly two full pages describing her intricate methods. Her language is almost as micro-detailed as the early collecting instructions offered by Elliot Coues; it certainly tops the American Birding Association's geographic codicils by multiple orders of magnitude:

> I would photocopy each page of the Monroe and Sibley 1993 checklist and attach it to a pre-prepared "grid" format, with vertical columns for each world region or area where I keep a list

and with horizontal lines following along the lines for lifer information that accompanies each species in the checklist. 11 × 17-inch sheets proved to be a perfect size. I attached each photocopied checklist page on the left, which allowed space on the right for my desired 16 regional/area columns, plus additional room at the extreme right on the horizontal lines for comments about any taxonomic changes. There was also space at the bottom to add new species. Thus, each species had a "box" in each regional column for a potential check mark (in my card-file color code, of course) if I'd seen the species in a given region of area.*

The only problem Snetsinger had with her system was a lack of appropriate graph paper—so she drew some: 336 sheets, over 5,000 perfectly straight horizontal lines. That small part of the project took months. Dad's notebooks are astoundingly detailed—he can go back to individual sightings and pick out splits and lumps—but his system is fundamentally to make a list. Snetsinger's tally had the quality of a religious tract; it wasn't just a count, it was doctrine.

FOR MOST OF HER BIRDING CAREER, Snetsinger's closest rival was Harvey Gilston, who managed to stay a few hundred birds ahead of her, and who beat her to seven thousand in 1988. (Snetsinger didn't

---

*Snetsinger's autobiography, *Birding on Borrowed Time,* was published by the American Birding Association in 2003; the book—along with interviews with her son, Tom Snetsinger—provided a large portion of the research for this chapter; those interested in a life as devoted to birding as my father's should pick up Snetsinger's memoir.

arrive at that goal until 1992.) There couldn't have been two more different ways of counting birds. Gilston simply marked the birds he'd been told he'd seen, using the same notebooks that he also employed to record the names of the pilots of planes he flew on, their registration numbers, and several other tallies of esoteric data that fascinated him.

Snetsinger knew birds—she was one of the most rigorously self-taught of the Big Listers—and wasn't afraid of having strong opinions on them. She had little patience for competitors who cut corners or counted softer sightings—when she saw something, she made sure she really saw it. She stopped submitting her list to the American Birding Association when that group began allowing heard species to be counted alongside seen ones. And she had a sense of posterity, advocating that a different way of measuring—by percentage of known species rather than plain numbers—might be better, for historical comparison. She proposed the method in an article she wrote for *Birding* magazine, titling it "Birding Planet Earth: Twenty-five Years Later," as a tribute to the story Stuart Keith wrote for the same publication in 1974. Keith had posited that seeing half the world's known species would be a reasonable goal; Snetsinger upped that limit to 85 percent. "I have now reached such a plateau that I can see that reaching ninety percent is impossible," Snetsinger said. Her own tally at the time was 84 percent.

Whether it was the desire to see more birds than she herself had deemed "impossible," or just the sense, following her cancer scares, that she had nothing to lose, Snetsinger continued to refine her goals. She wanted to become the first person to see every bird of a monotypic genus. (Simplified, this is a taxonomic classification containing a single genus and single species. In North America, a good example is the Northern Hawk Owl, found throughout most of Canada. It has no close relatives either currently extant or in the fossil record.) There are an estimated two thousand such bird species throughout the world.

Money wasn't an issue for Snetsinger, given her inherited fortune. But danger was. Constantly visiting remote locations, often far from medical help, often using substandard transportation, is a real hazard for Big Listers and their guides. Ted Parker, a bird tour leader who took Dad to Peru in 1988—he was considered the world's most gifted field ornithologist—died in a plane crash above the Andes in 1993. Another tour leader, David Hunt, spotted a Forest Eagle Owl in India's Corbett National Park on a 1985 trip. He rushed into the brush and was killed by a tiger (the animal was captured, but spared from destruction by the pleas of the birders Hunt had been guiding). When Dad and I were in Brazil, we heard of another birding tour in Africa that had been thrown into crisis by a client's disappearance on a jungle hike; it was assumed he'd encountered a wild cat. Snetsinger had the good luck to beat cancer three times, but she couldn't escape misfortune while birding: she was shipwrecked in Indonesia; survived a 7.0 magnitude earthquake in Costa Rica; and continued to bird even after she was raped in New Guinea. The setbacks never caused her to reconsider her pursuit, or her pace. (After the Costa Rica earthquake, during which the building where the group was staying partially collapsed, Snetsinger turned to the group—now standing on open ground—and said: "Well, we're outside. We might as well look for owls!")

BY THE LAST HALF OF THE 1980s, the race was in full swing. Snetsinger, the married Lambarth and Fisher, and Gilston were in the lead, with another group—Pete Winter, a decorated World

War II combat pilot; John Danzenbaker, who'd spent his entire career in the military; Dad; and several others—in pursuit. The two took entirely more regimented approaches than Dad did. All great birders are highly organized, but Dad's listing feels a bit more eclectic, rebellious; when he chose, once, to spend a weekend partying in Bangkok instead of following his birding group back into the field, the other Big Listers on his trip were aghast that he'd skip an opportunity for new species. "But it wasn't that big a thing—I knew I'd see the species later, and besides, I didn't mind shocking the other birders just a little bit," Dad says. His bond with Whitney was especially strong. He liked staying up late, trading stories, and drinking beers with the ornithologist. "Your old man," Bret told me, "is a real character." Dad was constantly preparing for his trips, waiting for packages to come from Buteo Books—the prime mail-order source for global field guides—and searching for foreign bird handbooks on stopovers in London. The rival listers were running into each other constantly; they were all aware of each other's count, but most of them avoided overtly competing, understanding that the game was one that you went in for the long haul and covered at your own pace. The atmosphere of "competitive non-competition" was enhanced by the fact that if you were on a trip with another Big Lister, you were almost certain to see all the same birds he or she would. Cliff Pollard, another Big Lister, described the chase to me as "the ultimate endurance event."

MOST OF THE BIG LISTERS FAVORED TRIPS led by Field Guides, the company Bret Whitney founded with several other ornithologists when he broke away from his mentor, Victor Emanuel. "They were getting a reputation for delivering sheer numbers," Dad says, adding with evident glee: "Incessant, nonstop birding." Standard bird-tour etiquette: up at three AM without hope for breakfast. Back at 10 AM, eat, sleep. Back out at 3 PM until after dusk, then dinner and several hours of list maintenance. Repeat every day for two, three, or four weeks, and don't dare think of doing something more typically touristic during your sojourn. (Even with my growing fascination for the culture of birding, I found myself bored during much of my trip to Brazil with Dad. I wanted to stop and look at the trees and the flowers; I wanted to visit native villages. These were blasphemous thoughts that no true lister would ever even conjure.)

Bird racers don't have time to pause. Dad remembers being amazed at Danzenbaker's persistence: "We'd be on an island that absolutely had only one bird, and we'd have seen it, and he'd keep looking." Dad was no less dedicated. He was on his way to South Africa and decided to take a long detour to Rio de Janeiro to get his first look at Brazilian avifauna. When he arrived, he was told he lacked the proper paperwork to enter the country. He did some quick calculations and boarded the next flight to Paraguay, where he could get his Brazilian visa and be back in a few hours. But he arrived late and was stuck in Ascunsion for the weekend. No problem. With his barely illustrated copy of Rodolphe Meyer de Schauensee's *A Guide to the Birds of South America*, he added twenty-three birds. On Monday, he returned to Brazil and added another twenty.

The listers were—each to their own individual degree—in competition with each other, but they also knew they formed an exclusive cadre. When Field Guides announced the first organized bird trip to Madagascar, nearly all the top birders came along. They all added the same birds to their lists, so there was no net change in the standings.*

DAD REMEMBERS THAT ON ONE OF HIS TRIPS with Snetsinger, she told him that birding was the thing that had kept her alive. "She thought there was some connection between her continued existence and continuing to count birds. It was almost a mystical thing," Dad recalls. I wondered if members of Snetsinger's family appreciated the birding—and the frequent absences it led to—as a life-giving force. I knew, from reading her autobiography, that her pursuit of birds had led to conflict. Her marriage nearly broke up (it was rescued through counseling), and there were some especially hurt feelings when one of the Snetsinger daughters announced a wedding date and Phoebe, saying it conflicted with a planned birding trip, skipped the ceremony. Oddly, I had a connection to Snetsinger's son Tom, who is the same age as me: He'd been the college roommate of my best friend in high school. I needed to talk to him for the book, but I also wanted to compare notes: Big Listers have plenty in common—do their children? An

---

*It was an excellent trip, but like all first visits, later excursions proved far more productive. An early 1990s Field Guides trip to the same island featured a stunning demonstration of that (and of Bret Whitney's superpowered hearing). Whitney had never been to the island, but he'd studied audiotapes, and as his group moved through the brush, he suddenly called for silence. A faint call echoed. "That's a new species," Whitney said. How did Whitney know that he was hearing the bird now called the Cryptic Warbler? Because the sound it made was unrecognizable. With every bird song in Madagascar committed to memory, hearing something that wasn't in his mental database was a guaranteed indicator of something that wasn't in anybody's database. Even for birders with whom quantity is job one, there's nothing like adding a bird to your checklist before it even has a chance to be included on a checklist.

introduction was made, and we spent a few hours on the phone. Tom told me that his family was always conflicted about Phoebe's obsession. They understood that with "the sword of Damocles" hanging over her, she had good reason to engage in all-out pursuit. "But that didn't keep feelings from being hurt many times," he added. One thing Snetsinger's son figured out long before I did was that you had to be a birder—on some level, at least—to reach a birder. Though they only went on one trip together, Tom Snetsinger's interest in avifauna has led him to a career as a wildlife biologist, working on a Spotted Owl restoration project in the Pacific Northwest. "It did bring us closer," he said.

There was one big difference between Phoebe and my father in terms what human connections were possible: Snetsinger hadn't chosen to isolate herself. "She just felt she had limited time," Tom Snetsinger says, "and wanted to pack in as much living as she could."

Snetsinger counseled her children to live life as aggressively as she did. When Tom Snetsinger wanted to join the Peace Corps, the only thing holding him back was a fear that his mother would die while he was away. "She told me the worst thing I could do for her would be to stay home because if she *didn't* die, I'd be faced with this regret of not having done what I wanted to, and I'd blame it on her." (Coincidentally, when I was considering the Peace Corps—at about the same time—Dad simply told me that it was a terrible idea.)

After I spoke to Tom Snetsinger, I wondered if the primary contrast between his mother and my father was motivation: Phoebe was driven by a ticking time bomb, and everybody knew it. A clean and simple raison d'être. Dad, on the other hand, didn't seem to be racing against anything. My first impression, in fact, would be that he was running *from* something (or perhaps from everything).

But that wasn't exactly accurate, either. Dad may have been escaping from family, or even from love, but he was in a chase, too: running toward an enduring dream, too long denied.

DAD WAS IN HOT PURSUIT, but I was still floundering. I'd quit graduate school and had no idea what to do with myself. I spent two years hanging around New York, doing very little. I got a job working in a basement storeroom at the New York Public Library. I could spend hours there, and nobody checked on me. There was an unused typewriter in my office and, as a way to fill time, I began writing. I made up story after story, badly imitating Paul Bowles, whose tales of misguided travelers who, at the moment they were farthest from home, were surprised to find that the world was cruel, resonated with me.

By the time Dad had reached four thousand, I'd stumbled onto a job as a reporter on a weekly newsmagazine. For the first time in my life, I felt like I was good at something. I quickly gained a reputation for dogged pursuit of recalcitrant sources. I'd become fixed on the hunt, not leaving the office, phoning my targets until they finally relented and spoke to me. I was good at finding out the home phone numbers of important corporate executives; I'd also been known to have them paged at golf courses and restaurants. When one shaken CEO called my boss to complain about my tactics—an interview with me, he said, "felt like somebody coming at you with a hammer"—I was proud. The job was more than an outlet for my anger; it was the anger itself, made poisonous and nearly irresistible. (It was a rage that I'd never outwardly expressed, so it made sense that I found a "legitimate" conduit for it, rather than figured out a way to genuinely take possession of it.) Though I'd been pretty much scared away from drugs in Europe, drinking was another story. One night, I ended up in a Brooklyn hospital, my chin sliced through, after a barroom brawl. When the wound got infected a week later, requiring minor surgery, Dad arranged to have it done at his hospital. I lied to him about what had happened.

I'd moved up in status—I had a career, at least—but I still felt like I was slowly losing. One weekend I went to visit my brother, who was living in Boston with friends, trying to make it as a rock guitarist. One of his buddies happened to work in a custom-bike factory, and when I arrived on Friday night, a group was gathered in his apartment, elated, after a few hours of racing along the dirt trails in the woods outside of town. Bikes had been my salvation as a teenager, but I hadn't ridden seriously in years.

One of the guys told me another ride was planned for the next morning, in a wooded park just on the outskirts of Somerville. There was a spare bike, if I wanted to come along.

By the next evening, my world had completely transformed. It was as if a box of treasure I'd hidden as a child and forgotten about had suddenly reappeared. I bought my own mountain bike a few weeks later. Each day I rode from where I lived, near the Brooklyn waterfront, to midtown Manhattan, where I worked. I rode loops around Central Park, entering at Columbus Circle, heading north toward Harlem and then back to midtown through the Upper West Side, at lunch. I'd pedal through Upper Manhattan and over the George Washington Bridge, methodically exploring every trail in the New Jersey Palisades. The more I rode, the more I wanted to ride. I began buying bike magazines, the covers of which always featured action shots of riders pedaling through the mountains and deserts of Southern California. When I called the editor of one of these magazines and offered some freelance story ideas, I was shocked by how quickly they were accepted.

New York was no longer agreeing with me. The hard-drinking,

aggressive lifestyle that seemed required for me to continue to be a good reporter was in direct conflict with my desire—my need—to ride my bike. I knew I had to get out. When an opening came up in my magazine's Los Angeles bureau—viewed as a remote outpost by the New York office—I begged for the job. My boss, warning me that the move would "wreck my career," reluctantly agreed. I was hoping it would. I didn't want to come at people with hammers anymore. I had a book that listed the hundred best mountain-bike trails in Southern California. My primary ambition was to ride every one. If my parents couldn't bother with me, I thought, I'd move far away. I'd do just fine bothering with myself. My dad had birds. I had my bike.

WHEN I LEFT NEW YORK IN 1990, I was certain I'd never have more than the most perfunctory relationship with Dad. But the distance surprised me. I missed him. Moreover, my best friend, Tom Huggins, who lived in Los Angeles and encouraged me to make the move, had given up a lucrative job as a television writer in order to study biology. Sometimes on our rides he'd bring butterfly nets; other times, he'd carry binoculars. Tom knew about Dad's pursuit, and saw him as a hero, somebody who'd dedicated his life to nature. (This surprised me, and it was ironic, since I saw Tom's dad as the hero. He was a well-known writer who'd written several novels and originated a score of legendary television shows.)*

---

*Roy Huggins created *The Fugitive, The Rockford Files, 77 Sunset Strip, Baretta,* and *Maverick*, and wrote for many, many other television series. He is generally acknowledged as the inventor of the modern detective drama on television, and was one of the most quick-witted and generous people I've ever met. Whenever I visited him, he always asked me about my writing, and was among the first to tell me that I needed to write about my dad. Roy passed away in 2003.

Slowly, I began to feel the same way. In 1993, Dad stopped in Los Angeles on his way to Australia. Southern California held a pair of nemesis birds for him: the California Gnatcatcher—a once-common coastal species whose habitat had been eroded by development; it was one Dad should have seen thirty years earlier, when we lived in San Diego—and the Mountain Quail, a bird I knew well because I occasionally saw it on my bike rides in the rugged peaks north of town (a nemesis bird, remember, isn't necessarily an uncommon one; it's just one that a birder hasn't seen through sheer bad luck). I was excited to see Dad—he'd never visited me in Los Angeles (and only has once, since)—and to try to show him a bird for a change.

The Gnatcatcher was first. We met Tom near the beach and methodically headed south, stopping at every tiny stand of coastal scrublands, the bird's habitat. Finally, on a bluff below the miniature mansions of Rancho Palos Verdes, we found it. We were walking along a dirt trail, passing a stand of yucca trees. Tom saw it first, flitting above the bushes, then vanishing. "Gnatcatcher," he yelled.

Patience. I remembered all the times as a kid that I had to be quiet and still while Dad was searching. After five minutes, the little bird appeared. Dad handed me his binoculars. He wanted me to get a good look. It was Number 5,991.

The next day, we planned to head into the mountains. Chantry Flats is one of my favorite spots in the Angeles National Forest. Nearly the same altitude as Denver, the area feels almost alpine. It's hard to believe that you're in a county with a population of 9.5 million people. I knew the Mountain Quail could be found there, but Dad double-checked with the staff of the nature center, who assured him that, since they always spread out a little birdseed in the morning, the Mountain Quail was almost a sure thing. (Did I resent that Dad didn't take my word for it? Maybe, then, but I've since learned that a lister can't help it: Nothing can be left to chance.)

This was one of the few birds I could definitely identify, even then. On lower-altitude bike rides, I frequently saw the California Quail, which looks almost the same, except it has a curled head plume. The Mountain Quail's plume is straight, so they're easy to tell apart. I'd probably seen one at least four or five times.

It was on that drive into the hills that Dad actually explained to me what a "nemesis bird" was. I thought the idea was astonishing, funny, and almost beautiful. We arrived just as dawn was breaking. The birdseed was waiting.

We waited, too. For hours.

Dad told me, as we sat there, how he was expecting to see his six thousandth bird in Australia (a week later, he'd get it: the Crested Bellbird, in New South Wales). I had no idea how rare a feat that was; he told me that seven thousand was an order of magnitude more difficult. "Do you think you'll make it?" I asked.

"That's years away," he said. "Who knows."

We didn't see the Mountain Quail. I thought this was strange, but Dad was more philosophical—almost superstitious—about it: "That's what makes it a nemesis," he said. (All birders know that no matter how much you work, or how long and boring a wait you endure, the only guarantee is that the law of averages will always dictate that you miss something.) One difference between a serious birder and a duffer (like me) is the ability to wait; we didn't leave until all hope was lost, hours after I'd become restless. I've seen similar behavior with the other Big Listers I've traveled with. Sometimes, the wait even pays off, with a sighting occurring just as you're packing up your telescope and getting ready to go home.

Dad left the next day. For the first time, I was sad to be apart from him, but happy to know what he was doing. I'd always understood how important birds were to him, but my own anger had created a sense of disdain toward the pursuit. I can't say that the visit completely stripped me of those feelings, but I was glad to see that, as he approached his sixties, he was finding something that truly fulfilled him—even if it was a solitary activity.

Dad's obsession was still his obsession. It still blocked out a lot of contact. But suddenly, I understood that I might be able to experience it with him: I'd never become truly interested in birds, but the chase? That was something that I could understand.

DAD SAID HE'D STOP AT FIVE THOUSAND. He said he'd stop at six thousand. "I said that," Dad says, "but I really didn't slow down at all." There were still so many more birds to see. And there was little else for him to do. He had his job, but he didn't have a girlfriend, and didn't want one. Judith had been over a decade earlier, and any relationship now would get in the way of his counting.

Pretty soon, he didn't want the job, either. In 1993, at age fifty-eight, he quit the emergency room. He had income from investments, and didn't see the point. "I didn't want to be a doctor anymore," he says. "I wanted to be a lister." And that was that.

After six thousand, the Big List gets tougher to expand. The numbers don't come as quickly, but the birds you see are real milestones; you're getting the exotics and rarities. The chase becomes more artful, the individual sightings more satisfying. In the Philippines, he saw what many believe to be the world's most spectacular avian species, the Philippine Monkey-eating Eagle. The bird is over three feet tall, with blue eyes, an oversized, sharp beak, and a war bonnet of head feathers. It speeds through the forest, making

seemingly impossible turns, as it searches for small primates.°
Dad's search for the eagle involved camping out on a mountaintop
on the island of Mindanao. Later that evening, while he was standing on his own, smoking, he saw another spectacular regional
species, the huge Philippine Eagle Owl.

Dad was still behind the other top listers, but he knew that
seven thousand was coming. Joel Abramson and he were both in
the six thousands, but Dad knew he'd reach the next level, probably by decade's end. Peter Kaestner was another birder who spent
the 1990s moving through the six thousands, but using an entirely
different method—living in one country for a year or two at a time,
first as a member of the Peace Corps, and then as a diplomat.
Kaestner didn't use guides, preferring to find birds at his own pace.
By 1990, when he reached six thousand, he was already in the
Guinness Book of *World Records* for being the first person to have
seen representatives of all 159 avian families. His no-guide approach put him in a strange and admirable place, somewhere between "ordinary" Big Lister and ornithologist (in fact, Kaestner has
discovered one new species, the Ecuadorian Cundinamarca
Antpitta). Even Snetsinger seemed to want Kaestner's life, describing him as her "role model." (The mutual admiration, however,
didn't extend to inconvenience. Unyielding birding schedules kept
them from ever turning their frequent correspondence into a face-
to-face meeting.)

Though birders often can't stop when they say they will, they all

---

°The regime of Ferdinand Marcos, which ruled the Philippines from 1965 through
1986, tried to change the bird's name to the more nationalistic "Great Philippine
Eagle." Jim Clements says that "while the birding community lamented the name
change," it was more accurate, since the bird's preferred meal was flying foxes, not
monkeys.

stop eventually. Harvey Gilston last reported his count in 1991, at 7,069. One tour leader told me that the fun had gone for the most numbers-oriented Big Lister: "It was good for Harvey when he could see dozens of species, but to spend all that time and money to just add one? It didn't make sense if you weren't really that interested in birds." Michael Lambarth retired with the death of his partner, Sandra Fisher, staying true to his vow to never count a bird the two of them hadn't seen together. Dad kept going.

Snetsinger saw her eight thousandth species—the Rufous-necked Wood-rail—in Mexico in September 1995. She saw her two thousandth monotypic genus in Peru in 1999. (A monotype is a bird with only itself as a relative, to put it in overly simplified terms; these are among the rarest category of birds, so cutting a list this way is an exercise in difficulty. Snetsinger's achievement in seeing every bird in this classification isn't quite as sexy as her Guinness-book accepted Big List, but scientifically, it is an astounding feat.)

She died not from cancer but on a birding trip, killed in the pursuit that she believed had saved her life. There's irony and tragedy and triumph throughout her two decades of leading the Big Listers. But in the end, it was just bad luck.

On the morning of November 23, 1999, Phoebe was in Madagascar with a birding tour, searching the scrubby underbrush for the Red-shouldered Vanga, a species that hadn't even been known to exist two years earlier. They'd tried for the bird earlier and failed. That morning, ornithologist guide Terry Stevenson played a tape of the bird's song. It appeared almost instantly. "It gave all of us a good look," said Paul Thomas, who was traveling with the group.

It was bird 8,450 for Snetsinger, and there was a good chance for a second lifer—Appert's Greenbul—later that day. They boarded a minibus and headed toward the Zombitse-Vohibasia National Park. On the way, the driver lost control of the vehicle, and the bus rolled; Snetsinger was killed instantly by the impact.

None of the other passengers was seriously hurt.

Phoebe Snetsinger left an astounding record. From the day she departed for Alaska after her first cancer diagnosis to the day she saw the Vanga near the shores of the Indian Ocean, she'd averaged more than one new species every single day for almost twenty-five years. Five years later, Phoebe's list—even without current splits factored in—is still hundreds ahead of her closest competitor's. Her ashes were scattered over the Grand Teton mountains. A small park near St. Louis—her hometown—bears her name.

Dad was shaken by the news of her death. Like the other Big Listers, Dad knew that Phoebe was the best; but his sadness was tempered by a realization that—because most birders are older— nearly every one of his rivals was, as Snetsinger put it in her book, birding on borrowed time. "They don't all go away as dramatically as Phoebe did," he told me. "They just stop showing up for the trips."

Dad didn't know he'd soon be fighting for his own life.

CHAPTER THIRTEEN

UP AND OVER

  ❝ *We were on our way to the INPA Tower, a fifty-foot-high birding plat-form in the Brazilian rain forest, where we'd see hundreds of birds from above, in a mad feeding frenzy. But we decided to make a quick stop on the dirt road that led to the facility—and it was well worth it: Bret Whitney quickly spotted a nest, high in a tree, and trained his telescope on it. Inside the nest was a baby Harpy Eagle. Like the Philippine Monkey-eating Eagle, this is a spectacular—and almost scary—bird, with a huge tuft of feathers surrounding its head, and claws big enough to lift heavy prey from the forest floor. Dad had already seen a Harpy eleven years earlier, in Venezuela, but he was excited for me. It was the first bird I'd ever made a note of seeing.* ❞

—For Dad, Harpy Eagle (*Harpia harpyja*),
February 24, 1988, El Palomar, Venezuela, #4706.
For me, September 21, 1999, Manaus, Brazil, #1.

IT WAS A COLD DECEMBER AFTERNOON, and with the thermostat near sixty—as it always was in Dad's house—I was freezing. I was in for a visit from Los Angeles, and we'd planned a mid-morning shorebird excursion. As cold as it was outside, I was even less enthused about standing on a windy beach, looking for seabirds. So it was more as a delaying tactic than an expression of true desire that I suggested tagging along to see Dad's seven thousandth bird.

His dismissal was withering.

"You wouldn't have fun. You don't like birding enough. And you can't afford it."

Over the years, I'd learned to persist when Dad came up with reasons to avoid contact. When he'd pooh-pooh a suggestion that he come and search for the Mountain Quail again, I'd simply ignore him and ask again a few days later. My fascination with his birding had increased, especially in 1996 and 1997, when I took a yearlong job in New York and spent weekends visiting Dad, marveling at his lists.* I no longer resented it when Dad wasn't home, when he didn't answer my phone calls. Sometimes I worried, though. One February morning, I tried to call Dad several times, but he didn't answer. It wasn't until late at night that I finally reached him. The evening before, he explained, he'd been informed that an Ivory Gull—a nemesis bird—had been spotted in Portland, Maine. He got in his car, drove ten hours to the dock where the bird had been seen, stepped out of his car, saw it, and then drove home. Bird Number 6559.

Despite my best efforts, my own life was beginning to look something like Dad's. Like him, I was capable of deep obsession, of withdrawing from contact with others. I seemed to constantly fail in relationships, to run from them, and especially—when they were getting too close for comfort—to throw myself into my own world of bike-riding and travel as a means of escape. But I was having adventures, too. I'd begun to make my living writing about distant places. In 1994, I became an editor of a bike magazine, and quickly understood that the best part of my job was the ability to send myself on trips to exotic places.

I began checking off the rugged parts of the world in my own way, sometimes even with birds. On a mountain-bike trip through

---

*At this point, Dad wasn't just counting birds. He was also checking off cheeses and beers, usually sampling new ones on his birding trips. And he was in the midst of an all-out attempt to read every single book that had won or been short-listed for the Booker Literary Prize. Many were out of print, but he eventually found them all, tallying 169 novels. There were rules—he had to finish a book, even if he didn't like it—but the best thing about this minor obsession was that he *blamed me for it*, owing to the fact that, when he asked me for a recommendation for some good fiction, I offered that being nominated for that particular British literary award was generally a good sign. He continues to keep his Booker Prize list current, usually ordering the publications from the U.K. as soon as the nominees are announced.

the Venezuelan Andes, I'd spent an entire day climbing into the mist. It was getting colder and colder, and wetter and wetter. I wanted to turn around several times—I was genuinely afraid of getting hypothermic on the long descent—but my own obsessiveness forbid that; just as Dad would never abandon the search for a nemesis species, I'll never quit a bike ride. Not when there's a summit to bag. When I finally reached the top, the clouds parted, and I saw, floating just a few feet above me, a huge bird with a wingspan wider than I was tall.

"Condor," I said to myself.

Andean Condor.

How did I know that?

I wasn't a birder, not by a long shot, but birds had been part of my life for so long because they were part of Dad's life.

The idea of going with Dad to see number seven thousand hit me that Christmas. By then, I was back in California, but since most of my magazine clients were in New York, I visited frequently. During my visits, Dad and I nearly always went out on a bird walk. I kept asking if I could come, and he kept saying no.

Then I realized that he didn't have a choice.

I'd gotten him to at least tell me what planned trip he'd be likely to see the milestone bird on: It would be a three-week excursion to the Brazilian Amazon, with Bret Whitney.

"I'm going," I said. And I meant it. Regardless of what Dad said.

"But what if I don't see it on that trip?" Dad said.

I knew that he knew exactly when he'd see it; he couldn't leave that much to chance. But I humored him: "Then we'll have a nice time together."

We hadn't traveled together since I was ten years old.

Dad continued to discourage me, but when I sent my trip deposit in and bought my airline tickets, things changed. I began to get packages from East Hampton, a handwritten list of books I needed to study. Then, details: specific birds I should practice identifying. My own, brand-new copy of Stephen Hilty and William Brown's 836-page *Guide to the Birds of Colombia*, the accepted guide for that part of Brazil. Dad had marked the relevant pages with Post-it notes.

I suddenly felt like I was back in Spain, sitting by the beach with him, reading Peterson's.

But that moment, burned in my memory, was a fantasy. It hid so much pain.

This was the opposite. What was about to be revealed, from the most secret corners, was love.

IN LATE SEPTEMBER 1999, I FLEW TO MIAMI and met Dad at the airport for our flight to Manaus. A friend of mine who worked at Varig Airlines had arranged a surprise upgrade to first class. Dad had always flown coach, and he marveled at the silly freebies—a face mask, a small bottle of cologne, flimsy disposable slippers. We arrived at three in the morning and Dad introduced me to two other Big Listers—Jim Plyler and Bill Rapp—and our trip leaders, Bret Whitney and a young ornithologist named Mario Cohn-Haft (there were five other birders on the trip, most of them in the low to mid thousands). You don't wait when there's birding to be done, so we started immediately, piling out of a cramped minivan a few miles from the airport to look for a pair of Great Potoos—a nighthawk-like bird—before heading into the rain forest.

A few weeks before the trip, Dad told me he'd been having nightly dreams about me and Jim. We were always young, and he was always happy. "Those were my favorite times," he said. "When you guys were so small." It was the first time I'd really understood how difficult the path he'd taken had been, how early his own fantasies had been revealed as impossible, and how much we had meant to him, even if it took him thirty years to tell me. I felt overwhelmed; I'd never before seen how his own dreams were interrupted—and how that, as much as his own obsessive nature, had kept him from seeing Jim and me as we truly were. What had been taken from him had also been taken from us, and it seemed that he was far more empty-handed from it than I ever was. "This can be a new favorite time for us," I stammered.

For the next ten days, we traveled up and down the Amazon. I can't say it was fun all the time. Obsession is filled with anxiety; Dad's persistent nervousness made relaxing with him next to impossible, and the difficulties in talking to him—like his constant changing of the subject when anything personal came up—was amplified by the fact that we were cooped up in a tiny cabin for over a week. I also hated the nonphysical nature of the trip: I'd expected we'd be walking great distances and traveling under our own power, but instead, we spent most of our time traveling by van or river to birding spots. The boat, especially, was trying for me, since there was almost no form of physical exercise to be had, other than the occasional leap into the dark waters of the Rio Negro. Dad wasn't exactly part of the group, either; his cigarette habit kept him apart, and some of the guests were clearly perturbed by his smoking, though he tried to maintain a distance from the other birders when he lit up. Worst of all, a lifetime of tobacco use was catching up with him. He had trouble walking even moderate distances, and often rested on a special cane he'd purchased, which doubled as a portable stool. I overheard one guest saying she was shocked when my dad told her he was only sixty-four: "He looks ten years older." And Whitney—who by then had been leading Dad on trips for a decade—told me: "Your Pop doesn't look right."

Whitney, who'd lost his own mother to lung cancer, added: "He's got five years unless he makes some changes." (Whitney pointed out to me later that one of the more bittersweet parts of his job is getting to know these Big Listers who are fulfilling their lifetime ambitions, usually as they're entering their advanced years. "I see so many of them," he said, "at the end of their lives.")

IN BRAZIL, THERE WERE THREE BIG LISTERS. Jim Plyler was a retired oil executive who'd caught the bug recently and was taking ten trips a year, building his list as fast as humanly possible. He was hovering around 7,200, having built his list in record time through constant birding and by spending record sums on both organized and custom birding excursions. Bill Rapp, who'd birded with Dad before, was just two or three trips away from his own seven thousandth. To one unenraptured by listing, these trips—whether you're with a beloved, but difficult, relative or not—can be maddening mixtures of tedium and delight. You're one of a dozen or so similarly equipped humans—Tilley Hats (which, as a "true" outdoors writer/snob/sometime adventurer, I'd come to despise as yuppie travel gear), khaki trousers, field shirts with epaulettes, a camera vest, binoculars, and the constant smell of high-strength insect repellent—searching for hundreds of birds over a period of weeks. Bird by bird, the guides position themselves and begin by playing generic tapes of the species they're hoping to see (or have just heard in the brush).

Once a target bird starts responding, the guides begin taping the specific song, and then play it back. When the bird is seen, everyone gets a clear look, and the process is repeated, dozens of times a day, as the group moves from site to site.

A peculiar vocabulary emerges.

"We're going to go to the side of the river and try to work that antbird," Whitney says.

"There's a Black-capped Becard," Mario shouts. "If anybody needs it!"

For the Big Listers, "needing" is especially important. Dad and Plyler spent a lot of their time strategizing, peppering the guides with questions. "Is there a chance for such-and-such on the next island?" There was a sense of rivalry between the two, but both subscribed to a fairly macho school of birding, and they found common ground in their rugged, less-conventional approach to the activity.

AFTER A LONG DAY OF BIRDING, we'd assemble in the dining room of the three-deck houseboat that was transporting us up and down the Amazon and Rio Negro, gathering around preprinted sheets of paper that catalog dozens of species in a check-off grid. Whitney and Cohn-Haft presided over the daily count, recollecting what was seen chronologically. It's up to the birders to decide whether or not they actually saw the species in question. (The temptation to simply tick anything seen by anyone is great: "It happens all the time," says Whitney.)

Some of the birds named during those sessions were in the process of being split. Dad decided not to count a potential new species separated from the Plain Softtail, but did—after reading a paper Whitney had recently published and brought along with him—accept a split of the Slaty-Antshrike into *eight* distinct species (he'd seen the bird in six of the areas where the split was being contemplated).

Whitney referred to those birds as "species in escrow."

As I was watching the tallying and listening to the discussion of potential splits, I had a somewhat wicked thought: Whitney had already pointed out that the birds had no interest in what we called them, or how many times we declared them related or unrelated. But the listers do. Ornithology is a unique science in that it is so wedded to a hobby that provides it with so many dollars (my biologist friend Tom Huggins, who spotted the California Gnatcatcher with us, studies creosote galls—tumbleweed—in the Mojave Desert. "Nobody is paying me big bucks to show them a bunch of twigs," he jokes). Splitting is real science, but on trips like ours, where the evening listing session resembles a frenzied auction, the hobby dominates. At such moments, it's easy to forget that all the splits are about something important—the definition of species, the heart of evolution—rather than the numbers. "No question," Jim Clements told me when I asked him who the splits benefited most, listers or ornithologists: "They're good for both," he said, "but great for the listers."

TWO DAYS BEFORE SEVEN THOUSAND, we had the longest hike of the trip—over a mile, to see a newly discovered species. We trod through dense, tropical canopy until we finally reached an open area: It had once been a farm, and wild sugar cane grew, forming a low hedge. Dad and I were right behind Whitney. It was a good spot; moments later, we became the second, third, and fourth people on Earth to see the newly described Yapacana Antbird. Even to a non-birder like me, that was cool. Dad shook my hand. He was grinning.

It was a slow walk back. As we neared the boat, I looked at Dad. He was pale and shaking. He braced himself against me. I asked if he was having a heart attack. "No," he said, and wrapped his arm around my torso. I helped him onto the boat. His breathing returned to normal. "Thanks," he said, gripping my arm. I took him to our room, where he sat on the bunk, falling asleep almost instantly.

The next day, I could tell that the walk had spooked Dad. He held back, while the group would head into the brush. I'd go with them, and run and tell Dad if any of his target birds appeared. It was a fairly workable system, though with my limited talents, I couldn't have been that helpful. We went to bed that night with the count at 6,997. Tomorrow would be the day.

IT HAPPENED FAST. We nabbed two birds quickly—the Brown-headed Greenlet and Cherrie's Antwren—from the deck of the boat. Then we pulled on our rubber boots and rowed to the tiny island, not much bigger than a baseball diamond, but dense with brush. We stepped just a few feet into the woods. The ground was soft and wet. I was wearing my backpack; inside was stashed a bottle of champagne, brought all the way from the Miami Airport.

Suddenly, Whitney raised his arm.

He'd heard something.

The night before, Dad had given me the names of a half-dozen potential life birds we were likely to see that morning.

"It could be a Black-Tyrant," Whitney whispered.

Neotropical birds always have interesting names, usually based on their behavior. Screamers scream; antbirds follow ants. (In fact, one of the best ways to find birds on your own in the jungle is to look downward, following the huge swarms of army ants that often form a somewhat eerie, moving carpet on the ground. As the ants travel, other insects jump out of their way, and dozens of birds swarm in to eat them. Ornithologists call this kind of frenzy a "bird party.") Tyrants are a kind of flycatcher known for their aggressive behavior.

But I couldn't remember if the bird we were now hearing was one of the birds Dad hadn't seen. I turned to ask, but Dad shushed me before I had a chance to speak. That's how I knew this would be it.

There was a moment of slow-motion silence. The jungle is a noisy place, but it can also be absolutely still: You don't hear planes or cars, voices or music, and the sounds of the birds and other wildlife sometimes seem to merge into a single, omnipresent hum that soon vanishes beneath the range of your hearing.

Whitney pointed his microphone and touched the RECORD button. The bird sang again. Whitney rewound the tape, then hit PLAY. One beat. Two. The returned call seemed a little angry; the bird was responding to the territorial challenge we were making. I looked over at Dad. He had a calm and intent look on his face; so did Whitney. They both knew that this was it, even before the bird appeared.

Dad was the first in our group to actually see it—a small, gray figure, deep in the brush, suddenly emerging into full view. It is a small bird. Some of the Tyrants have crests, but this one didn't. For a lister, not every bird can be special because of its physical characteristics, and even the dullest species can occupy an immortal spot on your tally.

Bret played the tape again. The bird came closer. This time, everyone saw it, and Dad stepped toward me and pointed my binoculars in the right direction, as well. I caught a quick glance, then reached into my backpack. We drank champagne; we took pictures. Dad threw his arm around me.

Then it was time to move on. There were, of course, more birds to see.

✿ ✿ ✿

BIG LISTERS ARE FASCINATING and passionate people. But they aren't necessarily easy to live with, or, I think, easy on themselves. When we returned from Brazil, my elation was tempered by fear. Dad was sick. I could tell. He'd gotten nearly 70 new species, bringing his life total to 7,041, but he was exhausted, and his voice had become progressively more hoarse. When I told him that I thought he needed a checkup and begged him to stop smoking, he was completely dismissive. I shouldn't have been surprised that our new intimacy had limits; to approach Dad, I still had to come through birds.

It turned out he knew how sick he was. Earlier that year—he'd taken four bird tours, and this was between excursions to Antarctica in February, and Bhutan in April—he'd briefly lost his voice. Before Brazil, he'd visited his doctor, who found nodes on his vocal cords. "I knew I'd have to have a biopsy," Dad says. "I knew something was wrong."

But he didn't tell anyone. Instead, he went to see his seven thousandth bird. And he kept smoking. Was it a foolish choice? Maybe. But we were already planning our trip, and I'd like to think that he made that decision not just for himself, or for the list, but also for me.

My article was supposed to be a straightforward account of the trip. But Dad and I were talking. I found myself asking more and more questions about the list, about the birds he'd seen, about the places he'd been. He'd kept records. The details were easy, and they contained something he'd never have otherwise told me: his life story. I spoke to friends—childhood buddies, army pals—and asked them about my dad. (I even reached Will Astle, who was ninety-two years old. He told me a story about taking Dad on a birding trip to Florida. It was a great yarn, but it never happened. Astle probably had Dad confused with another young birder, but most of the details he got right.) It was astonishing to find that they were describing a person I barely knew existed: somebody open, passionate, full of ambition, and optimistic.

It was during this process that Bret Whitney called to tell me that Phoebe Snetsinger had died. I was still worried about Dad's health, and I was sad—in a slightly selfish way—that I'd never get to interview her. The other Big Listers were forthcoming to varying degrees. I couldn't find Stuart Stokes. Gilston and Lambarth didn't respond to requests for interviews. But Joel Abramson, Jim Plyler, and Pete Winter were happy to talk about their birding exploits. (When I told Abramson that Dad had passed seven thousand, he replied, "He beat me! That rascal!" Only he didn't use the word *rascal*.) I spoke to Peter Kaestner, who cut an entirely different profile than any of the other listers.

On January 4, 2000, Dad smoked his last cigarette. He checked in to Southampton Hospital. I flew out from Los Angeles to be with him. The doctors knew as soon as they saw the tissue samples. Dad told me in his hospital room. I don't think I was terribly stoic, but I didn't break down until after I got outside, to the hospital parking lot. He had throat cancer.

Dad forbade me to mention his illness in my magazine account of our trip to Brazil. He didn't want the world (and especially his fellow Big Listers) to know he'd been weakened. But the prognosis was good—his treatments were noninvasive, and the only major side effect was that they made his voice quite hoarse. But we kept talking, and when the story finally came out, Dad was immensely pleased—and so was I.

I felt like it was the first time he'd ever really been proud of me.

✿   ✿   ✿

DAD'S DIAGNOSIS DID NOT DETRACT from his goals: There was still birding to do.

He took another trip in April, this time to Morocco; in July, he went to the Canary Islands. His life list was now at 7,080. He'd booked a major birding trip for that coming November, to Argentina, again with Field Guides. That didn't surprise me. What did surprise me was Dad's somewhat hesitant request that I come along.

"I thought you might like it," he said.

He even offered to pay. I was astonished.

In September, I was on assignment at Disney World, doing a story for a travel magazine. I'd spent the whole day "working" (riding roller coasters) and was feeling almost completely exhausted when Jim called me—Dad had had a heart attack. I had to get to New York, fast. I arrived just as he was going into surgery; when I next saw him, after his triple bypass, he was in intensive care. He looked weak and fearful; tubes and breathing apparatus surrounded him.

I felt the same way: absolutely helpless, terrified.

"I think you should cancel Argentina," he said.

After the surgery, I spent almost a month in East Hampton, helping Dad recover. For a person who craves order as badly as Dad does, being incapacitated for that long is miserable. When he asked me to do things for him, he'd specify exactly what steps I needed to take: "Go get a wrench from the toolbox," then come back, he'd say. When I returned, I'd get the next piece of the task: "Now, go out to the swimming-pool filter."

He was still listing.

I'd never thought of Dad as particularly strong or brave, but over the next six months, I saw a tougher side of him emerge. But his ordeal wasn't yet over. A routine checkup revealed that Dad's throat cancer had recurred. My brother Jim and I were initially dismayed—there was a strong possibility that Dad's refusal to quit smoking at his first symptoms and his delayed biopsy had rendered the radiation treatments ineffective (though there was no absolutely certain way to know).

A patient who has failed radiation generally has one option: a laryngectomy, the brutal procedure that removes the vocal cords through the neck. Dad asked not to know the clinical odds. When I looked them up, I was staggered: With or without the surgery, it was less than five years. But that turned out to be moot; because of his recent heart attack, his doctor was afraid to perform the operation. "He thinks I'll die on the table," Dad said.

Jim was heroic. He insisted that Dad see a specialist in New York. Dad was initially against the idea, but he gave in. The specialist told him about an experimental procedure being done in Boston. The vocal cords would still be removed, but they'd be burned away, using a laser aimed down the throat. Dad was accepted to the program, and the first night we'd roomed together since our trip to Brazil was spent in a Holiday Inn a block from Massachusetts General Hospital. We went out to dinner, but everything about the night felt listless, dark. We reminisced about Brazil. "I think that was my last trip," Dad said.

Now I was the one who didn't want to listen.

Dad's medical problems continued for another year; he needed several follow-up laser treatments. The biggest miracle—next to the surgery itself—is that he can talk. Patients who lose their vocal cords are taught to attempt a technique that allows them to speak by vibrating the air in their throat. A speech therapist told us before the operation not to expect much. "Many people can't do it," she said, "even with training." Dad didn't even need the training;

ten minutes after surgery, he was croaking out lists of things I needed to do for him.

DAD STILL OCCUPIES THE WORLD TOP TEN. But other names have changed. Jim Plyler, with whom Dad developed an e-mail friendship, and who was approaching eight thousand birds at breakneck speed, was stricken with lung cancer the same year Dad had his heart attack. He died a few months later. Dad was genuinely grief-stricken; in Plyler, he had found a kindred spirit, somebody who seemed as hard-living and driven as he was. Plyler's polar opposite, Peter Kaestner—who birds slowly and is about twenty years younger than any other member of the 7,000 club—is now at 7,958. There's one birder ahead of Kaestner: Tom Gullick, with 8,114. Pete Winter is at about 7,800; John Danzenbaker is just behind; Jim Clements is at about 7,200, and he's still trying to clean up Peru.

Dad hasn't gone on a single birding trip since 2000. His list is now above 7,200, but the increase is all due to splits, which he follows avidly. I keep trying to get him to come to Los Angeles, to find the Mountain Quail, but so far, he hasn't.

"I can't explain it," Dad says, "but I'm not so interested in birds."

The places he really wanted to go, Colombia and Indonesia, are now considered too dangerous for travel. He's got a tentative want—or need—list for those countries that could easily push him toward 7,500, but it's all just speculation. "The truth is," Dad says, "that I did what I wanted to do."

BESIDES, THERE'S SOMETHING NEW. Dad's medical odyssey has continued. He's had multiple surgeries on his throat to burn away scar tissue that might have prevented him from breathing. He was diagnosed with and received treatment for prostate cancer. As I was writing the first parts of this book, he needed to have an additional operation to repair an aortic aneurysm. He's stronger and fitter (now that all those problems are fixed) than he was back in Brazil, but he's still nervous about traveling too far, about adding to his total of fifty-nine birding trips in seventeen years.

He still watches for new yard birds, though he won't say whether he thinks he'll make it to two hundred.

But now most of his time is spent in a new kind of pursuit.

In the summer of 2001, the local natural-history society sponsored a butterfly walk. Dad went along. Afterward, he bought a butterfly field guide and a pair of closer-focusing binoculars—essential for insect work.

But there's something different.

"Staying local was part of it," he says, "but that's not the only reason. Seeing and learning about butterflies felt good. It helped me regain a sense of wonderment I had about birds during the earlier years." He pauses. "With butterflies, I don't have to be a maniac, addicted lister."

Yes, he keeps a list. When I visit him, we go looking for new butterflies and moths, and when we get home, he writes them down.

But he's not counting—or so he says.

"I know what butterflies I'd like to see," he says. "But I couldn't tell you how many I've seen."

He's looking into the future.

Nothing could make me happier.

A DIFFERENT WAY TO COUNT

IN EARLY 2004, I flew to Brazil to meet Peter Kaestner. There wasn't a single Big Lister or ornithologist guide I'd spoken to who—if they knew Kaestner—didn't think that he was the one most likely to break Phoebe Snetsinger's record. Kaestner had spent the past several years as a consular officer at the U.S. embassy in Brasilia, and was about to be transferred. He'd invited me to come along on his last weekend of birding in South America. His goal: to see twelve new birds, which would bring his life list to 7,950. One of Kaestner's habits, he explained, is that he "likes round numbers. It keeps things neat."

We flew, together, to Manaus, to the same airport where Dad's attempt to reach seven thousand began. From there, we took a tiny commuter plane to the isolated village of Borba, deep in the rain forest. Kaestner didn't want to relax. He didn't want to check in to the tiny hotel in the Amazonian village. He didn't want to get water. Instead, he quickly assembled his kit—binoculars, telescope, and audio recorder—and ordered Nathan, the driver who had met us, to speed through the midafternoon heat, rumbling down a dirt road, until we reached a barely extant trail into the jungle. Kaestner leapt out of the car. I followed behind, trying to keep up, trying to keep quiet. We stepped over thick, twisting strangler fig vines and gingerly crossed through a swarm of army ants. We could hear the movement of other insects, leaping out of the way, as the ants crawled, by the millions, from tree to tree. The ants were a good sign: The same creatures that were trying to avoid them would attract birds—dozens of them, ten or more different species. The jungle is a difficult place to see birds: dark and thick, with little room for maneuvering and short lines of sight. Kaestner scanned the flock. "Maybe," he said. He dropped a cassette into his tape recorder and hit the PLAY button. He'd seen something I hadn't caught. Rewind. Playback.

Again.

Again.

Suddenly, it appeared. The tape contained the recorded voice of the Pearly Antshrike, a distinctive bird—there are dozens of antshrike species, but only this one has large white wing spots— and just one of the dozens of bird songs Kaestner had assembled just for this trip. He quickly raised his binoculars and confirmed the sighting.

"We did it," he said, clapping his hands. "We broke the ice!"

THE FIRST TIME I MET KAESTNER was at his job. I took a taxi from the airport in Brasilia to the U.S. embassy. The complex sprawls across the oddly manicured plain that houses Brazil's answer to the "city of the future." The country's capital was built from scratch in 1960, and it seems that way—as if it were lowered from outer space onto the vast, cleared jungle (art historian Robert Hughes called the city a "utopian horror"). After passing through several checkpoints, I was escorted to Kaestner's office. He holds a high State Department rank, and I found myself wondering whether this very buttoned-down professional could really be the future of birding. Most top birders possess both eccentricity and drive. In Kaestner's case, I soon concluded, his drive *is* his eccentricity.

Kaestner and Dad both have excellent birding skills, but they have completely different styles and motivations. Dad birds for himself; the activity feeds a need that, for most of his life, seemed nearly unquenchable. Kaestner's impetus seems much simpler: "I want to win," he told me.

Kaestner grew up in Baltimore. His mother passed away when he was young, leaving his father to raise seven boys and three girls. "It was a competitive environment," Kaestner says. Instead of a regular allowance, Kaestner's father would throw quarters onto the floor of the TV room. "We'd have to fight for them," he says, and the smaller ones—Kaestner is the third-youngest—had to be really tough. The family remains aggressive in everything: "Play tennis with them," says Kimberly Kaestner, Peter's wife, "and you play for blood." Kaestner definitely looks the part; he's got an aggressive glint in his eye, and he's constantly scanning his surroundings. In fact, I found it a bit hard to believe that, at over six feet tall and broadly built, with Nordic good looks—blond hair, blue eyes— Kaestner could successfully blend into the jungle surroundings we'd soon be visiting.

Kaestner began birding at age ten, with his older brother, Hank. The two instantly became rivals, and, as they grew up, began look- ing for ways to get to the world's most bird-rich countries.

Hank became a spice importer, which allowed him to travel to remote parts of the world (and bird). Peter joined the Peace Corps, then became a diplomat, specially requesting remote postings— New Guinea, the Solomon Islands, Guatemala—where the birds were plentiful. Kaestner has a master plan that, because his birding is integrated into his day-to-day life, is entirely different from any other Big Lister's. He's got everything counted out, years in advance. He'll probably reach eight thousand at his next posting, in Cairo. Eighty-five hundred? Five years, he says. And he's going to do it in Brazil. He's already got the trip planned.

"Time," he says, "is my weapon."

FOR THREE DAYS, WE BIRDED. We were working from a two-sided printout of a spreadsheet that listed sixty-two birds, arranged by common and scientific name. This "want list" included sixteen birds in boldface (those are ones he's never seen), along with highlighted birds (ones found near Borba, whether he's seen them or not); italicized (birds he doesn't have tape-recorded songs for), and plain text (he's seen them, but not in Brazil; like most big-time birders, Kaestner keeps a separate country list). Birds with a letter E next to them mean he wants them on *this* trip: They're the birds that will bring us to his hoped-for round number. There are twelve of them.

Kaestner doesn't *need* any single E-ticket bird more than the others—he plans to get them all, and that's that—but all of them are exotic. There's the Buff-cheeked Tody-Flycatcher, a species that hadn't been seen in the wild for 150 years and was believed to be extinct until it was rediscovered in the early 1990s; the extremely rare Pale-faced Antbird; and the White-tailed Cotinga, which has become a nemesis bird. "That bird is jinxed," he says. We begin walking back to the road; we stop once, and Kaestner trains his telescope on a long-tailed Paradise Jacamar, with shiny, blue-black feathers. The bird spins off its perch, somersaults, grabs a flying insect, then revolves back to the branch. Kaestner continues,

"Maybe you can be my good-luck charm for the Cotinga," he jokes. "Somebody has to."

Kaestner spent weeks preparing for this trip, gathering information on where his target birds could be seen and studying—over and over again—the recorded bird songs he'd obtained for the species on his want list. He's warned me to bring my own food, to expect to be in the field for hours, and—especially—to not get in the way. But I find him surprisingly generous with his knowledge; a few times, I find myself wondering how interested I'd be in birds if Dad had been this way. Kaestner takes time to show me birds he's seen a dozen times. He even instructs me in proper binocular technique (you locate the bird with your unaided eyes, then lift the binoculars to your gaze, so you can focus on the same spot).

"Are you just being nice to me because you think I'll bring you good luck with the Cotinga?" I ask, half-serious (it probably has more to do with his natural gregariousness and diplomatic skills).

"Absolutely," Kaestner says.

A few moments later, we reach the trailhead. We're nowhere near done for the day, but we're going to move to a different spot. As Kaestner is putting his telescope in the car, he takes a last glance up and sees it, flying across the dirt road, from one section of canopy to the other. "White-tailed Cotinga," Kaestner shouts. He grabs the telescope and aims it toward a branch. He's literally jumping for joy, now. "We got him! *We got him!*" He slaps me on the back.[*]

The celebration lasts another four seconds. Then it's back to the chase.

---

[*]I was struck by how animated Peter was when he finally got a bird, especially compared to Dad, whose outward displays of emotion were limited.

❀   ❀   ❀

THE NEXT MORNING, we paddle slowly down the Mapiá River—an Amazon tributary—in a creaky, leaking, dugout canoe. We woke up at 3 AM and drove into the forest; Kaestner shined a giant spotlight into the woods, and we saw the flashing eyes of spiders and potoo (related to a common California species, the nightjar). We ended our first day with three new species, and Kaestner is still thinking he'll get his dozen. Dawn was breaking by the time we reached the river. A Big Lister is always used to big numbers, but Kaestner has been going at an especially frantic pace for the past two years. His original plan was to stay in Brazil until 2007, but his wife, who also works for the State Department, had a career opportunity in Egypt. There are good birds there, and throughout Africa, for him, but the change involved some restructuring of his master plan. "I accelerated things," he says. In 2003, he saw over a thousand new species. Up until his departure from Brazil in June 2004, he'd added over eight hundred new birds to his list.

Kaestner networks heavily, collecting what British birders call "Gen"—short for "general information"—that gathers location data, directions for finding, and other key information on target birds. (For tour leaders, many of whom work for competing companies, personal Gen is often kept as secret as a good fly-fishing spot. Kaestner is trusted with this information. "They know I won't tell," he says. "I'm used to dealing with sensitive data.") After gathering his resources, Kaestner prepares a trip, mapping his routes, finding places to stay, and finally generating the master want list. The spot where we're paddling right now is a bit of a tricky place; we're on the border of an indigenous reservation, home to the Mundurukú Indians. Under Brazilian law, nobody is allowed to enter such reserves, so we pull up to shore and head into the bush on a path that just skirts the area.

The key to finding birds in the jungle, I'm quickly learning, is to find the ant colonies. It's no coincidence that the most common bird families in the Amazonian tropics are species called antbirds, antpittas, or antwren. When you walk in the jungle, you see an ant or two, at first. But if you focus, two will turn into two hundred, and then two million. In a true swarm, the trees and the leaves themselves seem to be dripping insects, or even moving themselves. We focus into the brush and watch, on the jungle floor, as other insects—beetles and cicadas—leap off the ground to avoid the marauding ants; birds swoop in to eat them.

In a few minutes, we've got seven of the twelve.

It's only 10 AM on the second day. We've still got hours. "Do you think we'll do it?" I ask.

Kaestner is quiet. He believes it, but even saying so could be bad luck. Better to keep birding.

THAT BUSY MORNING WAS THE BEGINNING of a twenty-four-hour dry spell. Kaestner was already recalculating, trying to figure out if he could squeeze another day in somewhere near Brasilia. It would be tight. At that point, I didn't need to ask what the point was. I knew that he could easily leave Brazil with just nine, and still reach eight thousand in plenty of time, and still be number one. Barring accidents, all that was pretty much preordained. But Kaestner wanted that nice, round number—7,950—and I understood.

"It would be neat," he said.

We headed toward the river one more time. Our guide waded in and began dragging the canoe toward shore.

Truthfully, neither of us was terribly confident. Of the birds we needed—Flame-crested Manakin, Crimson-bellied Parakeet, and Brown-chested Barbet—only the parakeet was likely to be seen on open river. But we didn't have time for another jungle walk. There's only one reason we'd see the other birds: if they were chasing something.

There were bugs everywhere, flying around us, above the trees.

A Flame-crested Manakin shot out from the trees and snatched one.

Kaestner, as I mentioned, is a very buttoned-down guy. You don't get to the highest echelons of the foreign service by being a wild man (at least, not if you can't contain how wild you are until you're in the middle of the jungle in avian ecstasy).

"Holy freakin' cow!" Kaestner screamed, although he didn't use the word *freakin'*, and the final word was a scatological reference, not a bovine one. *"Holy . . . !"*

Three expletives, probably the first three Kaestner had spoken all year (in fact, when I later published an article about the trip and repeated the actual words, Kaestner wrote me, slightly chagrined).

It was a good thing we were on the water because twenty minutes later, and less than a hundred yards from where we saw the Manakin, the parakeet we wanted flew across. Not as unusual, but still . . . Kaestner sounded like a sailor.

One to go.

One day left.

IN PETER KAESTNER'S FINAL FEW HOURS OF SEARCHING the Amazon, we saw many amazing things. We came upon a family roasting manioc, the staple grain of Brazil (in a different form, we use it for tapioca pudding), on a huge, open burner. They'd planned to eat roast pig, but an eagle had grabbed the animal, so they were making do with what they had. Still, they shared some small bits of cake, wrapped in banana leaves, with us. We saw my favorite bird: the magnificent and bizarre Harpy Eagle, with Mohawk tufts on its head, capable of flying at over 50 mph—including right-angle turns—through thick forest. Before dawn, we saw several shooting stars. We saw a family of howler monkeys, moving along the treetops.

And we saw the Barbet.

It skirted, just as the sun was rising, across the trees. It wasn't a good look, but the Barbet is an unmistakable species, with a chunky body and odd feathers. Even in silhouette, you'd know one. Kaestner knew.

Birders have to be sure to add a species to their list. You can be sure in several ways. A good, solid look in a telescope or binoculars is best. Song response is also a legitimate means of verification. Without song, and without a good look, you're left with pure deduction. There's only one kind of Barbet in this part of Brazil, and what we saw was definitely a Barbet.

7,950.

Anticlimactic? "The rules," says Kaestner, "are the rules. I'd like to see it better, and one day, I will. But I get the check mark today."

THERE'S NO DOUBT THAT KAESTNER will soon hit eight thousand, that he'll soon be number one. He may set a record that, except for splits, is unbreakable. The one question remaining is why: Why birds? Why try to see them all?

Kaestner has fashioned his entire life to deliberately revolve around birds. Not just a few years, like a professional athlete, and not just a few times a year, like a mountaineer or a marathon-runner. Every spare minute Kaestner has is spent looking for birds, or getting ready to look for birds. What I realized in watching him and Dad, and learning about the techniques of the other Big Listers, is that they really do prepare for the excursions—whether it's a weekend alone or a month in the bush with a group—as if they were athletic events. To see thousands of birds, you don't have to train—Harvey Gilston didn't. But to gain the respect of your competitors, whipping yourself into shape is essential.

In this context, there's no birder more "athletic" than Kaestner, who sees it more as a sport. Why?

"Because it's a goal," Kaestner says.

Because he wants to win.

Win what?

I wanted him to answer, but I knew he couldn't. When you're that obsessed, you can't see your obsession (if you could, you'd probably be unable to continue). For the same reason, Dad could never explain why he was obsessed. Even I didn't begin to see the bigger questions until his physical trials began: Why does obsession exist? Is it to fill our empty spaces? Does it work?

I don't think it does. Not for Dad, not for me, and probably not for any of the Big Listers.

I think the answer is related to a more direct concern, held by the counters and the backyard birders. It was what motivated the shotgun-toting collectors of a century ago, and it motivates the species-splitting ornithologists of today. What makes a species? Or, more broadly, what makes life? Birds show us, and have always shown us, what nature is. Not just physically, but as an idea. As something we love, something we value. The clue is in the naming, in the counting. The birds don't have any need for the names we give them; they'd still fuss in the trees and fill the skies. But in the listing, in the categorizing, in the identifying—whether at the backyard feeder or deep in the rain forests of Brazil—we untangle the web of creation. We don't name birds, we don't number birds, for birds; we do it for each other. When we do, we get, just briefly, to soar alongside them.

BIBLIOGRAPHY

Alden, Peter, and John Gooders. *Finding Birds Around the World.* Boston: Houghton Mifflin, 1981.

Barrow, Mark V., Jr. *A Passion for Birds: American Ornithology After Audubon.* Princeton: Princeton University Press, 1998.

Bull, John. *Birds of the New York Area.* New York: Harper & Row, 1964.

Chapman, Frank M. *Autobiography of a Bird-Lover.* New York: D. Appleton-Century Company, 1935.

———. *Handbook of Birds of Eastern North America.* New York: D. Appleton-Century Company, 1939.

Clements, James. *Birds of the World: A Checklist.* Vista, California: Ibis Publishing Company, 2000.

Coues, Elliot. *Key to North American Birds.* Boston: Estes and Lauriat, 1884.

Cruickshank, Allan D. *Birds Around New York City.* New York: The American Museum of Natural History, 1942.

Cutright, Paul Russell, and Michael J. Brodhead. *Elliot Coues: Naturalist and Frontier Historian*. Chicago: University of Illinois Press, 1981.

Davis, William E., Jr. *Dean of the Birdwatchers: A Biography of Ludlow Griscom*. Washington, D.C.: Smithsonian Institution Press, 1994.

Devlin, John C., and Grace Naismith. *The World of Roger Tory Peterson*. New York: New York Times Books, 1977.

Dunn, John L., et al. *ABA Checklist: Birds of the Continental United States and Canada*. Colorado Springs: American Birding Association, 2002.

Griscom, Ludlow. *Birds of the New York City Region*. New York: The American Museum of Natural History, 1923.

Hilty, Steven L., and William L. Brown. *A Guide to the Birds of Colombia*. Princeton: Princeton University Press, 1986.

Kastner, Joseph. *A World of Watchers: An Informal History of the American Passion for Birds*. San Francisco: Sierra Club Books, 1986.

Kaufman, Kenn. *Birds of North America*. New York: Houghton Mifflin, 2000.

Kieran, John. *A Natural History of New York City*. Boston: Houghton Mifflin, 1959.

Levine, Emanuel, ed. *Bull's Birds of New York State*. Ithaca, New York: Comstock, 1998.

Meyer de Schauensee, Rodolphe. *A Guide to the Birds of South America*. Wynnewood, Pennsylvania: Livingston Publishing Company, 1982.

Peterson, Roger Tory, ed. *The Bird Watcher's Anthology*. New York: Harcourt Brace, 1957.

————. *Birds Over America*. New York: Dodd, Mead and Company, 1964.

————. *A Field Guide to the Birds*. New York: Houghton Mifflin, 1934, 1947, and 1980 editions.

————. *A Field Guide to the Birds of Texas*. New York: Houghton Mifflin, 1960.

————. *A Field Guide to Western Birds*. New York: Houghton Mifflin, 1992.

Remsen, J. V., Jr., ed. *Studies in Neotropical Ornithology Honoring Ted Parker*. Washington, D.C.: The American Ornithologists' Union, 1997.

Sibley, Charles G., and Burt L. Monroe, Jr. *Distribution and Taxonomy of Birds of the World*. New Haven, Connecticut: Yale University Press, 1990.

Sibley, David. *The Sibley Guide to Bird Life and Behavior*. New York: Alfred A. Knopf, 2001.

————. *The Sibley Guide to Birds*. New York: Alfred A. Knopf, 2000.

————. *Sibley's Birding Basics*. New York: Alfred A. Knopf, 2002.

Snetsinger, Phoebe. *Birding on Borrowed Time*. Colorado Springs: American Birding Association, 2003.

Stresemann, Erwin. *Ornithology from Aristotle to the Present*. Cambridge: Harvard University Press, 1975.

Villani, Robert. *Long Island: A Natural History*. New York: Harry N. Abrams, 1997.

ABOUT THE AUTHOR

Dan Koeppel is a well-known outdoors, nature, and adventure writer. He's a contributing editor at *National Geographic Adventure* (which has published over a dozen of his stories) and a frequent contributor to *Audubon, Men's Journal, Backpacker, Popular Science,* and *Bicycling* magazines. His work has also appeared in the *New York Times Magazine, Outside, Wired, Forbes, Elle, Martha Stewart Living, ESPN: The Magazine, Metropolis,* and *Sports Afield.* He is coauthor of *The Tour de France Companion.*

Koeppel has been writing outdoor adventure stories since 1993, when he became the senior editor of *Mountain Bike* magazine (Rodale Press). That job took him on off-road excursions to Turkey, Venezuela, Chile, and Costa Rica, as well as throughout North America. In 1995, he was part of the team that became the first to pedal the interior of Mexico's Copper Canyon; he's since returned there four additional times to map and explore that remote area. The Copper Canyon experience led him to be invited as official writer/observer on an archaeological team that explored Mexico's remote Piaxtla Canyon in 2001; an account of the team's discoveries will appear in *National Geographic Adventure* in 2005. He continues to write "Hug the Bunny," a monthly column that has appeared on the back page of *Mountain Bike* since 1995. Dan Koeppel was a commentator for Public Radio International's "Marketplace," and wrote episodes of *Star Trek: The Next Generation* for Paramount Television. He cowrote *The Lost Words*, a feature film that won the Silver Medal Award at the International Festival of Cinema (Lisbon, Portugal, 1995) and the First Feature Award at the Münich Film Festival (1995).

He grew up in Queens, New York, and attended Hampshire College (Amherst, Massachusetts, 1983). He later studied creative writing and nonfiction at The New School (New York City) and Santa Monica College, as well as archaeology at California State University (Northridge). He was elected to the Mountain Bike Hall of Fame, based in Crested Butte, Colorado, in 2003. He lives in Los Angeles, California.